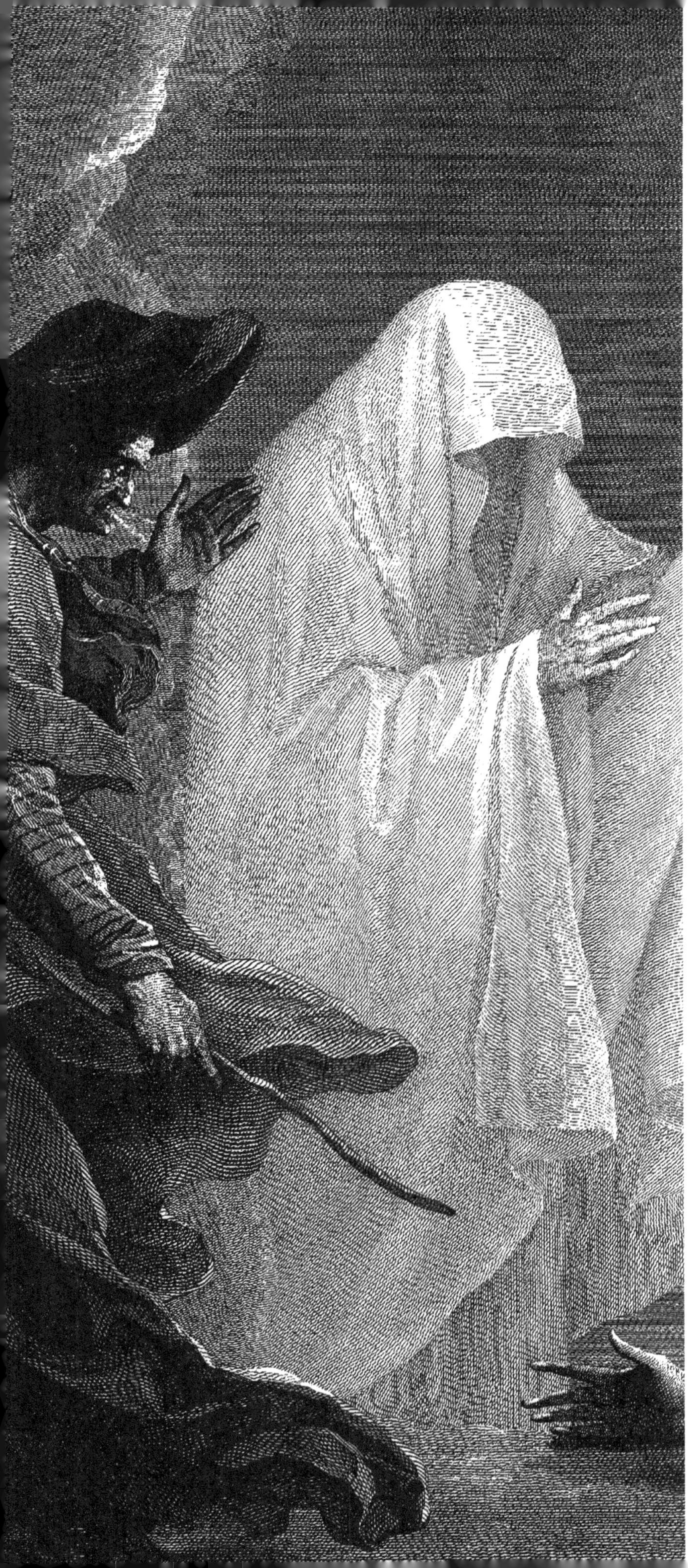

VOLUME NUMBER ONE

AF256617

WITCHES & WIZARDS

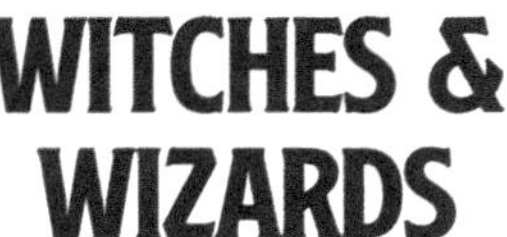
AN IMAGE ARCHIVE FOR
ARTISTS *And* DESIGNERS

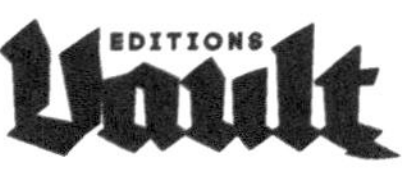
EDITIONS Vault

INTRODUCTION

For centuries, witches and wizards have haunted the edges of the human imagination — figures of fear, fascination, and forbidden power. From the conjurers of ancient myth to the sabbath scenes of the early modern period, these archetypes have inspired some of the most dramatic and viscerally compelling imagery in the history of Western art.

Witches & Wizards, an Image Archive by Vault Editions is a celebration of this dark and enduring artistic tradition. This collection brings together over 100 meticulously restored vintage engravings, etchings, and woodcuts, showcasing the extraordinary ways artists have depicted magic, sorcery, and the supernatural across five centuries. Featuring works by masters including Albrecht Dürer, Francisco Goya, Hans Baldung Grien, Eugène Delacroix, and Arthur Rackham, the collection spans biblical sorceresses and classical enchantresses — Medea, Circe, the Witch of Endor — through Shakespearean witches, fairy-tale hags, and the teeming chaos of the witches' sabbath.

Whether you are a graphic designer seeking richly atmospheric assets, an illustrator searching for reference material, or simply a lover of dark and historical art, this book offers an inexhaustible source of visual inspiration. Each image has been carefully selected and restored to ensure that the detail and character of these timeless works are preserved and ready for modern use.

Additionally, we've included a unique download link granting access to all images featured in the collection. These high-resolution files are perfect for use in your art and design projects, allowing you to bring the atmosphere of centuries of occult imagery into new and imaginative contexts.

Explore five centuries of bewitching art with *Witches & Wizard, an Image Archive* by Vaut Editions.

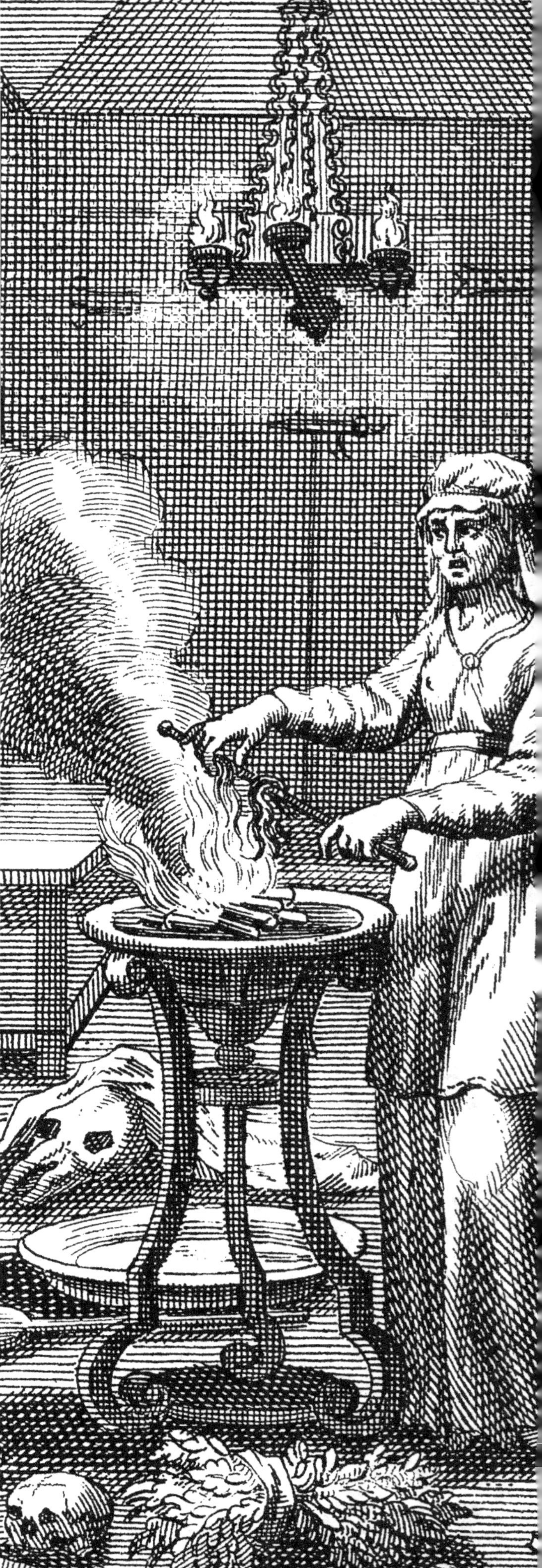

PREFACE

There is something about the figure of the witch or wizard that has always resisted easy explanation. Across cultures and centuries, these archetypes have embodied our deepest anxieties about power, knowledge, and the boundaries of the natural world — and artists have returned to them again and again, producing some of the most charged and inventive imagery in the Western tradition.

This book was born from a fascination with that imagery and a desire to gather it into a single, usable archive. In curating this collection, I sought to bring together a wide range of subjects and moods — the biblical drama of Saul and the Witch of Endor, the classical menace of Medea and Circe, the grotesque carnival of the witches' sabbath, the quiet menace of the fairy-tale hag, and the theatrical witches of Shakespeare and Romantic painting. Together, these works trace five centuries of artistic engagement with the occult, from the woodcuts of Dürer and Baldung Grien to the book illustrations of Arthur Rackham and the etchings of Goya.

Witches & Wizards, an Image Archive is is a resource for the modern creative. Whether you are designing a book cover, building a collage, seeking references for your own illustrations, or simply drawn to the atmosphere of this imagery, this book is intended to inspire and support your work. With the included downloadable images, you can take these works beyond the page and into your own projects, giving new life to some of history's most bewitching art.

It is my hope that this collection serves as a practical tool and an invitation to engage with a tradition that remains as vital and unsettling as ever. The artists represented here were grappling with questions of fear, belief, and the unknown — and in their work, something of that tension survives.

Enjoy the journey.
-Kale James

DOWNLOAD YOUR FILES

Downloading your files is simple. To access your digital files, please go to the last page of this book and follow the instructions.

For technical assistance, please email:
info@vaulteditions.com

Bibliographical Note

This book is a new work created by Vault Editions Ltd.

ISBN: 978-1-922966-77-3

01

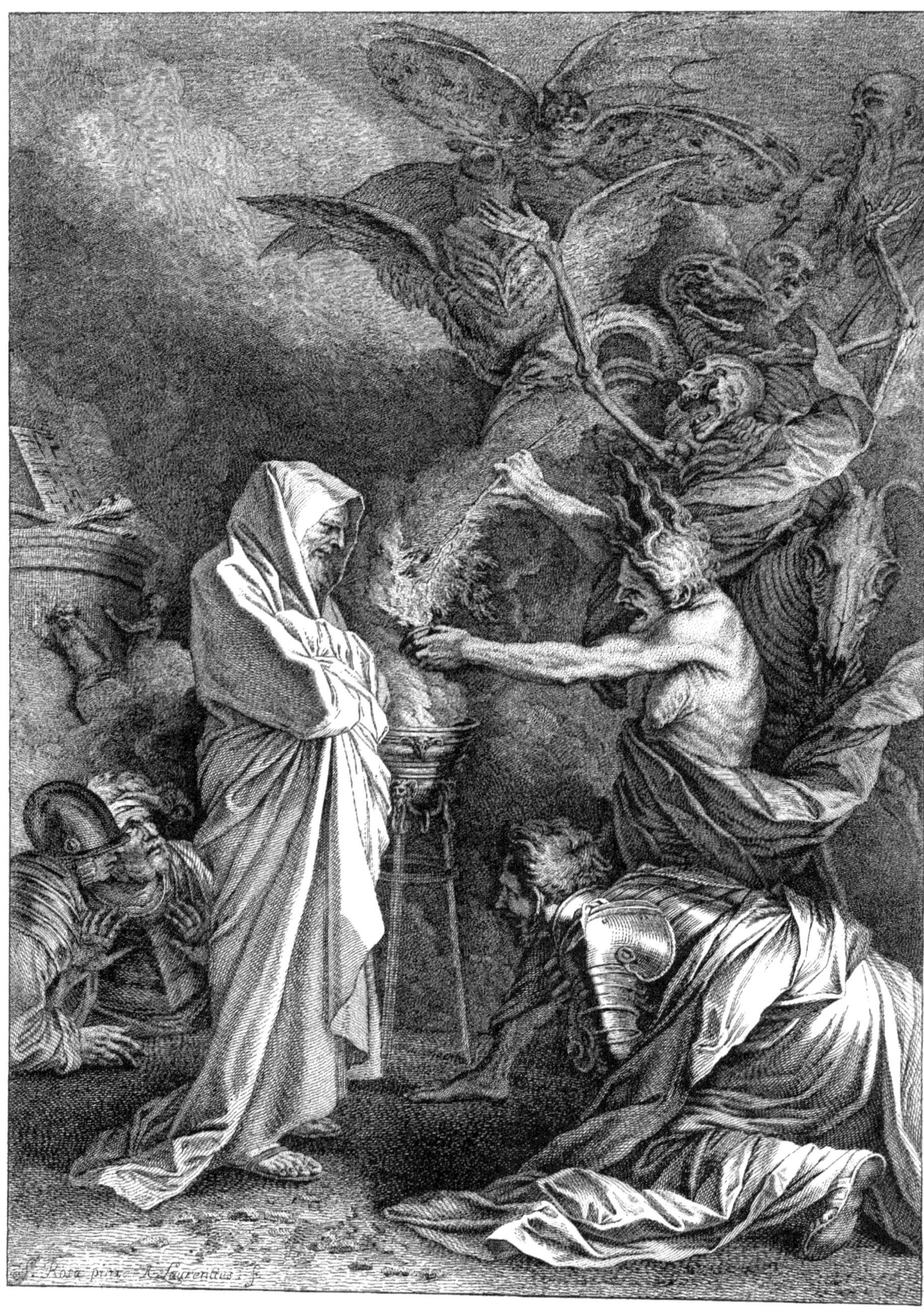

01. Saul by the witch of Endor, Caspar Luyken,
1712

02

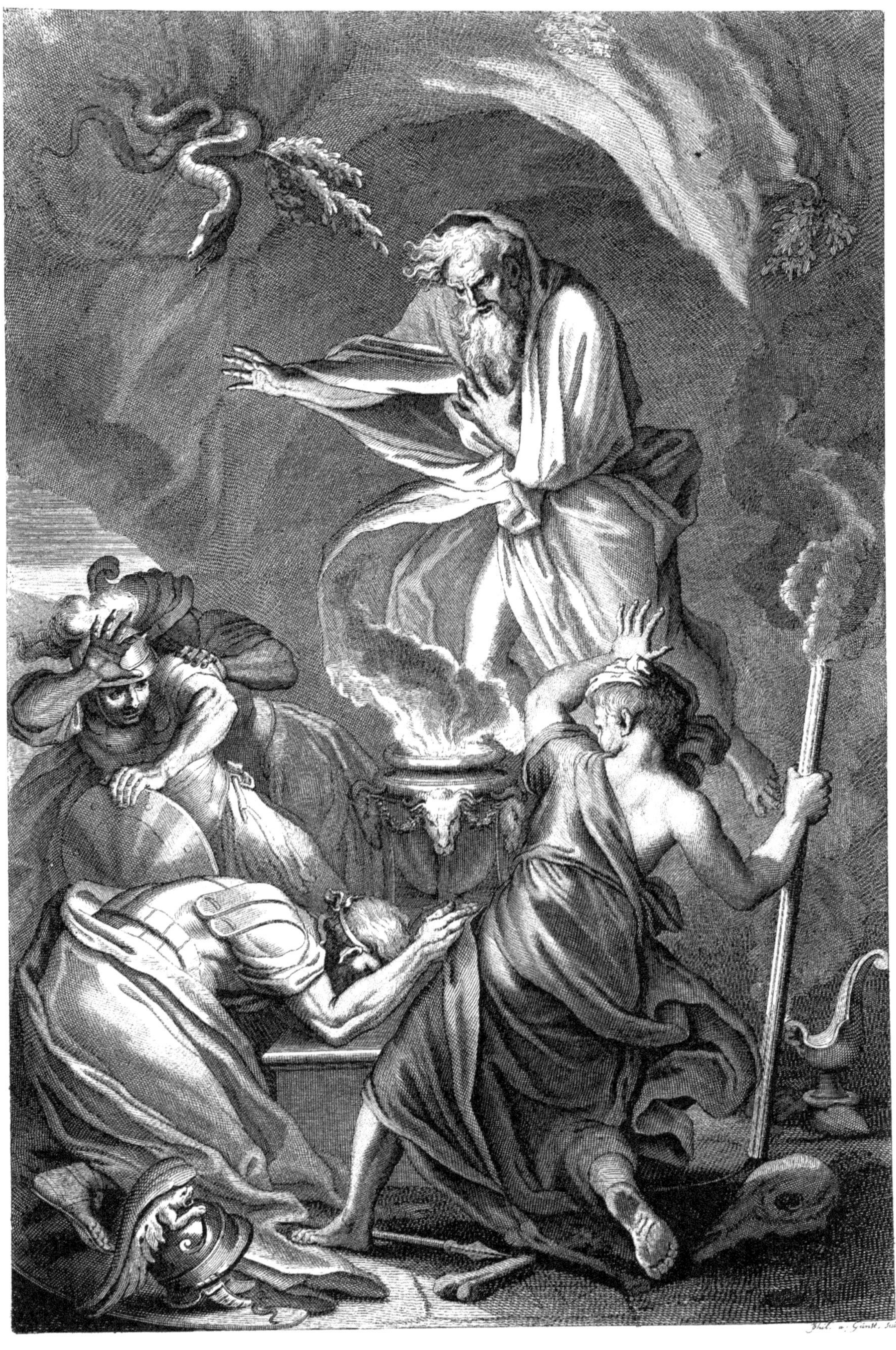

02. Saul by the witch of Endor, Philip van Gunst
(on object), 1685 – 1732

03

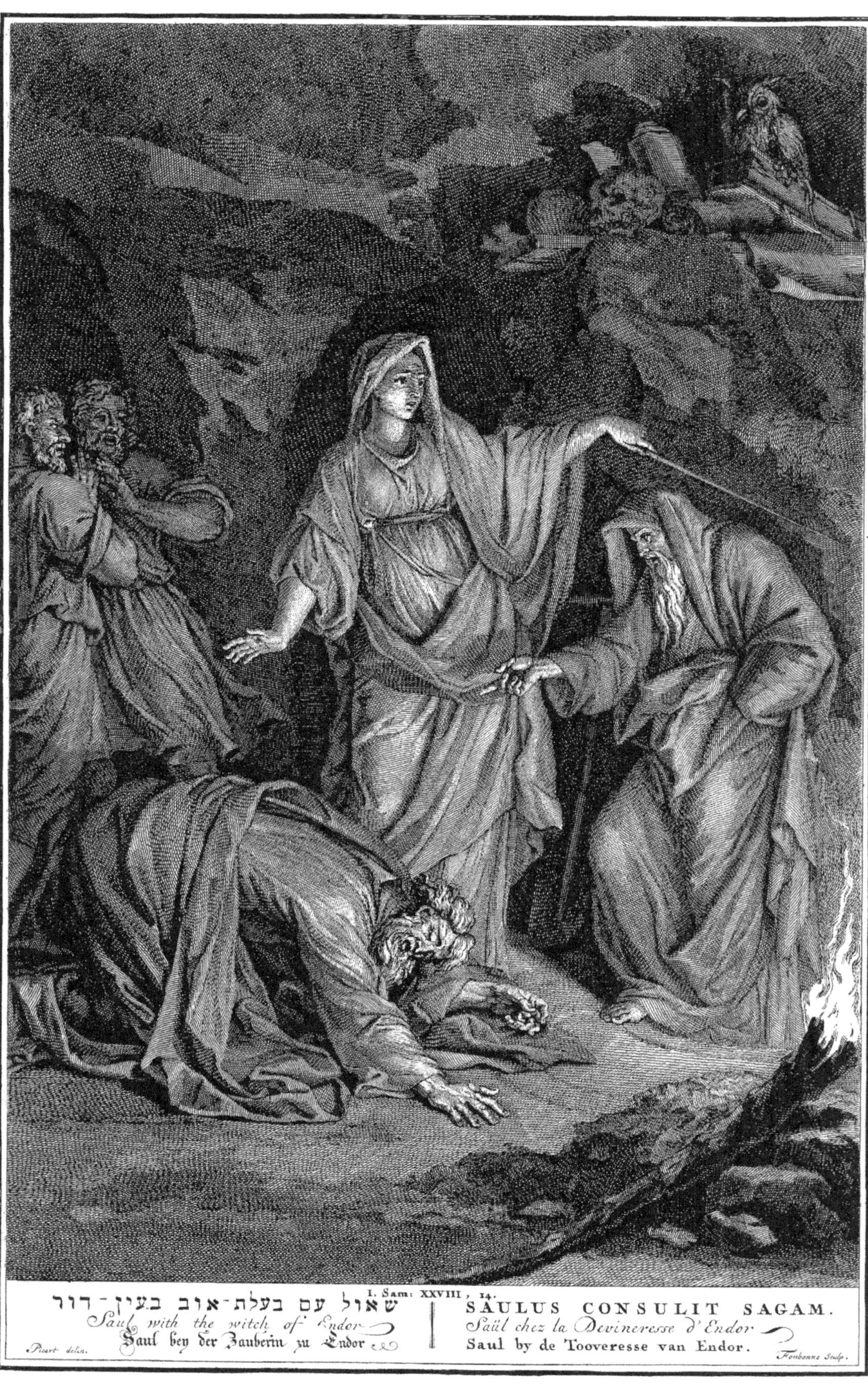

03. Saul by the witch of Endor, Quiryn Fonbonne
(mentioned on object), c. 1690 – c. 1757

04

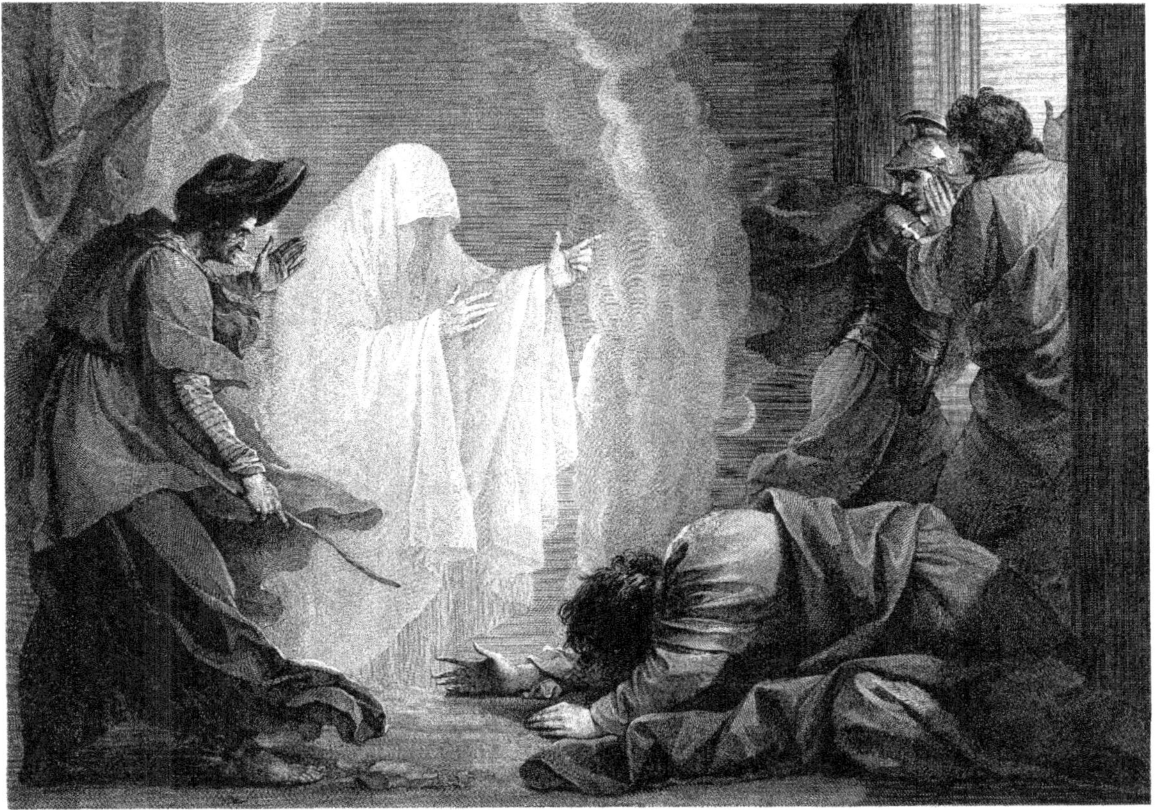

05

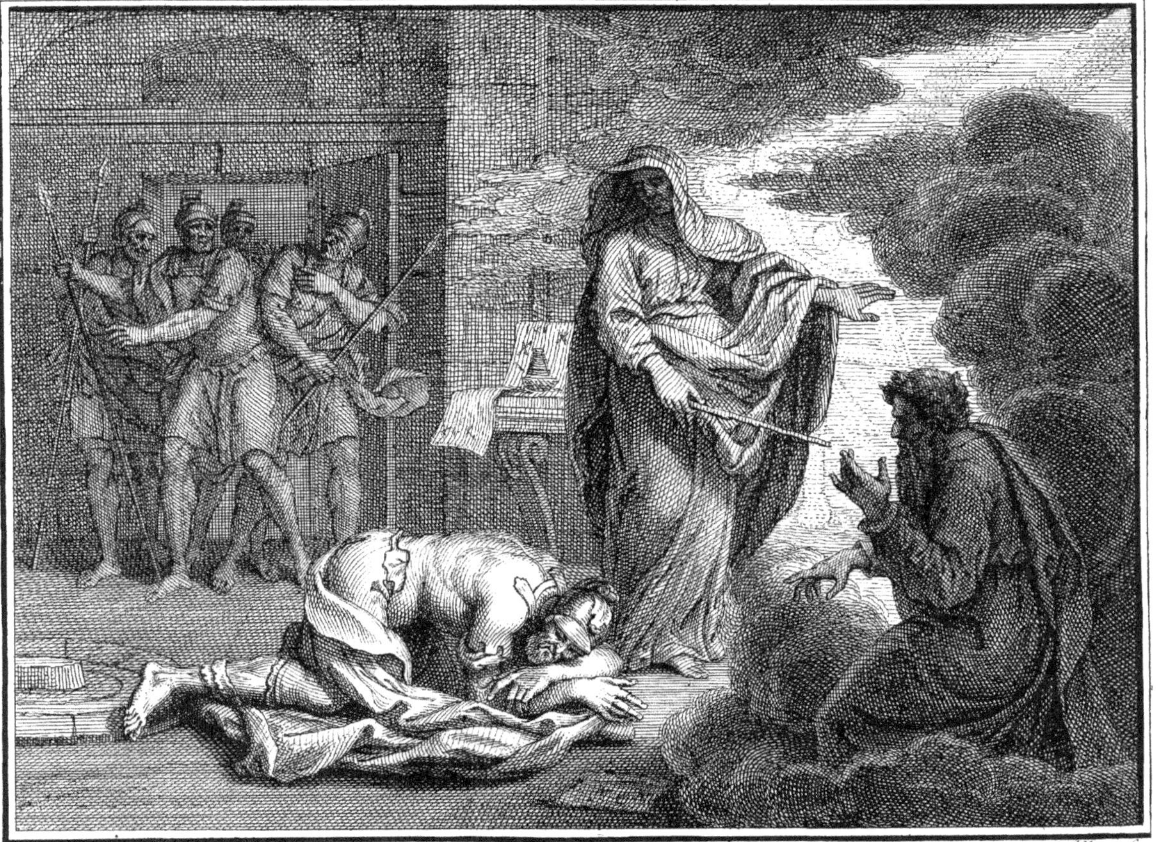

04. Saul and the witch of Endor, William Sharp
(on object), 1788

05. Saul by the witch of Endor, Jacob Folkema
(on object), 1791

06

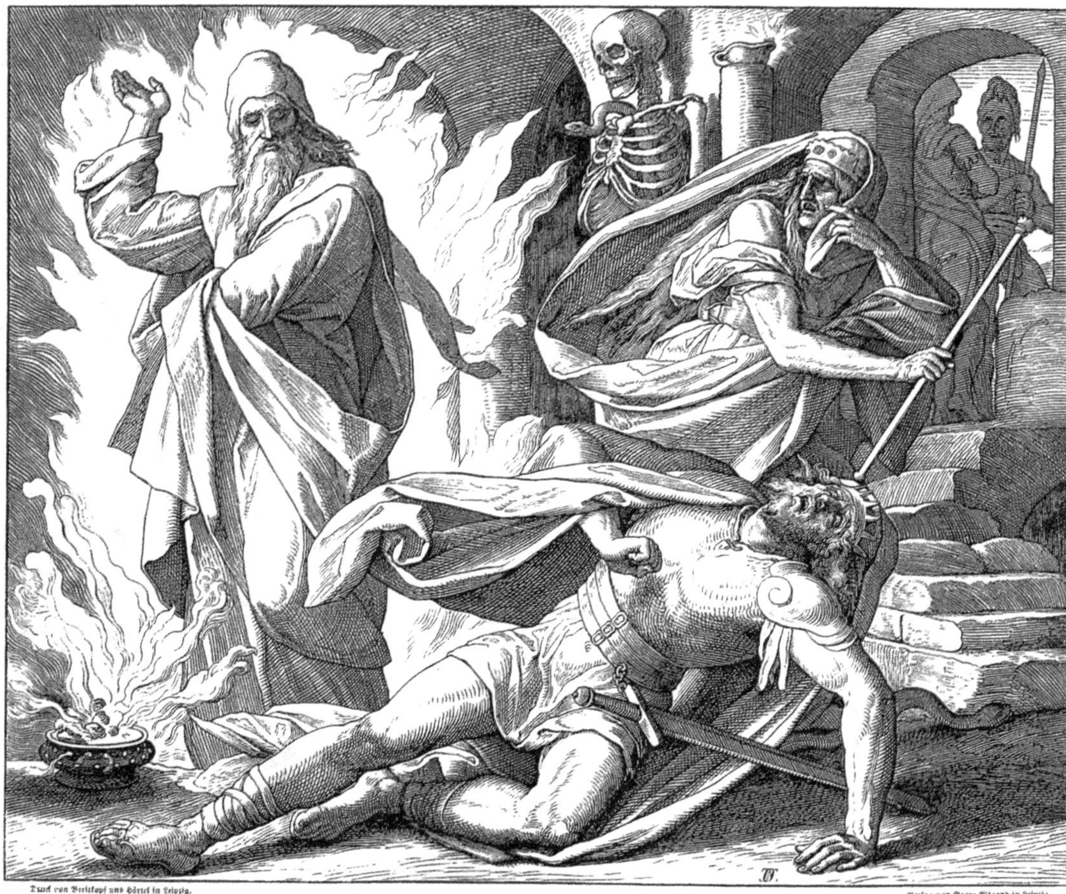

07

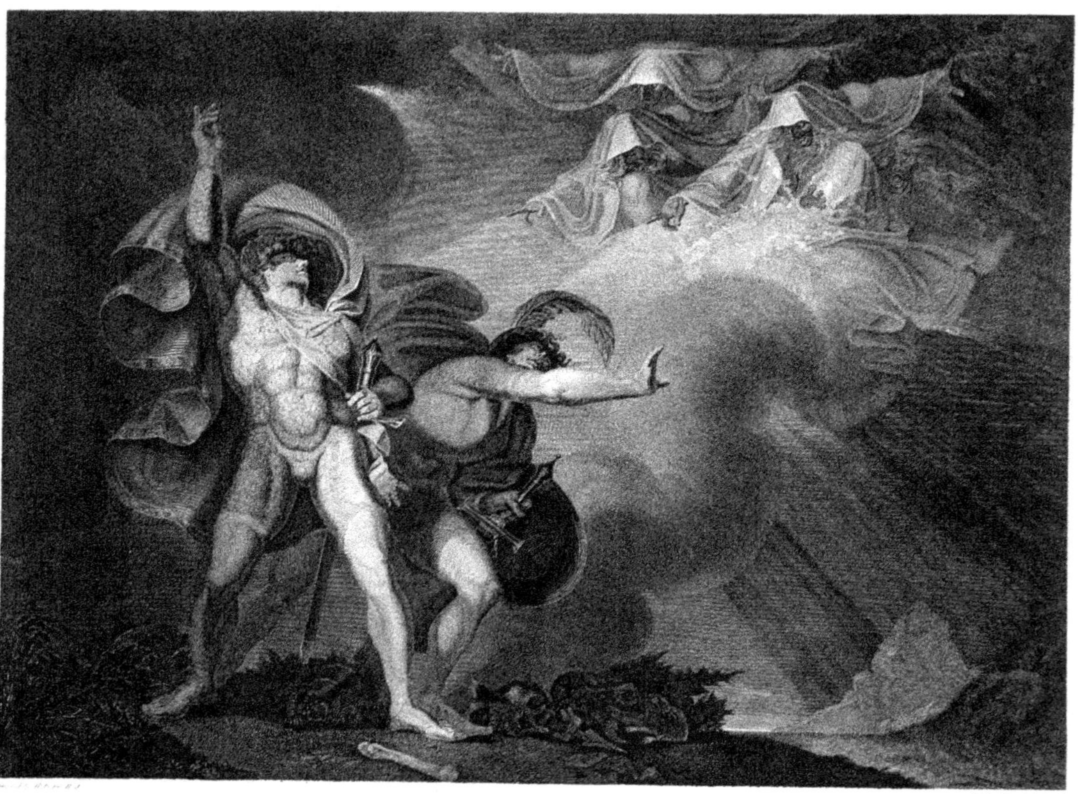

06. Saul collapses as the witch of Endor
conjures Samuel from the dead. Wood engraving
after Schnorr von Carolsfeld, Julius, 1794–1872

07. Three witches appear to Macbeth and
Banquo, James Caldwall (on object), Thomas
Trotter, 1798

08

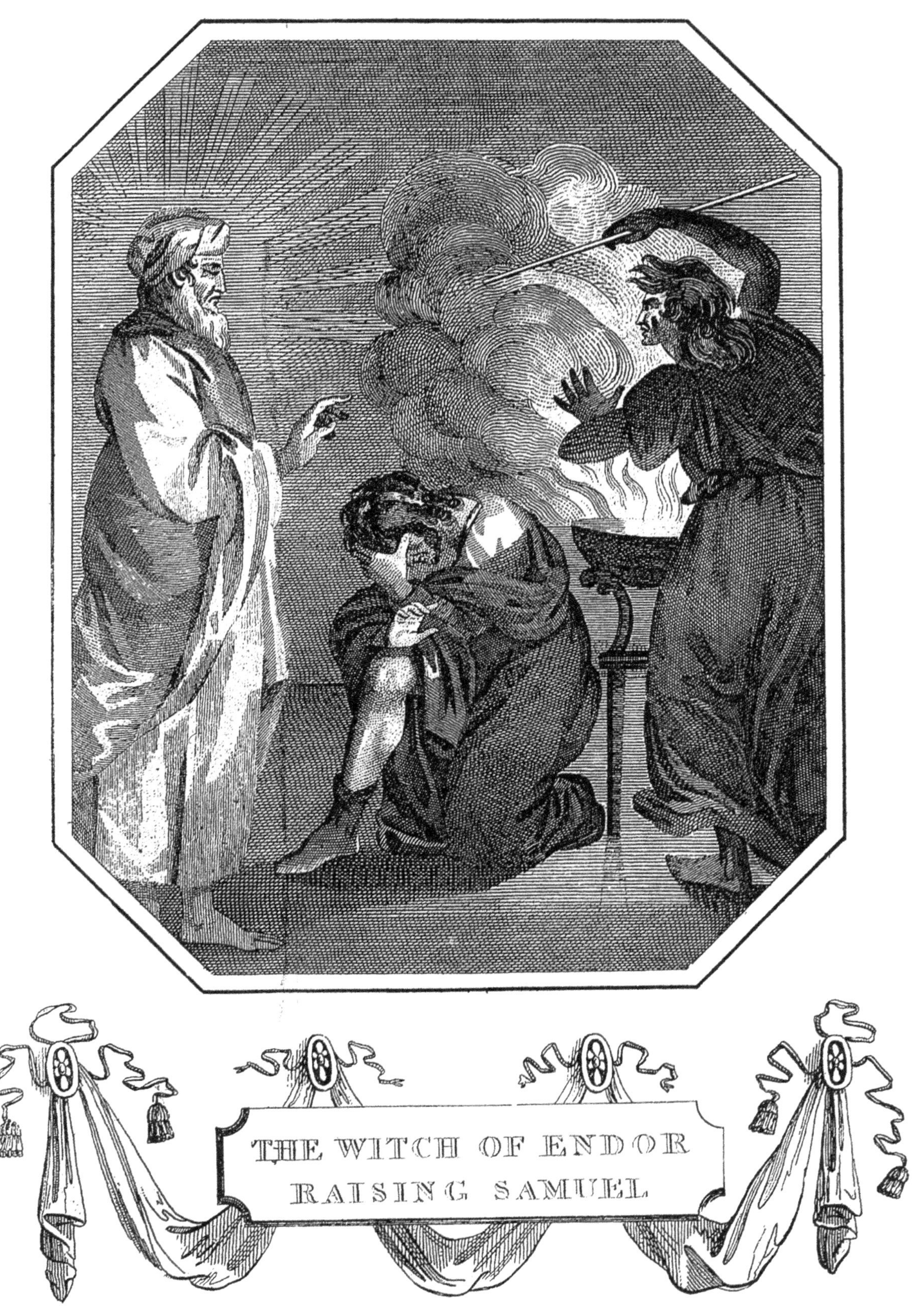

08. The witch of Endor conjures the ghost of
Samuel; Saul bows before him on the right.
Etching, 18th century.

09

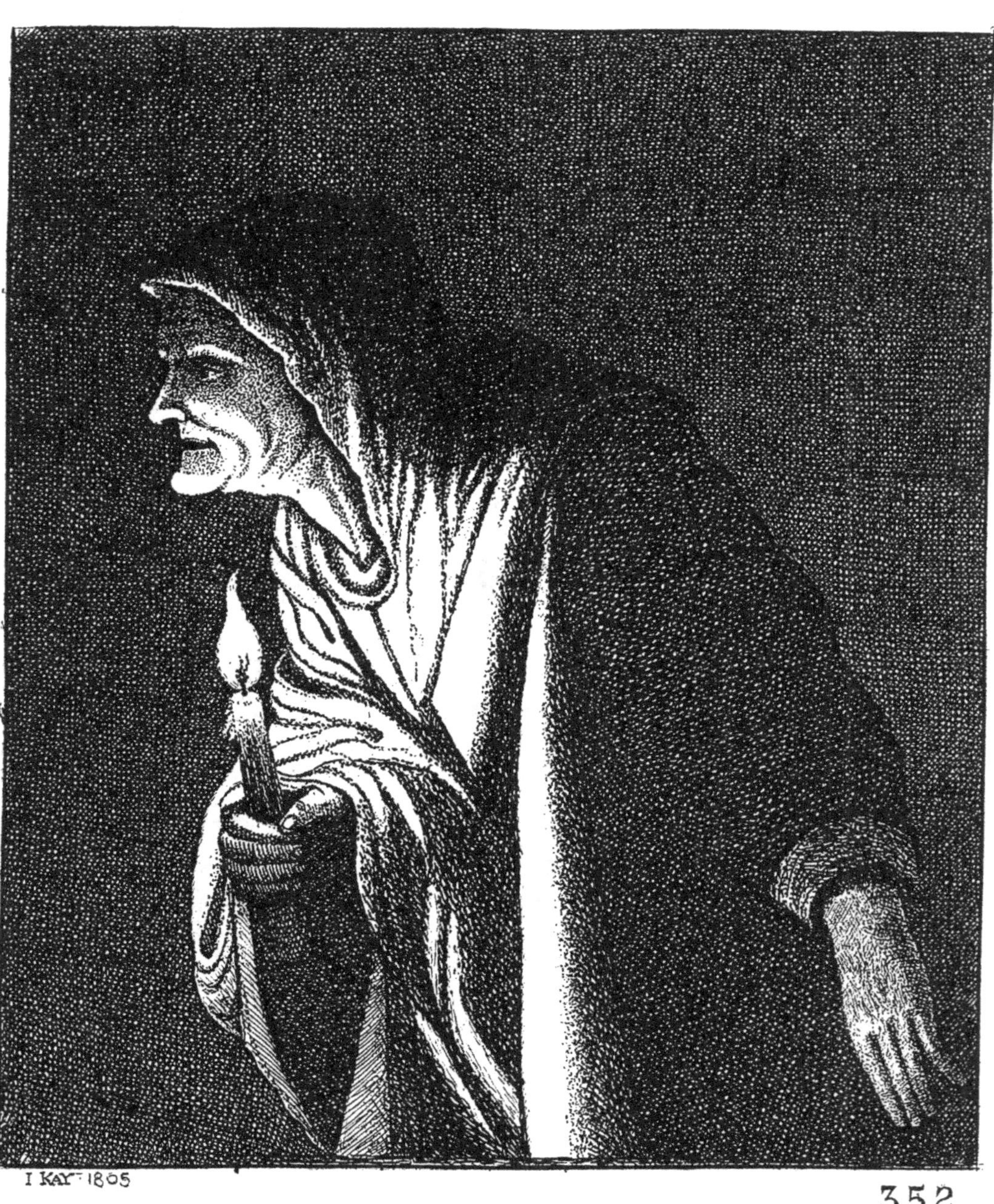

09. The witch of Endor with a candle. Engraving
by J. Kay, 1805, after A. Elsheimer. Elsheimer,
Adam, 1578–1610.

10

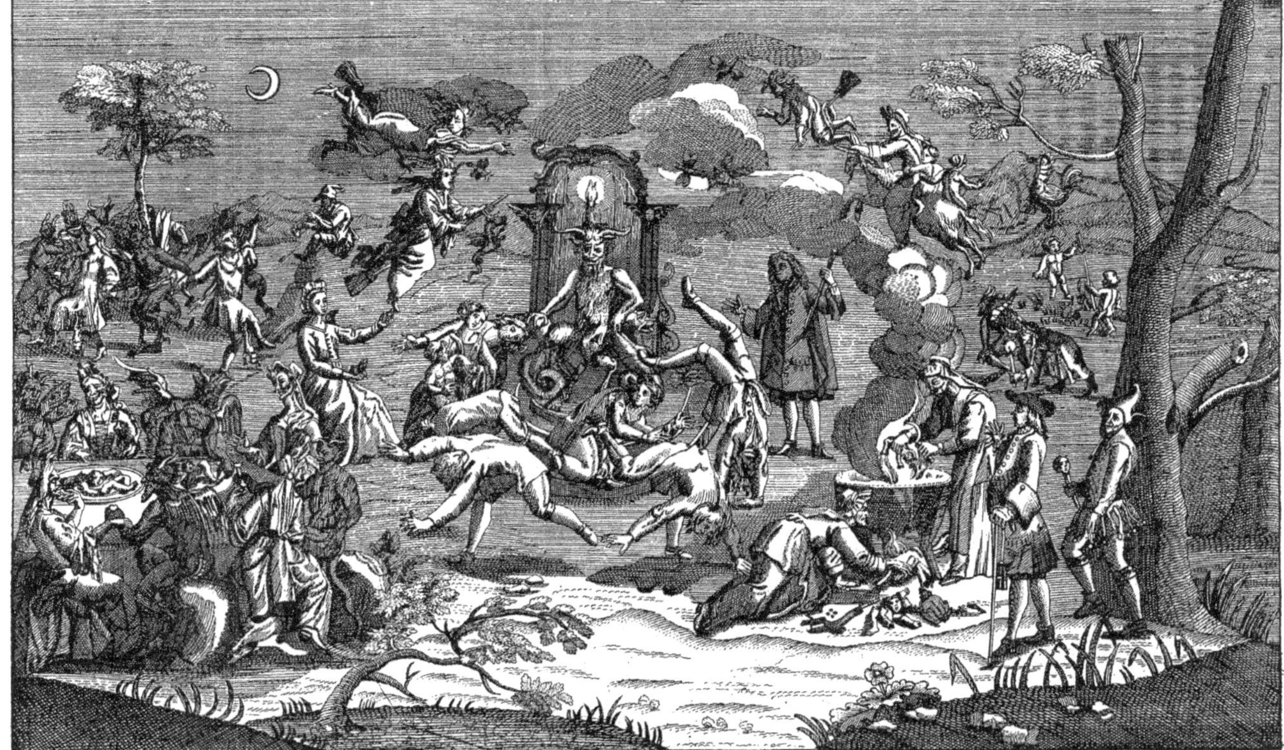

11

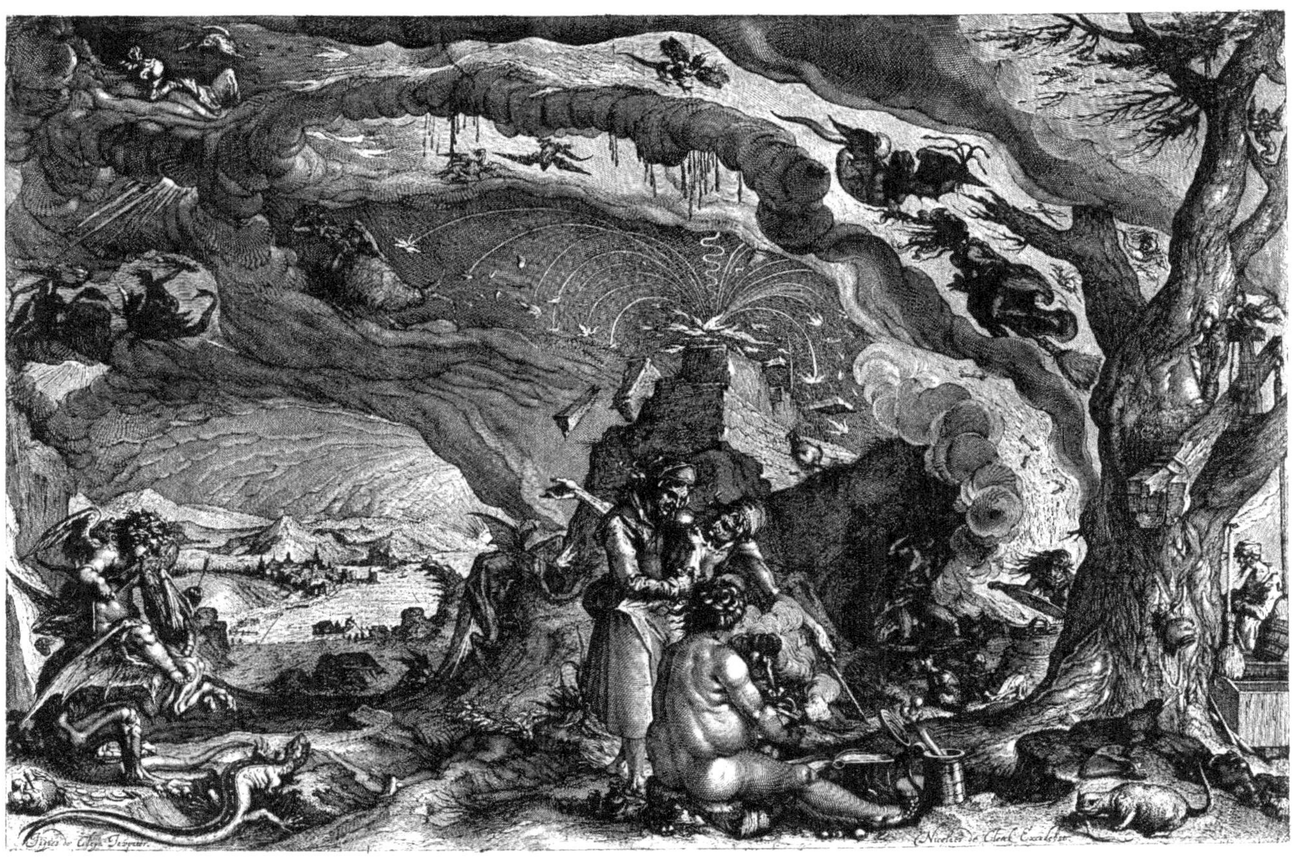

10. Witches Sabbath, Spranger II

11. Witches Preparing for Sabbath Andries Stock
Netherlandish

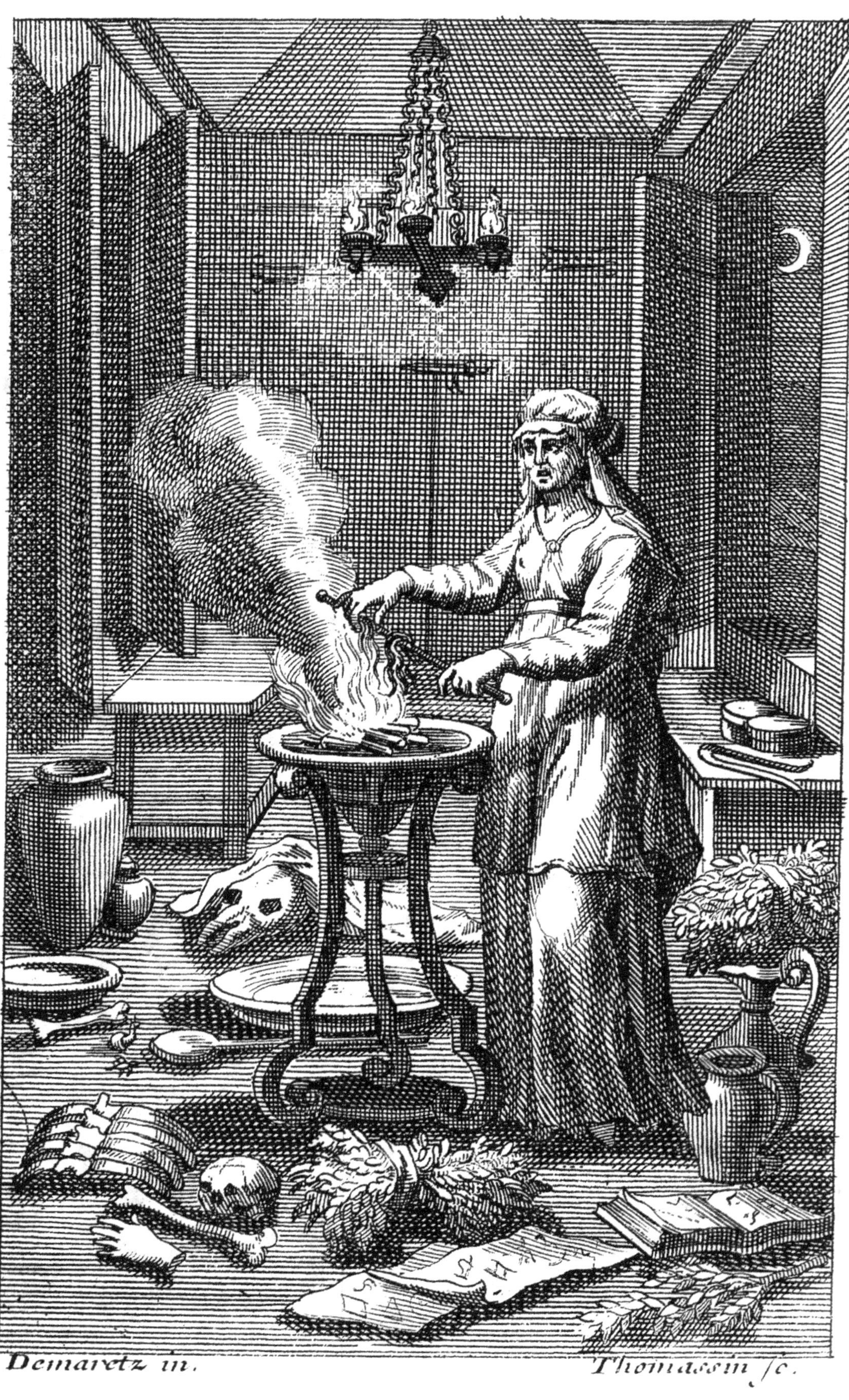

12. A witch casting spells over a steaming
cauldron. Engraving by H.S. Thomassin after
Demaretz.

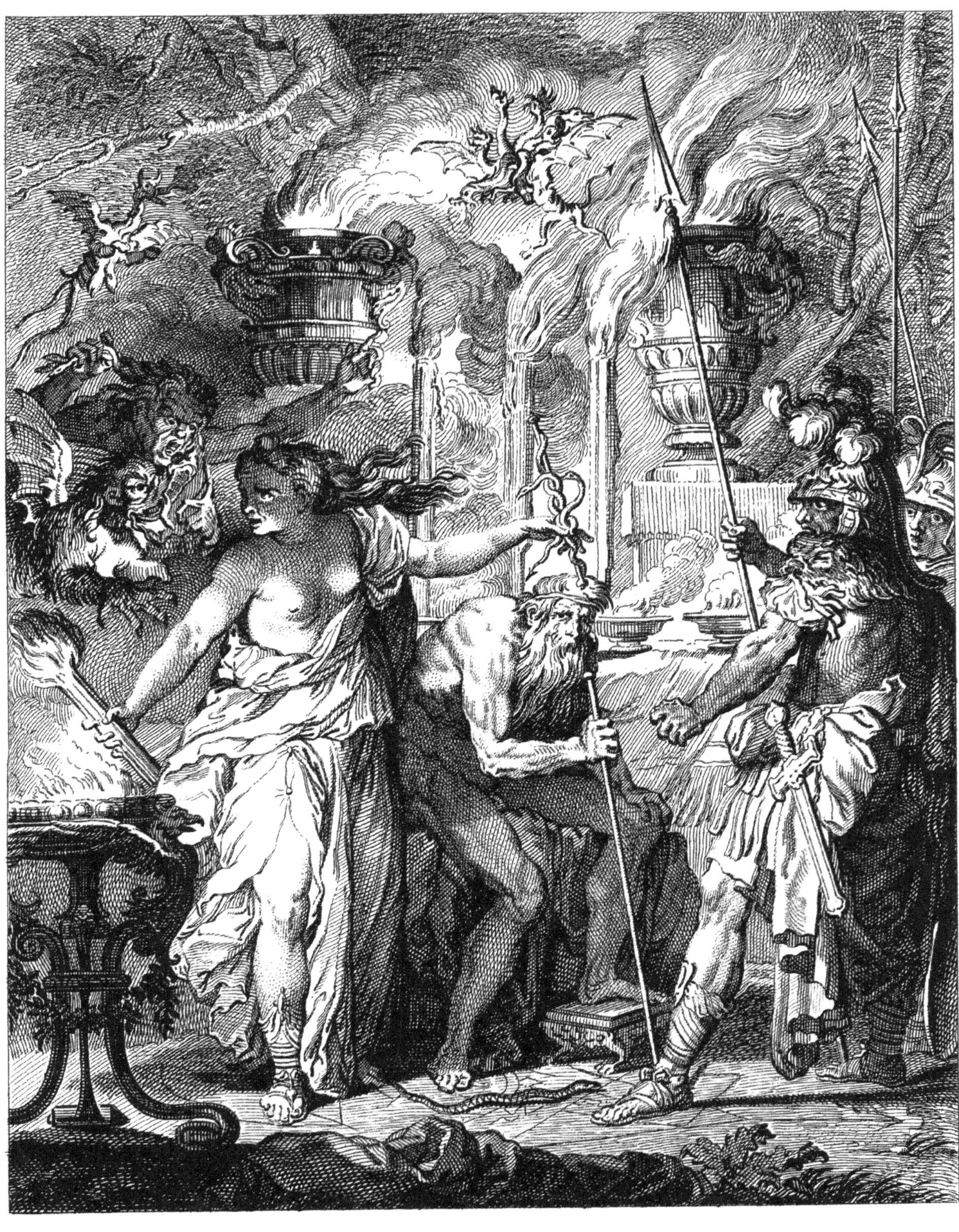

13. Medea the sorceress, Louis Desplaces (on
object), 1692 – 1738

14

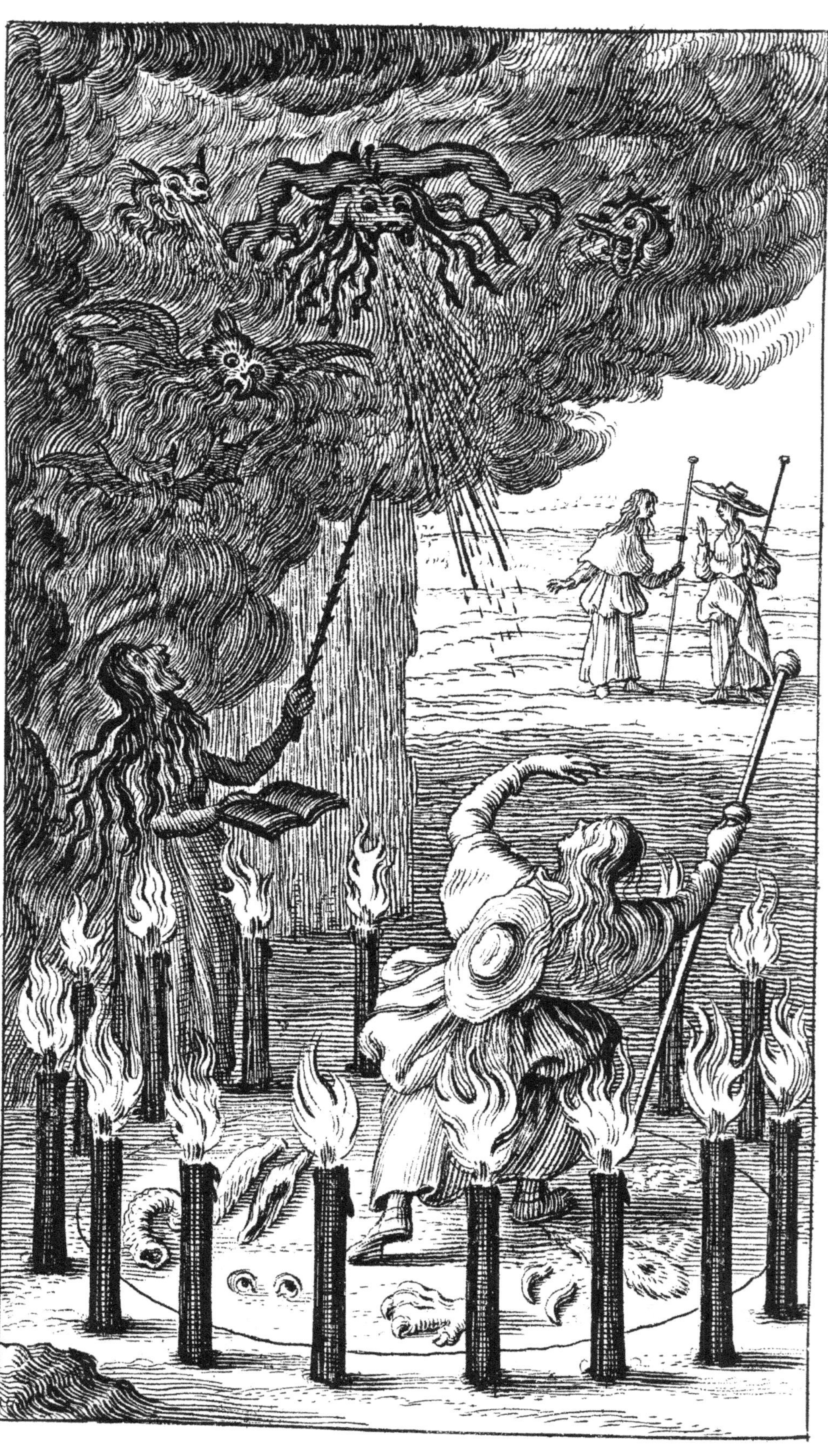

14. Witch conjures demons for Willemynken,
Boetius Adamsz. Bolswert, 1590 – 1627

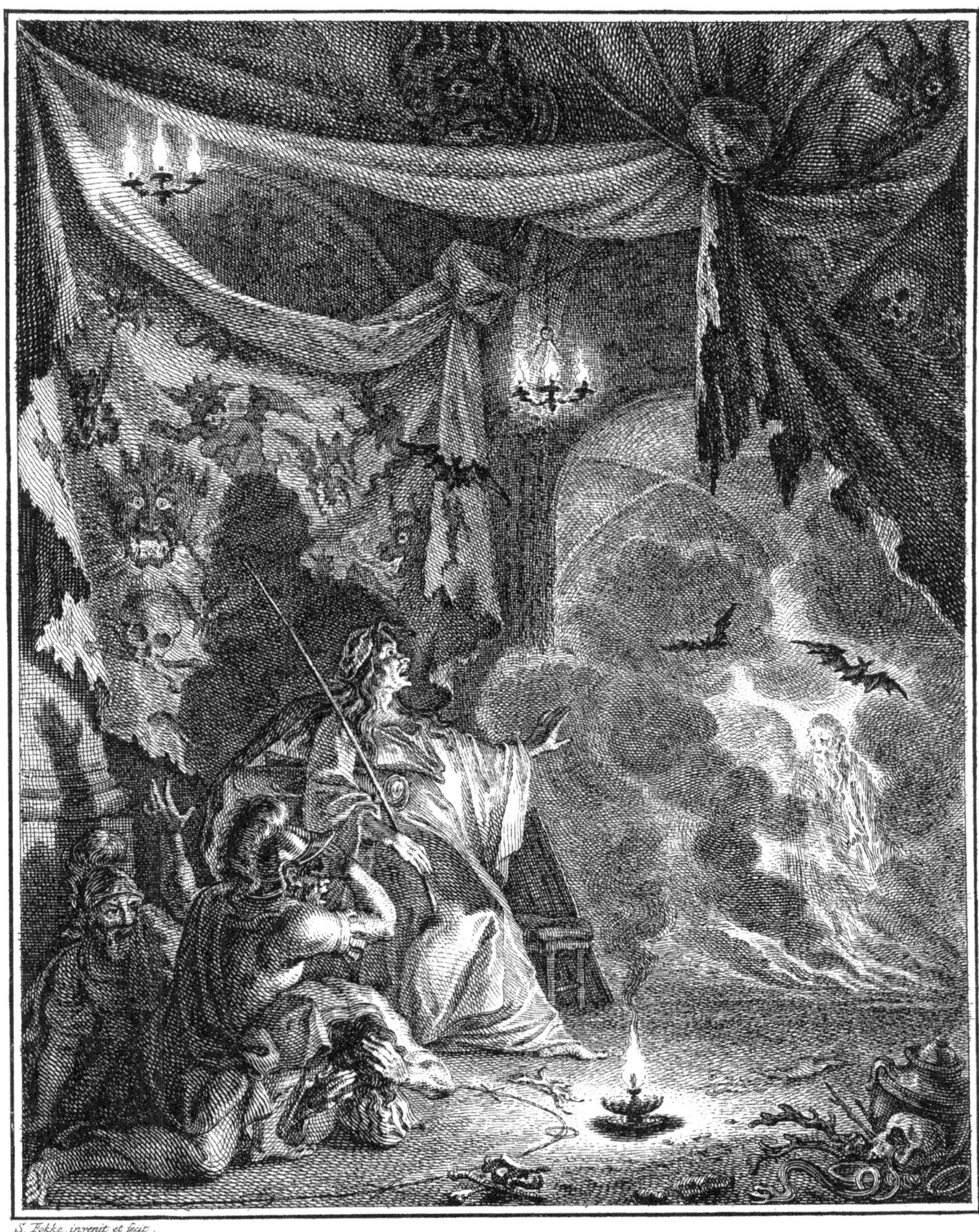

15. Saul by the witch of Endor, Simon Fokke (on object), 1766.

16

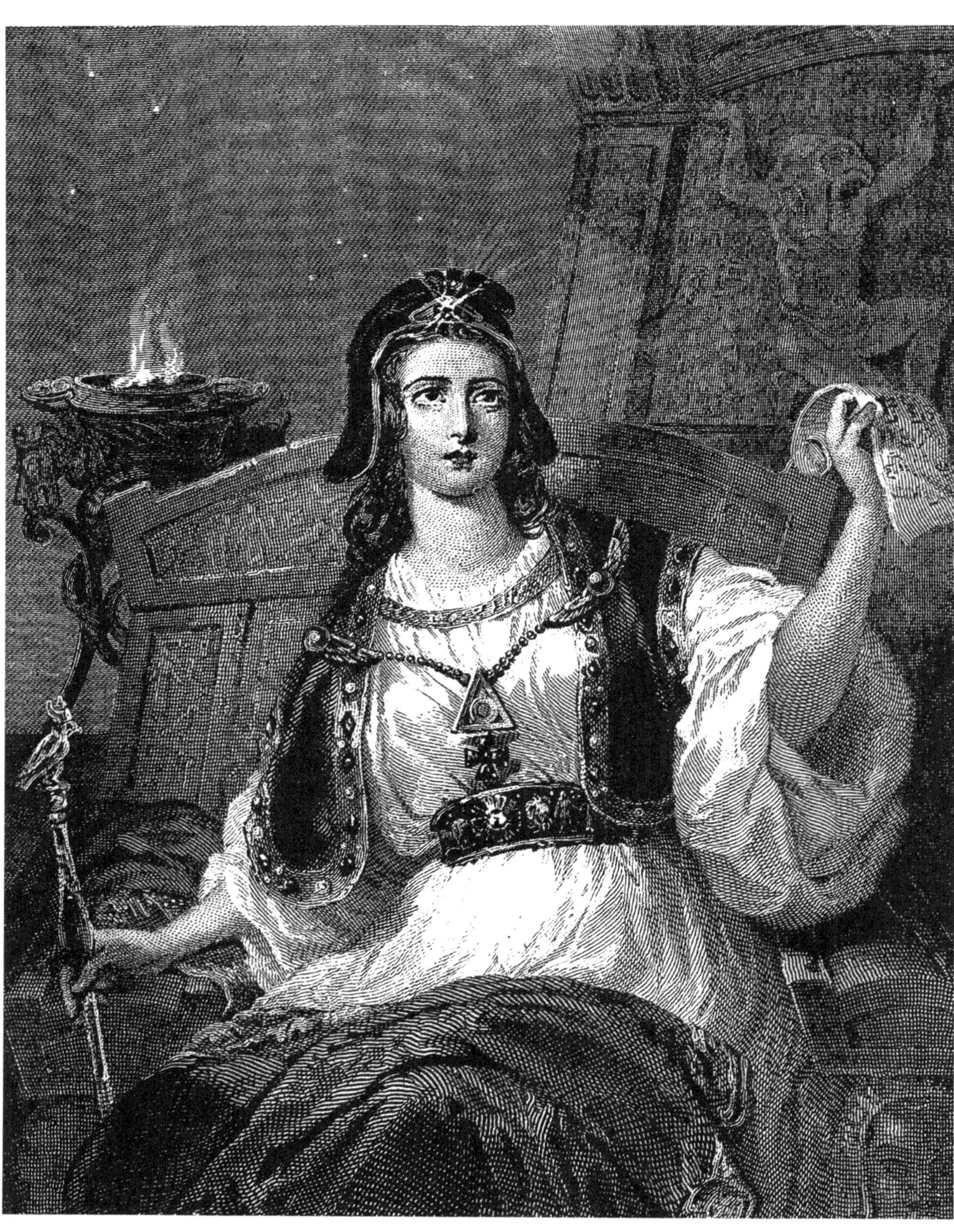

16. A sorceress. Engraving by G.A. Periam, 1837,
after F. Corbaux.   Corbaux, F. (Fanny)(1812–
1883.)1837

17

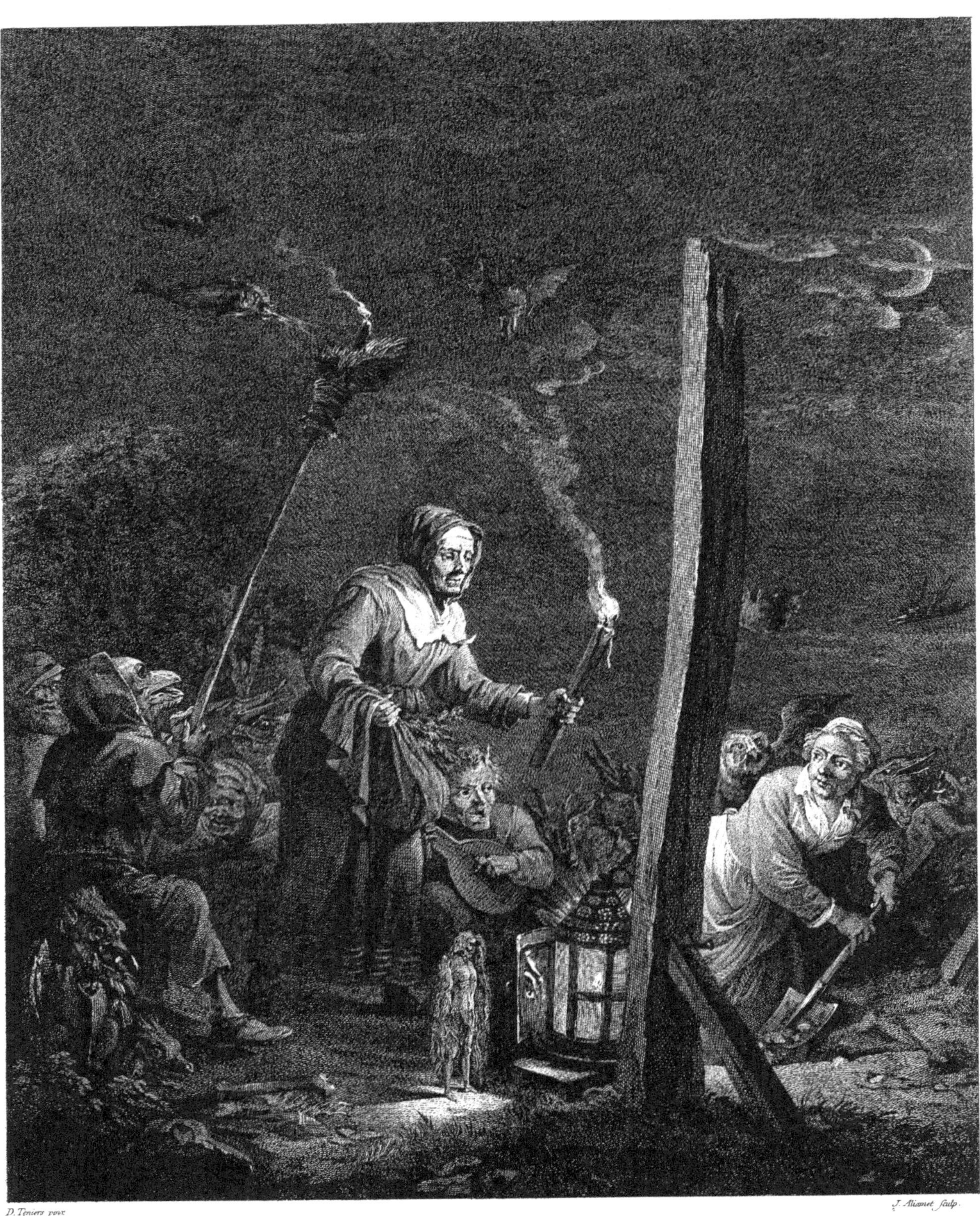

17. Arrival at the witches' sabbath, Jacques
Aliamet (on object), 1755–10

18

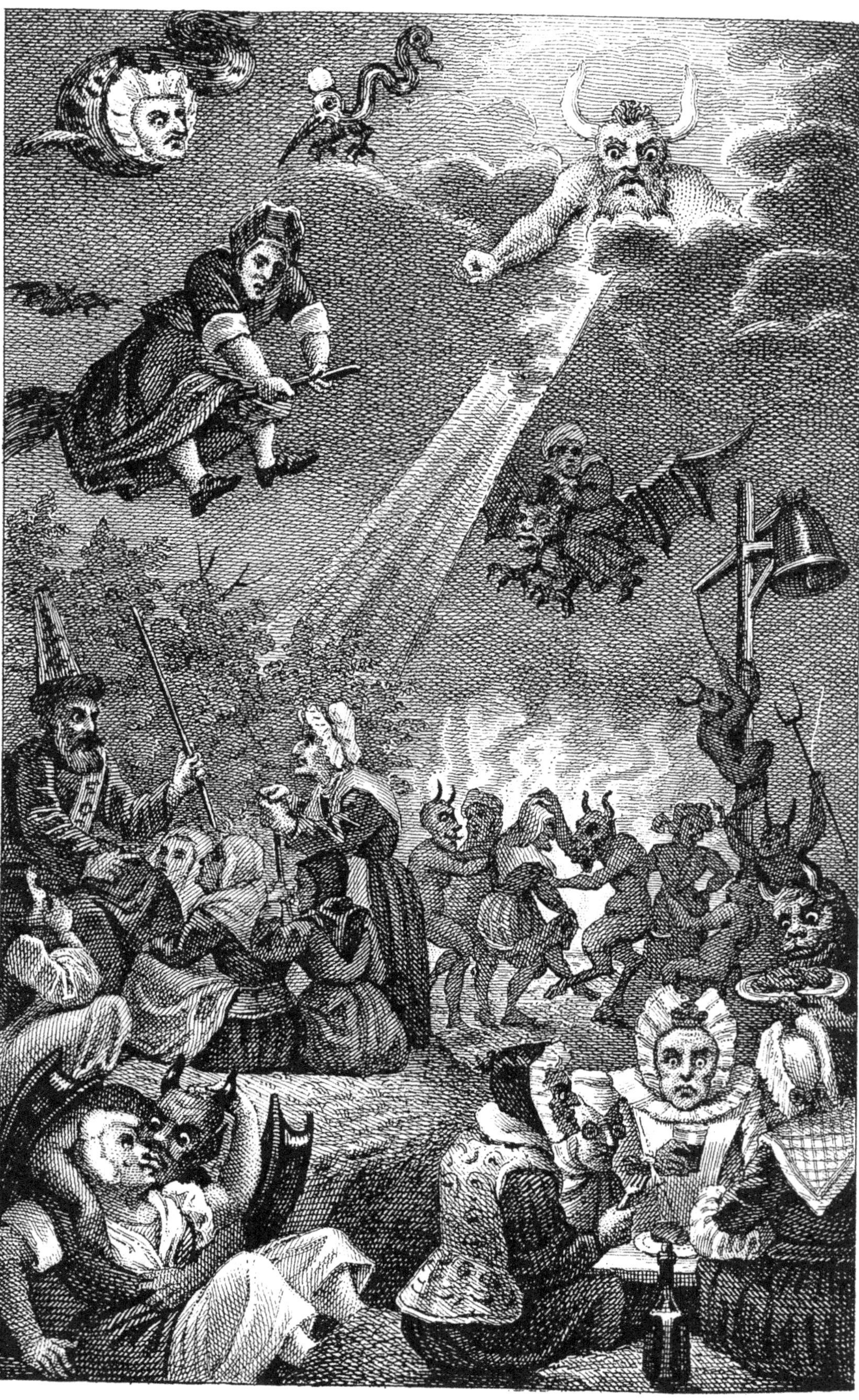

18. Le streghe, frontispiece, 1830

19

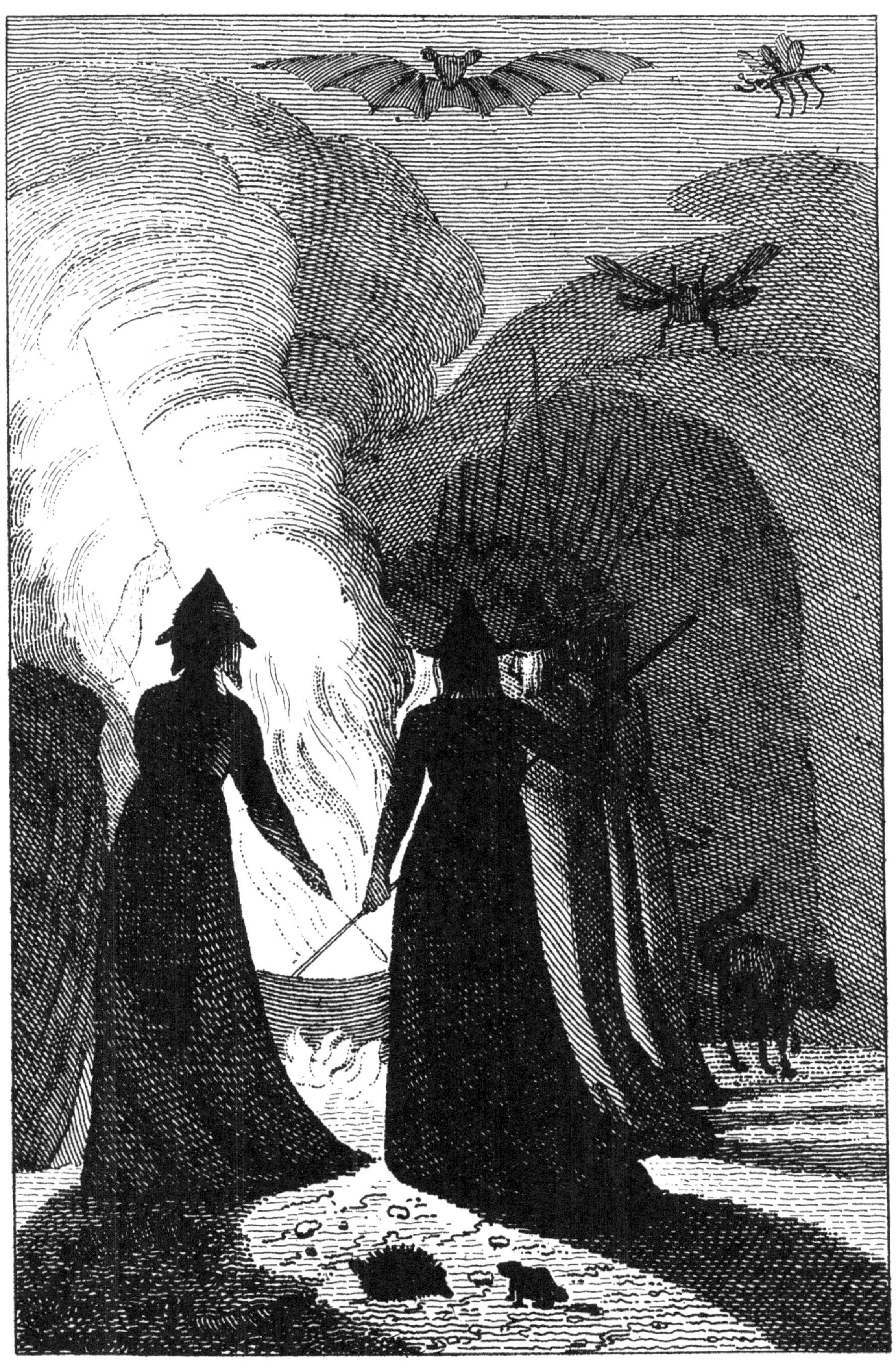

19. The Witches' Cauldron, 1810

20

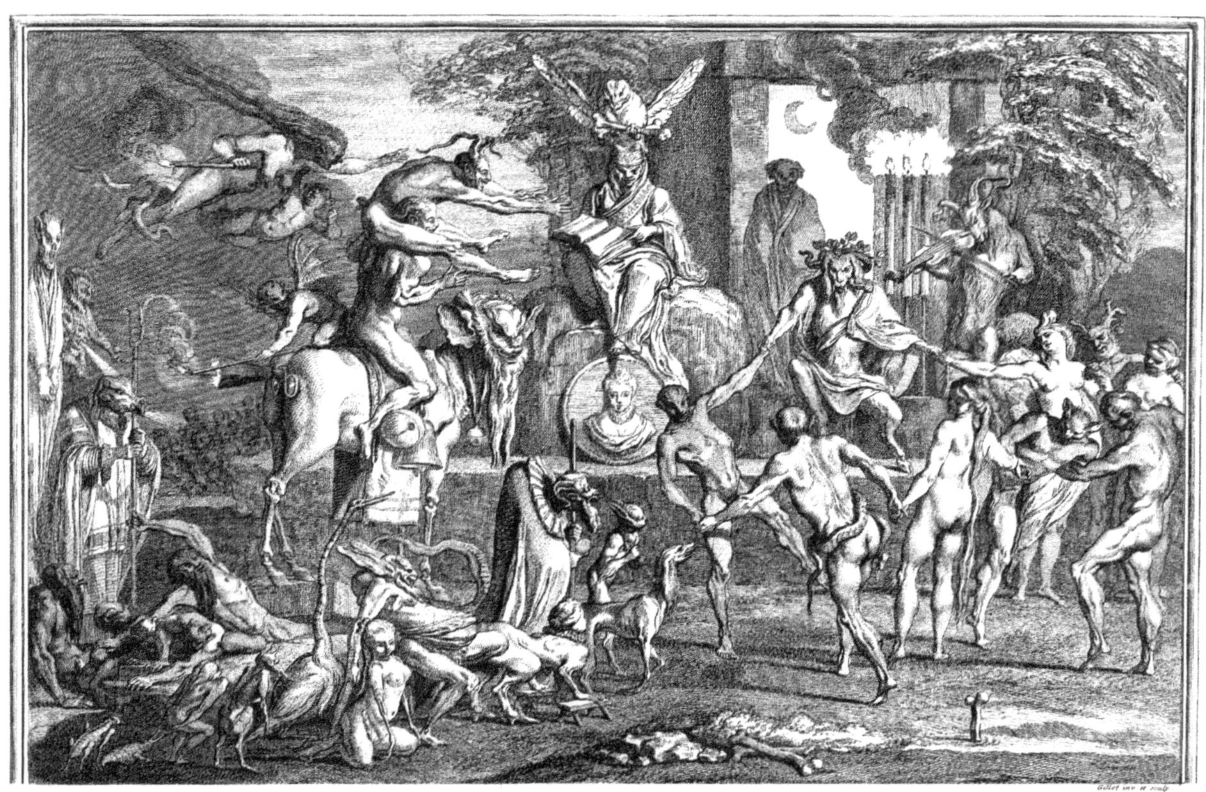

21

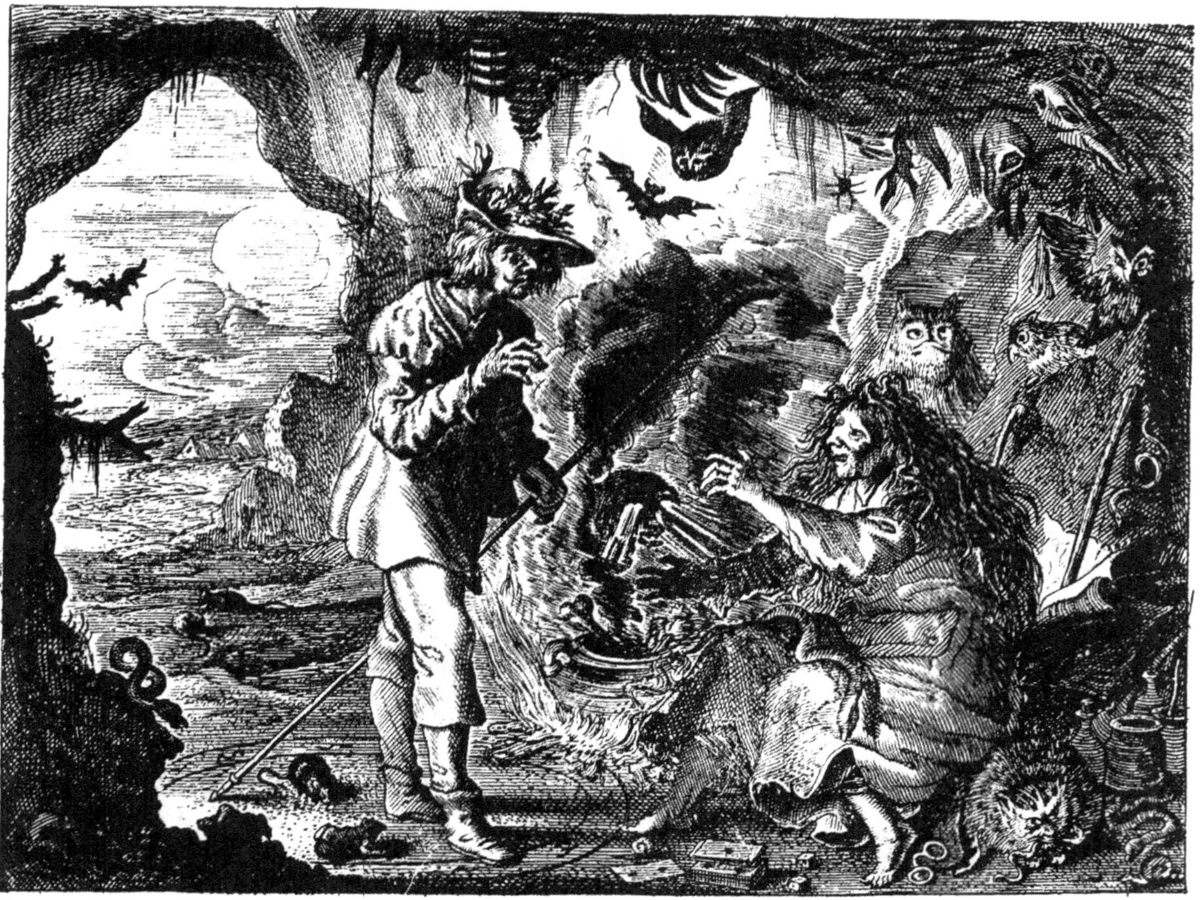

20. Witches' sabbath, Claude Gillot (on object),
1683 – 1722

21. Damon visits the Lodippe witch, after design
by Adriaen Pietersz van de Venne, 1637

22

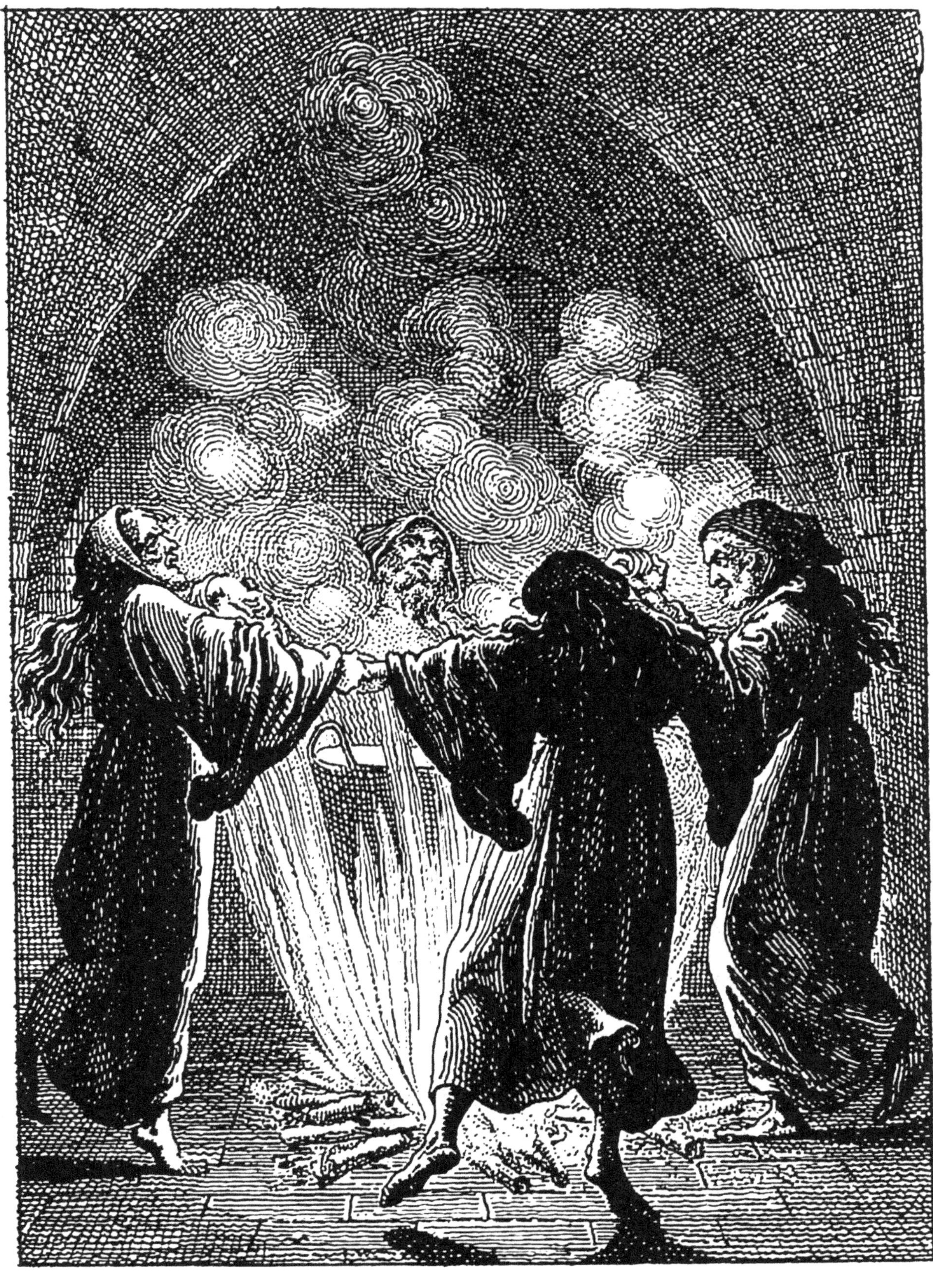

22. Witches dance around the kettle, Daniel
Nikolaus Chodowiecki, 1784

23

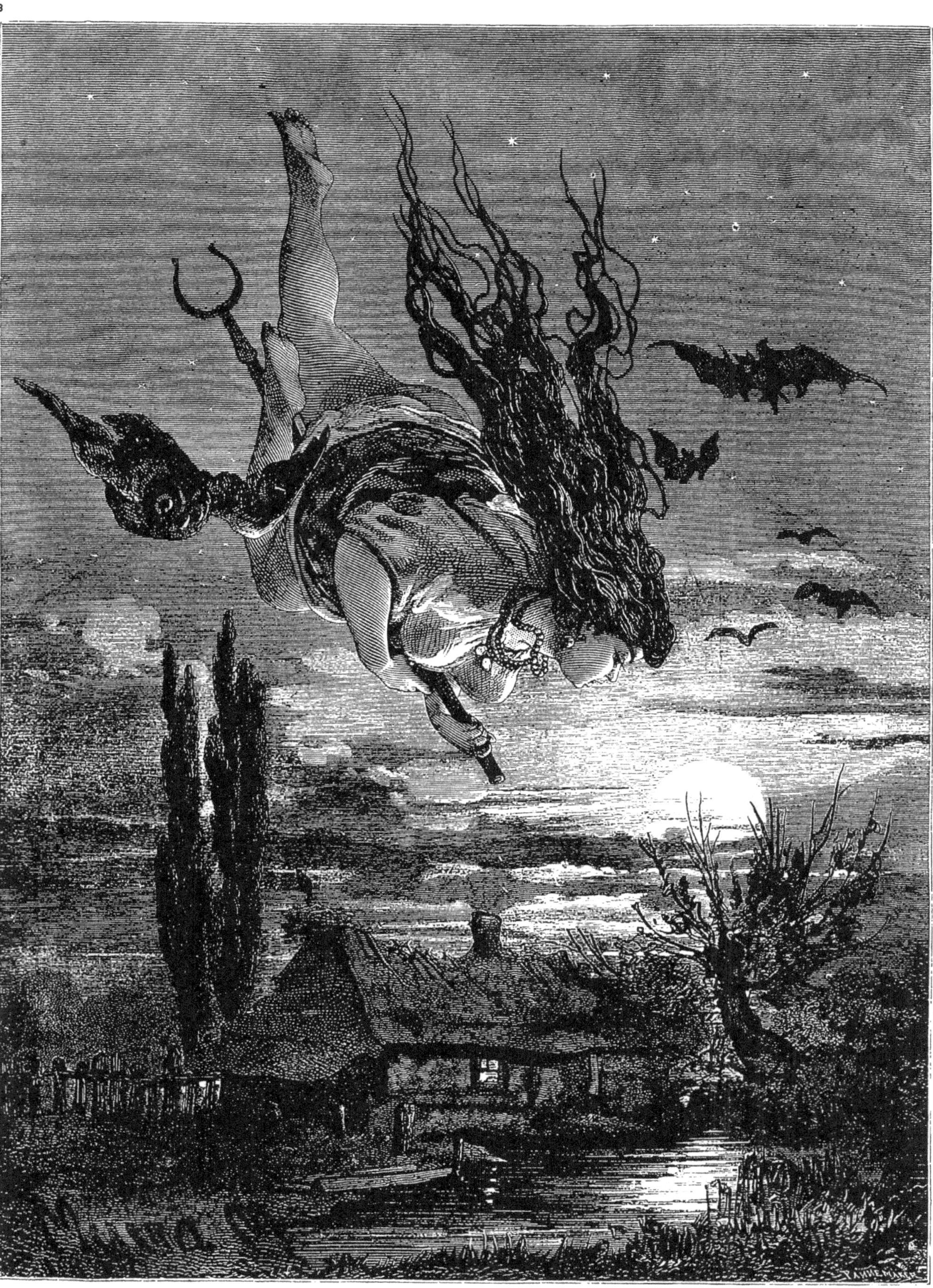

23. Witch, Unknown, 1897

24

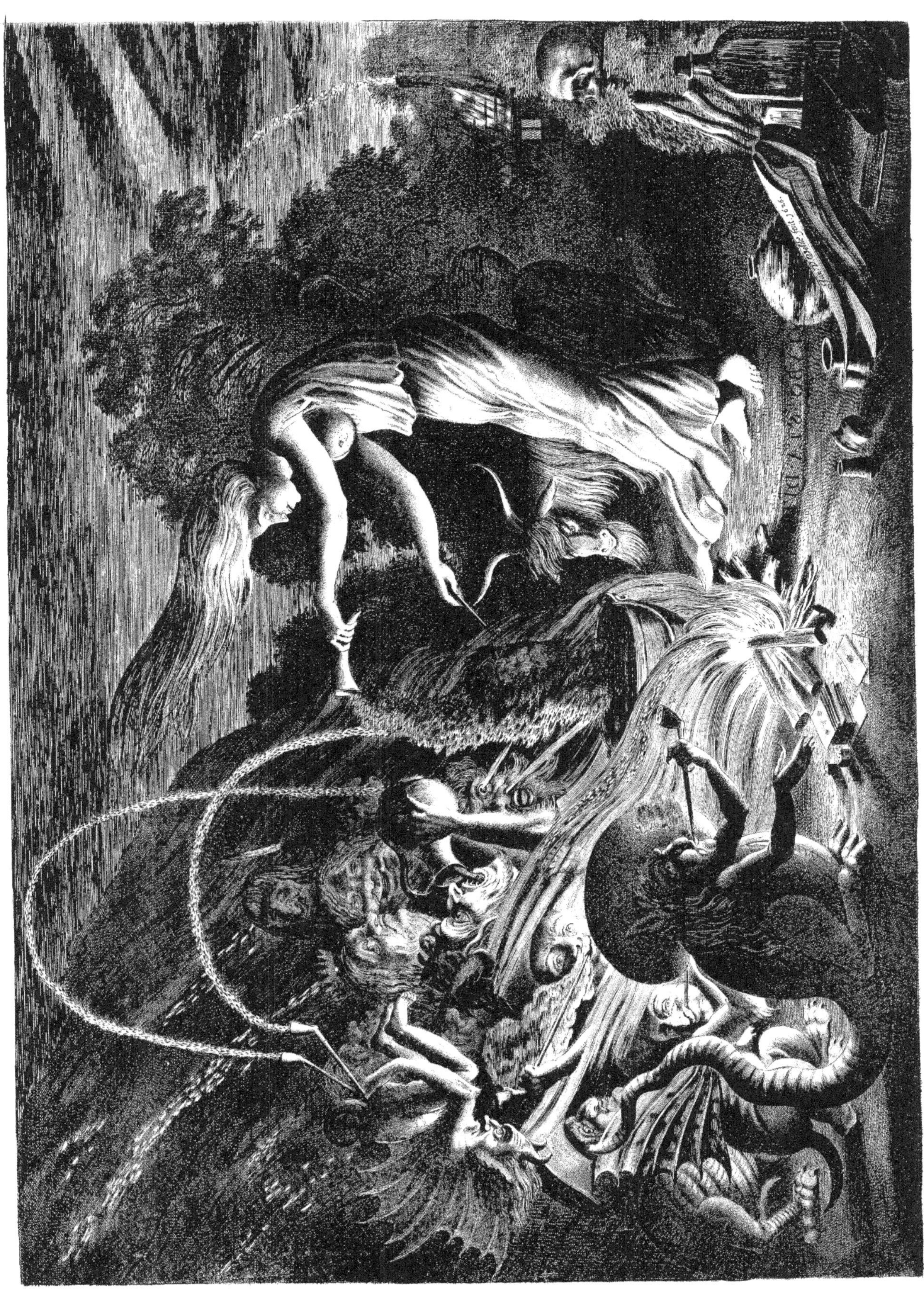

24. Witch Jan van de Velde (II), 1626

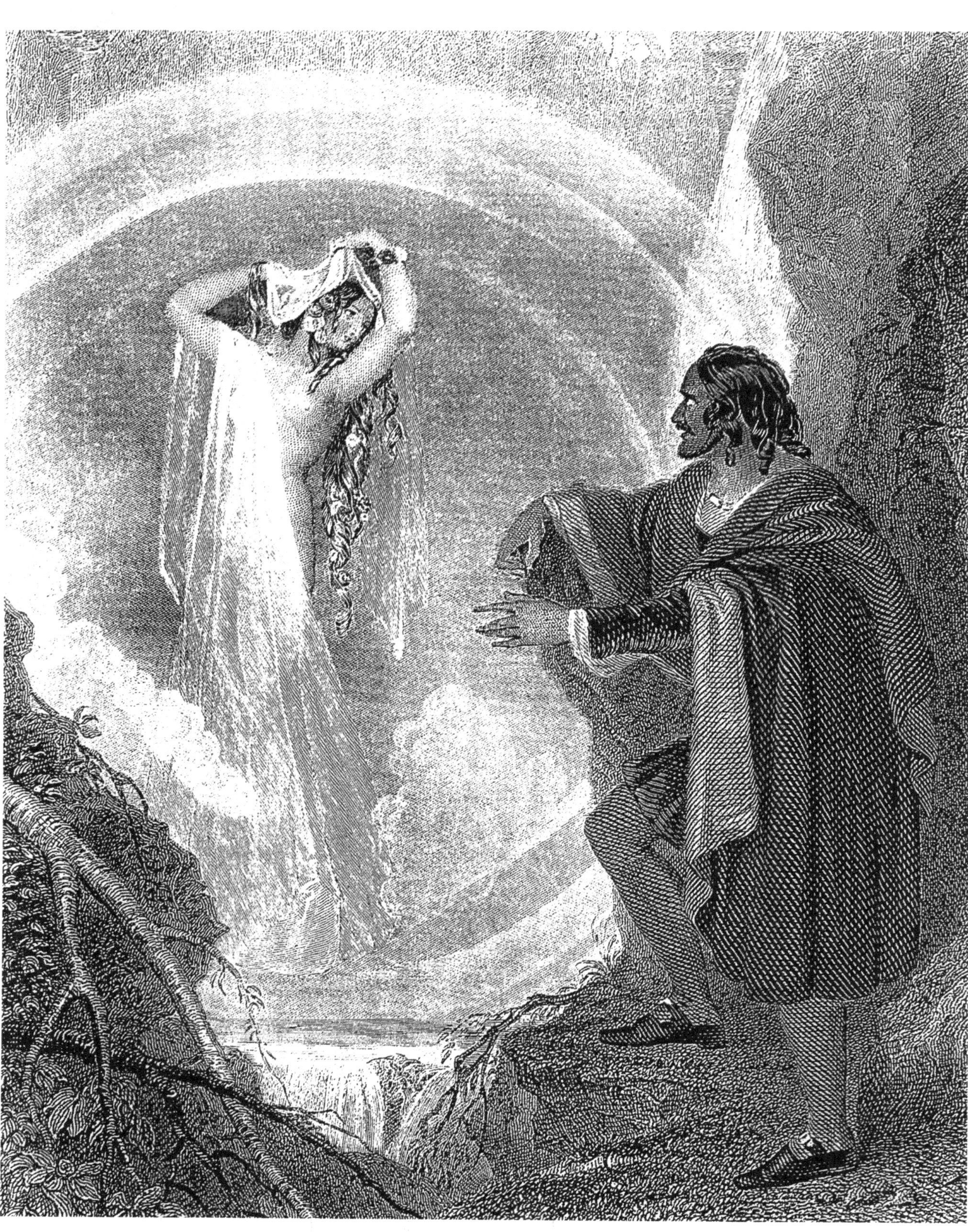

25. A traveller being entranced by a witch
disguised as a beautiful woman in the Alps.
Engraving by T. Stocks after F. Meadows

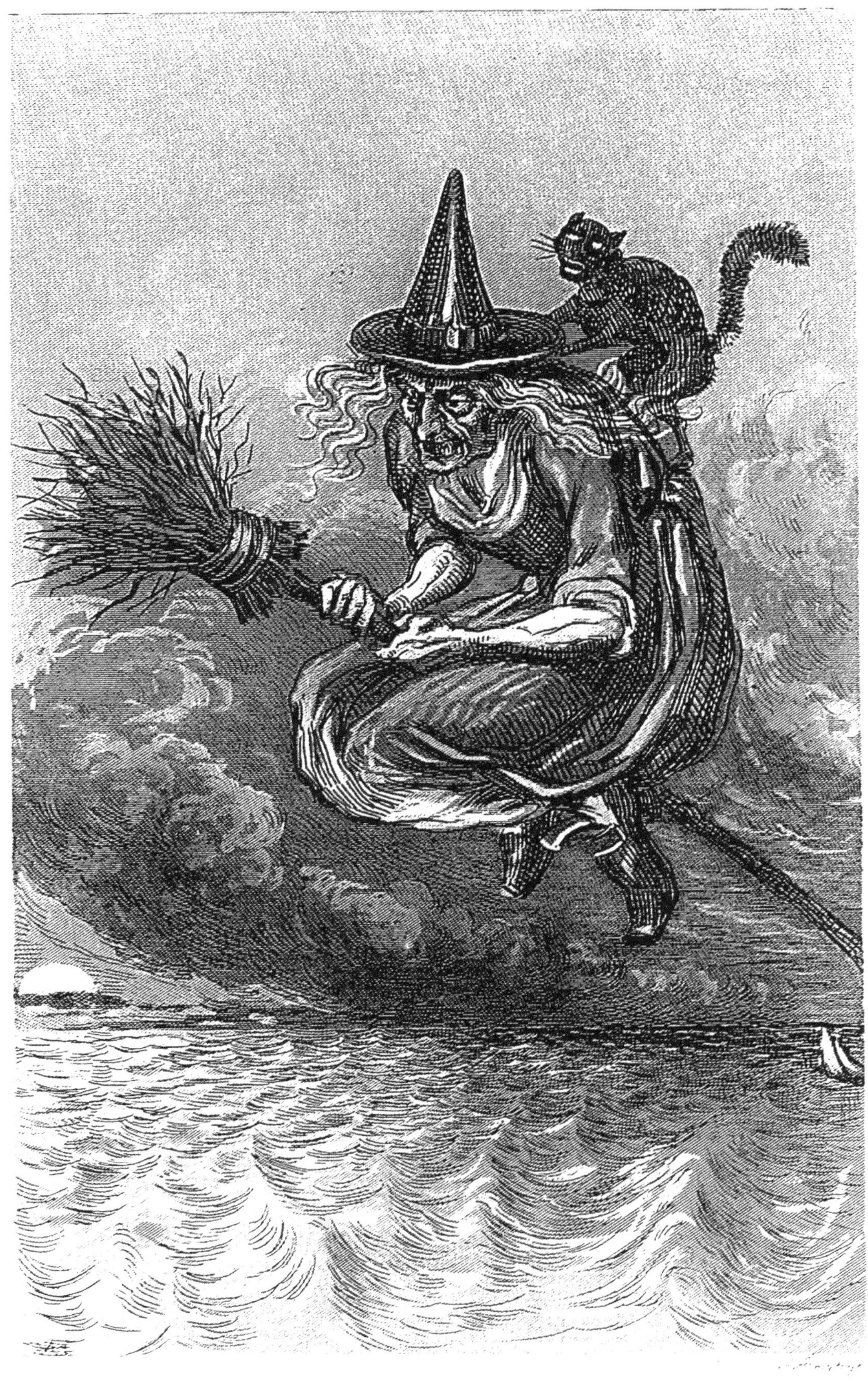

26. Illustration of a witch from Walter Scott's
1830 book, Letters on Demonology and
Witchcraft.

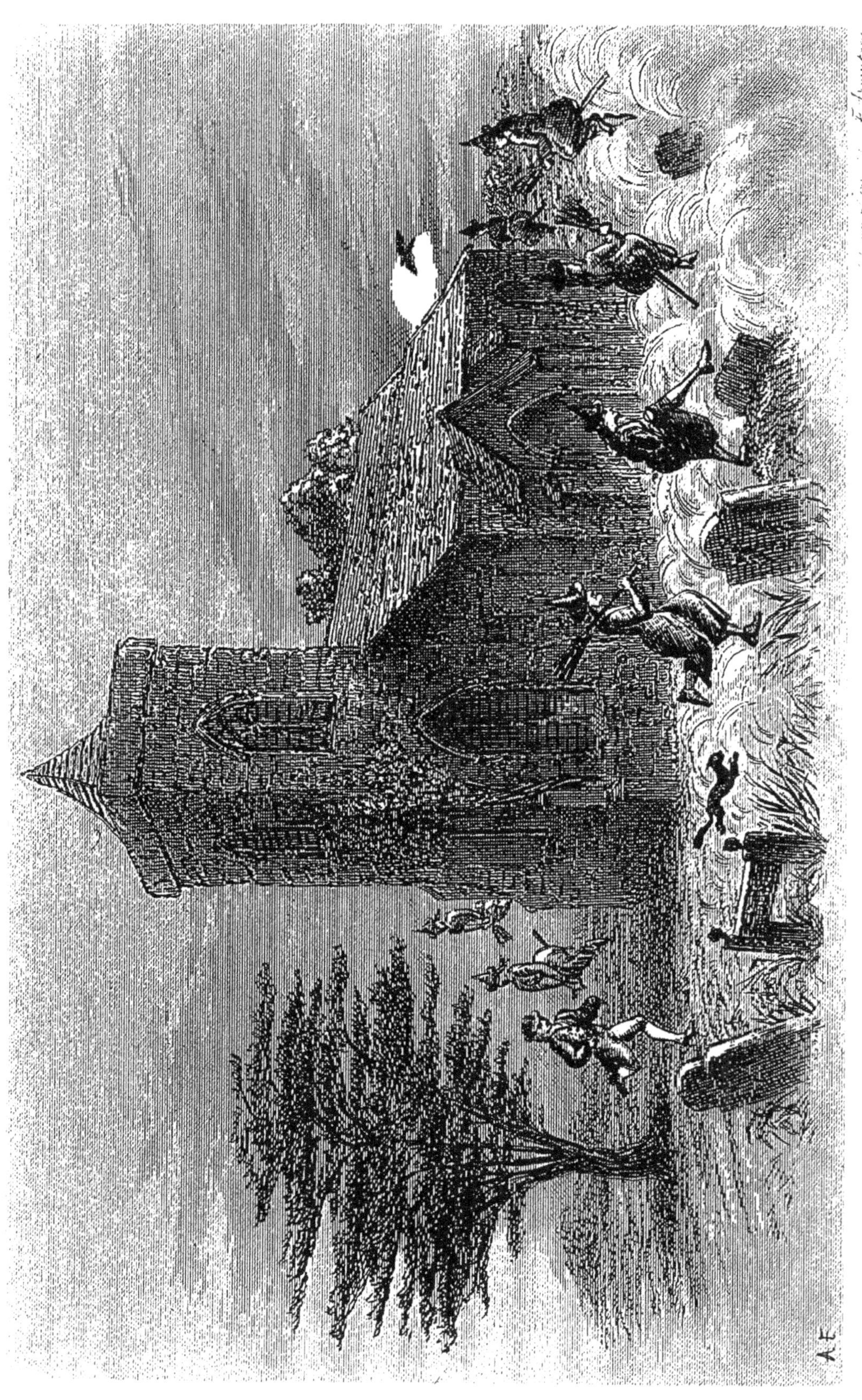

27. Illustration of Witches circling a church from
Walter Scott's 1830 book, Letters on Demonology
and Witchcraft.

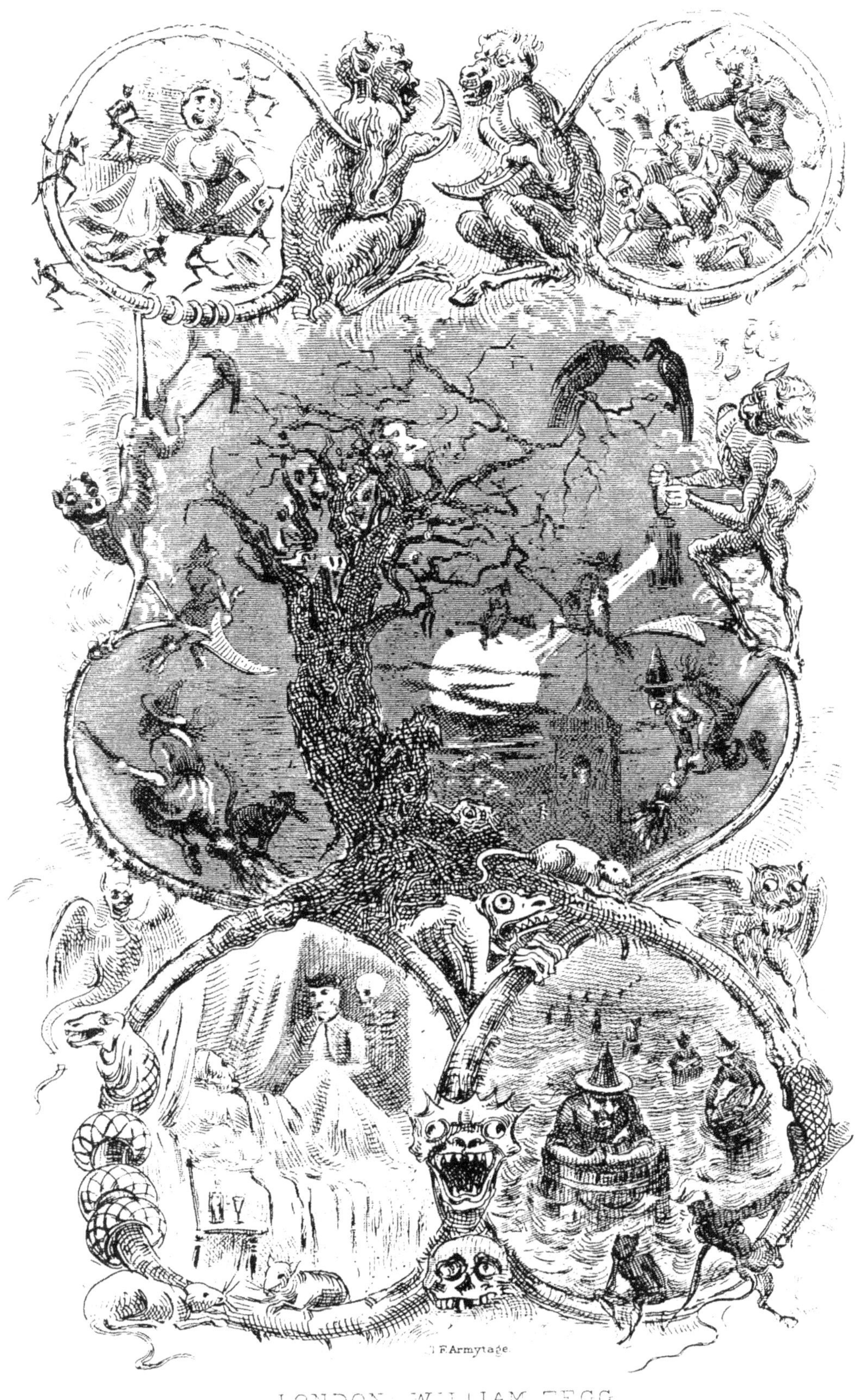

28. Illustration from Walter Scott's 1830 book,
Letters on Demonology and Witchcraft.

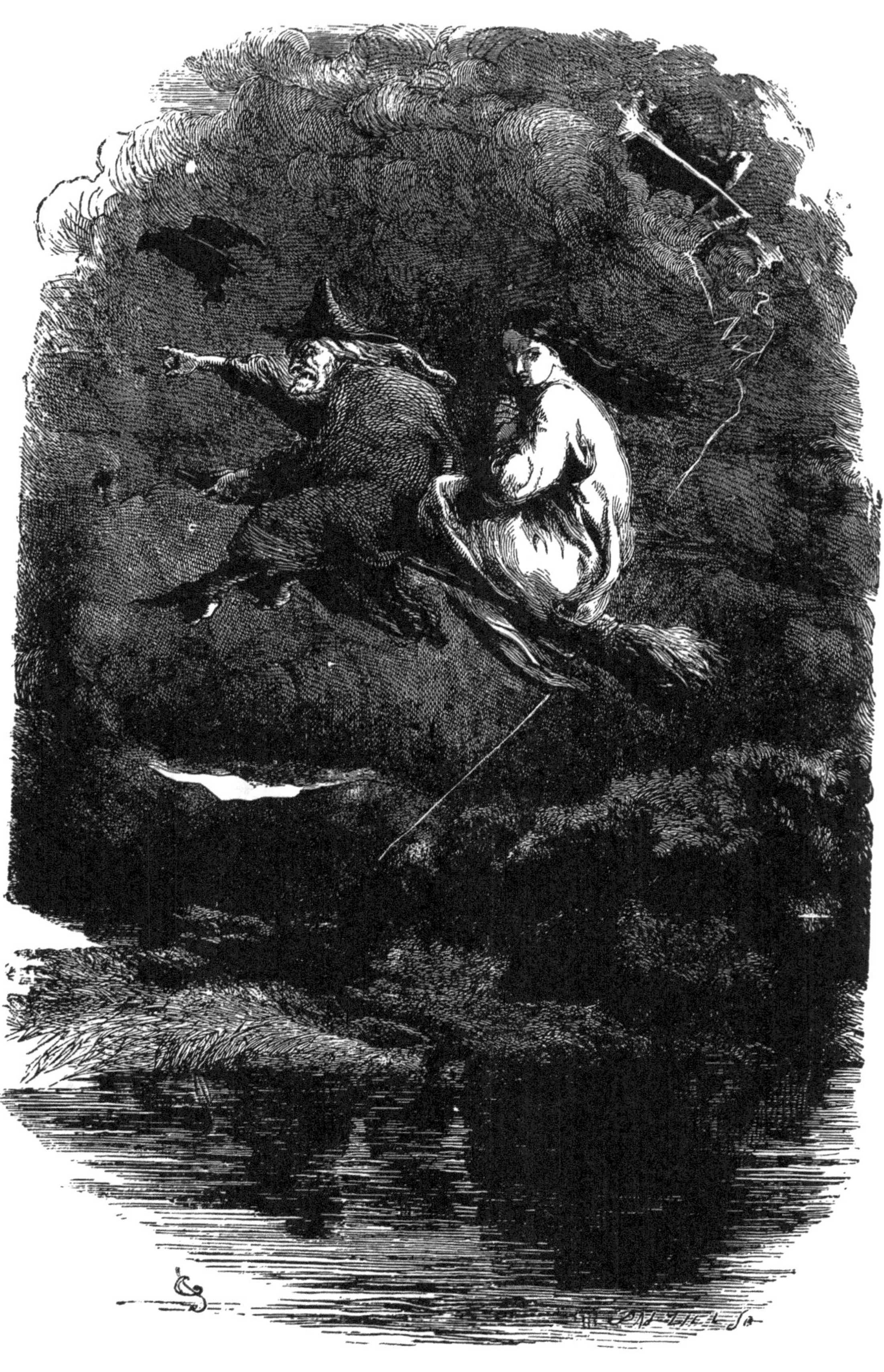

29. Witches 4 'The Ride Though The Murky Air,
The Lancashire Witches, A Romance of Pendle
Forest by W.H Ainsworth, J. Gilbert, 1897

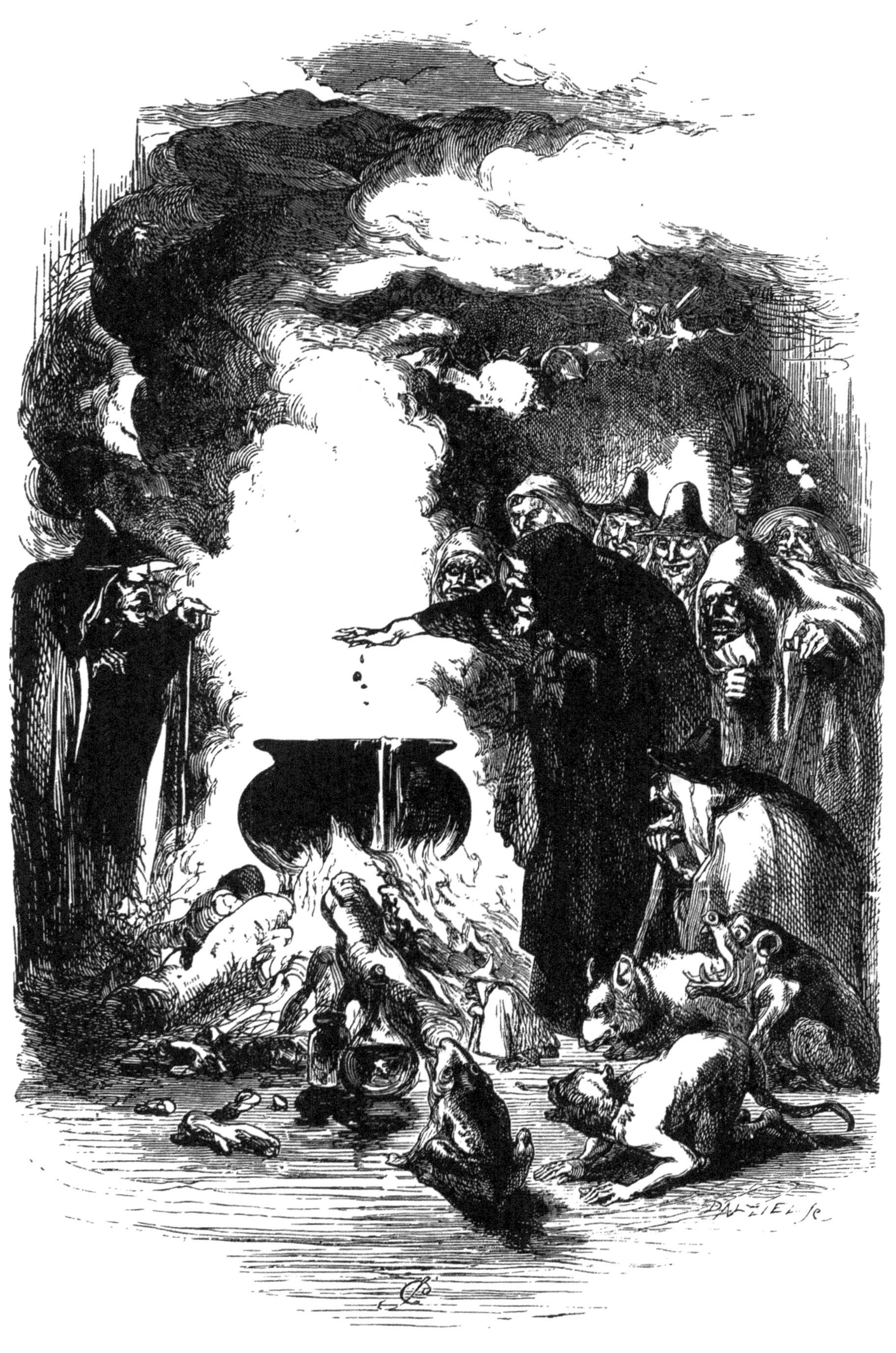

30. Witches 4 'The Incantation', The Lancashire
Witches, A Romance of Pendle Forest by W.H
Ainsworth, J. Gilbert, illustrator, 1897

31

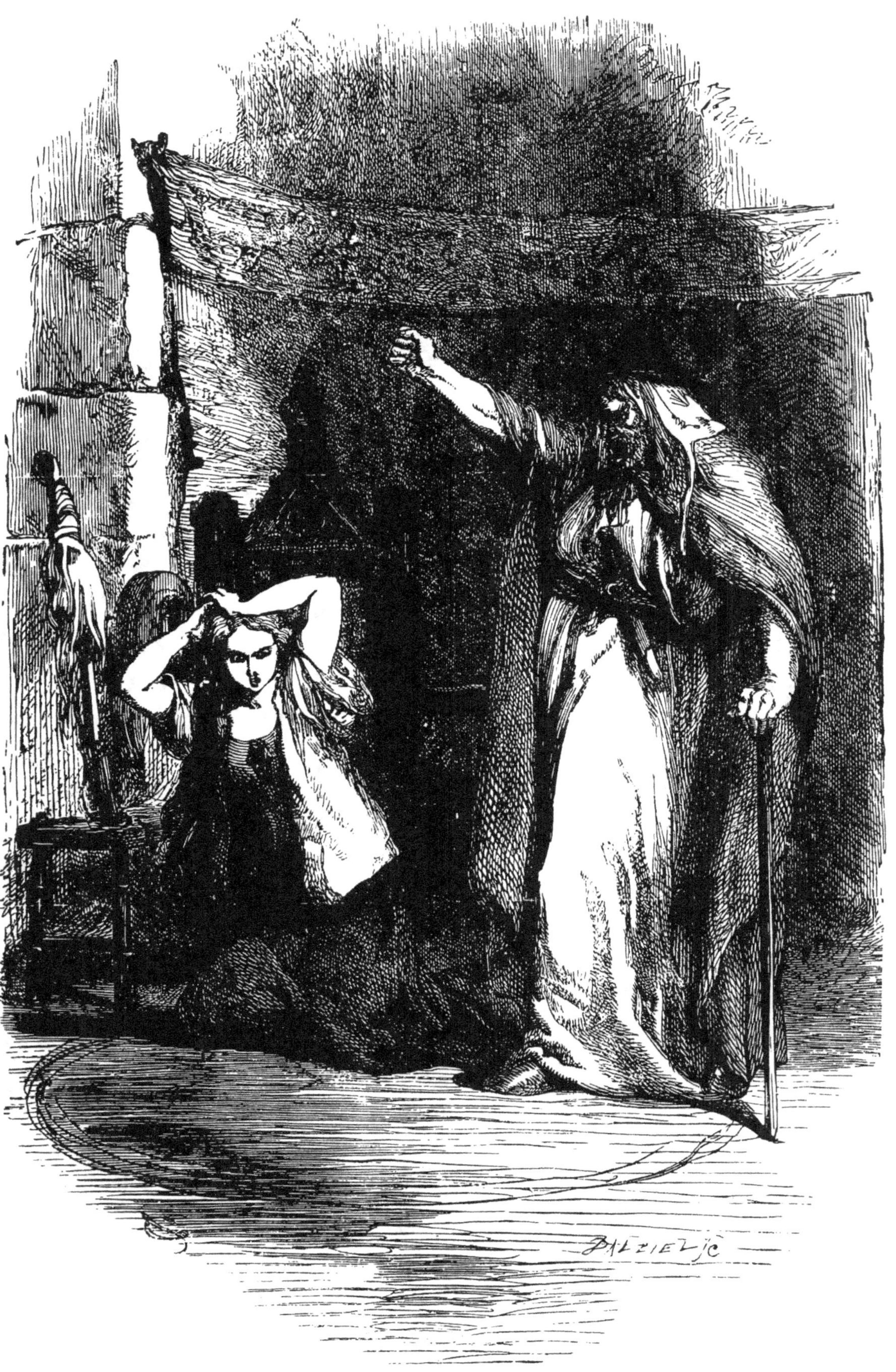

31. Witches 3, The Lancashire Witches, A
Romance of Pendle Forest by W.H Ainsworth, J.
Gilbert, illustrator, 1897

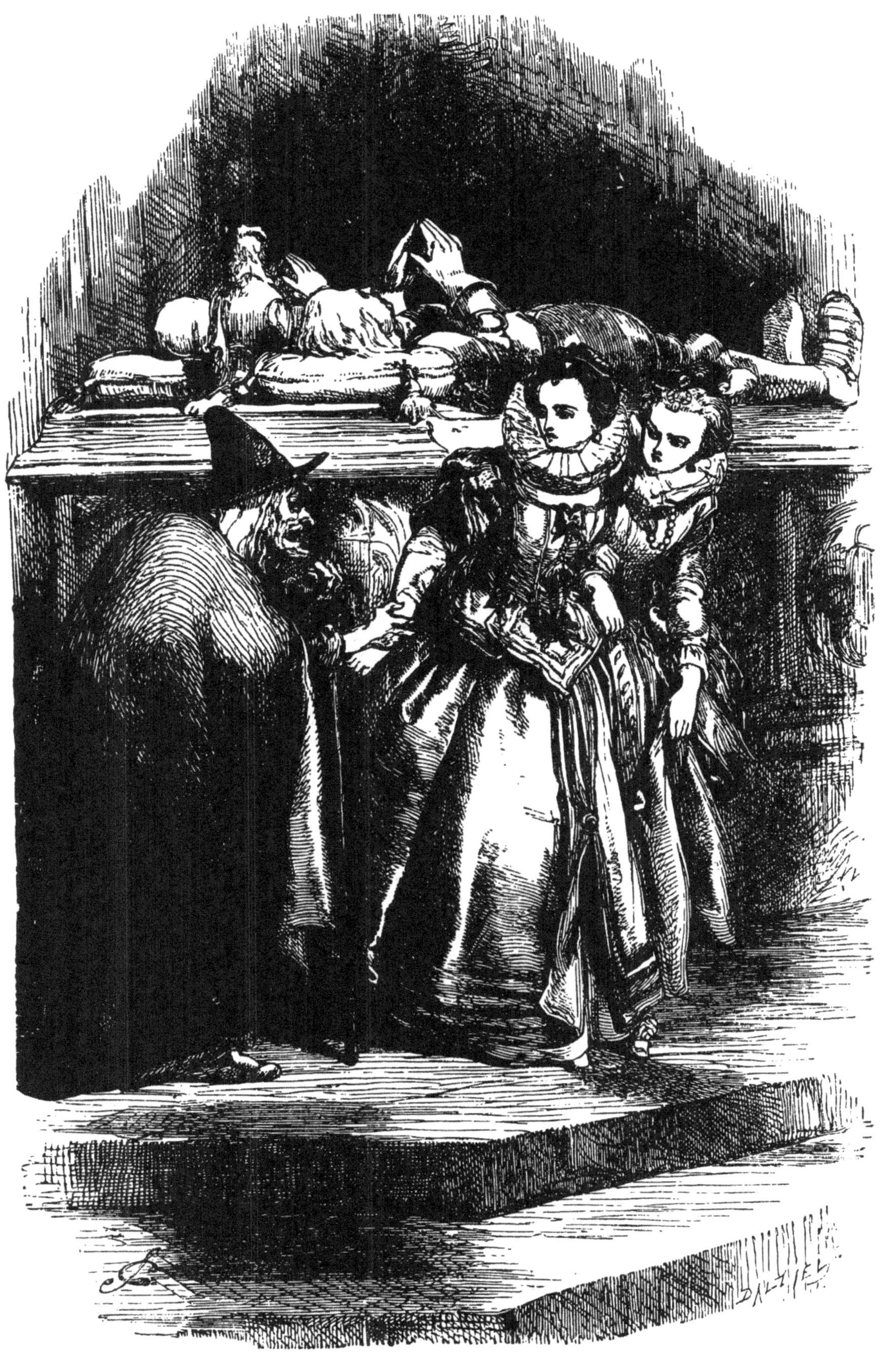

32. Witches 1, The Lancashire Witches, A
Romance of Pendle Forest by W.H Ainsworth, J.
Gilbert, Illustrator, 1897

33

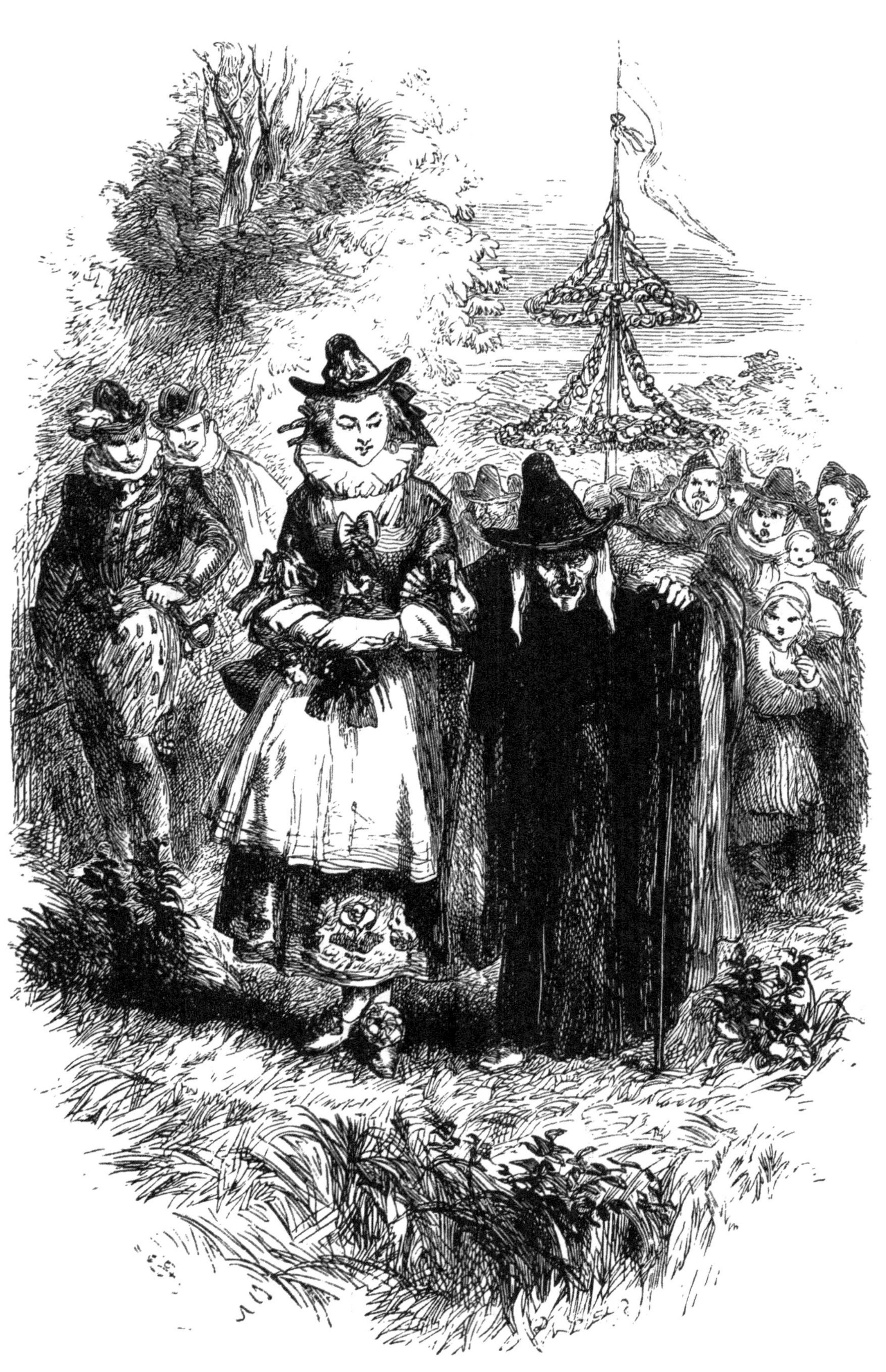

33. Witches, The Lancashire Witches, A Romance
of Pendle Forest by W.H Ainsworth, J. Gilbert,
illustrator, 1897

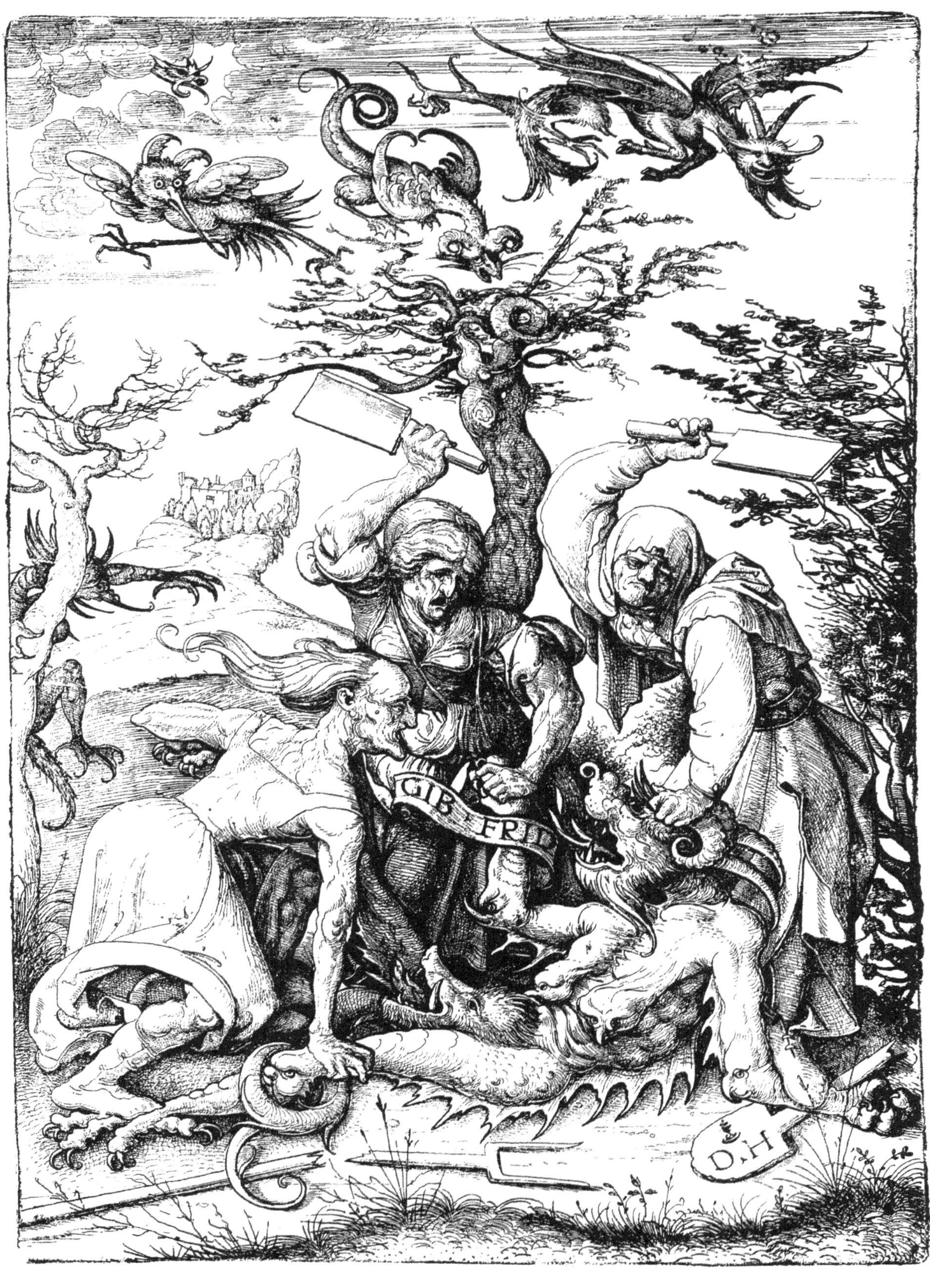

34. Three witches attack the devil, Daniel Hopfer
(I) (on object), 1505 – 1536

35

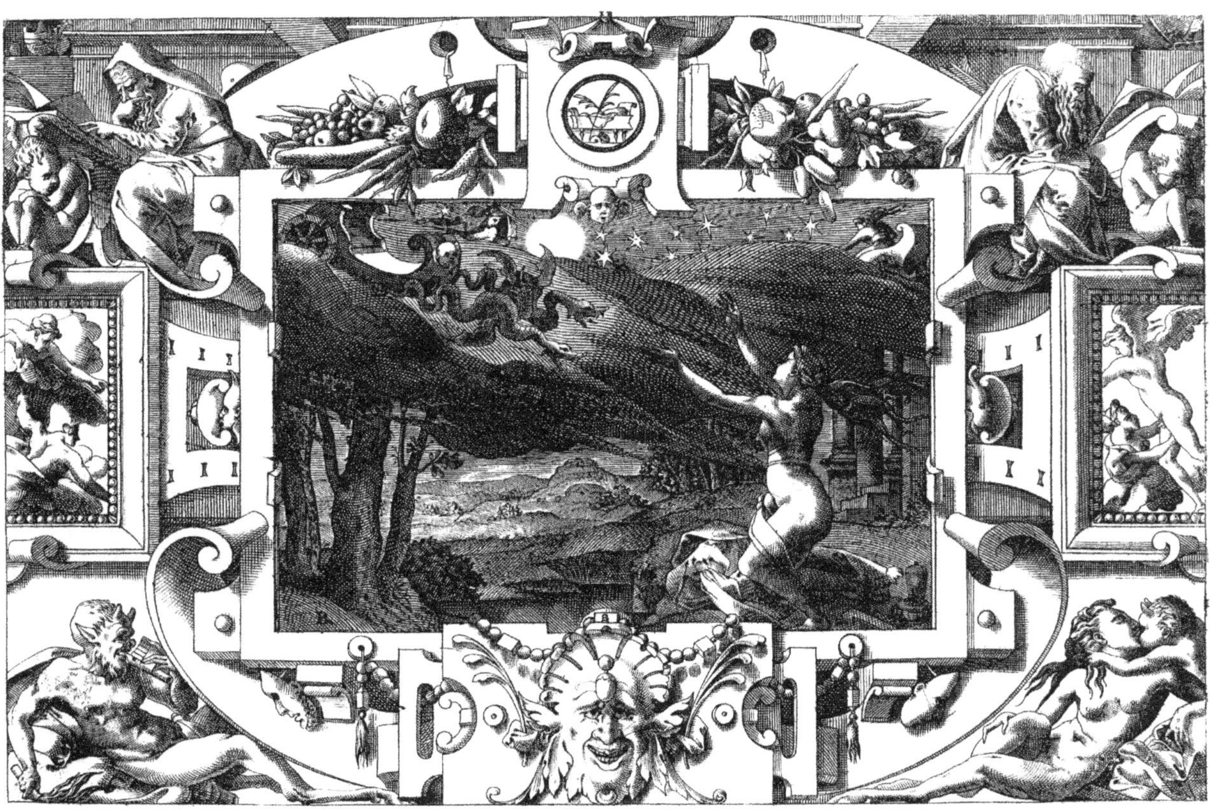

36

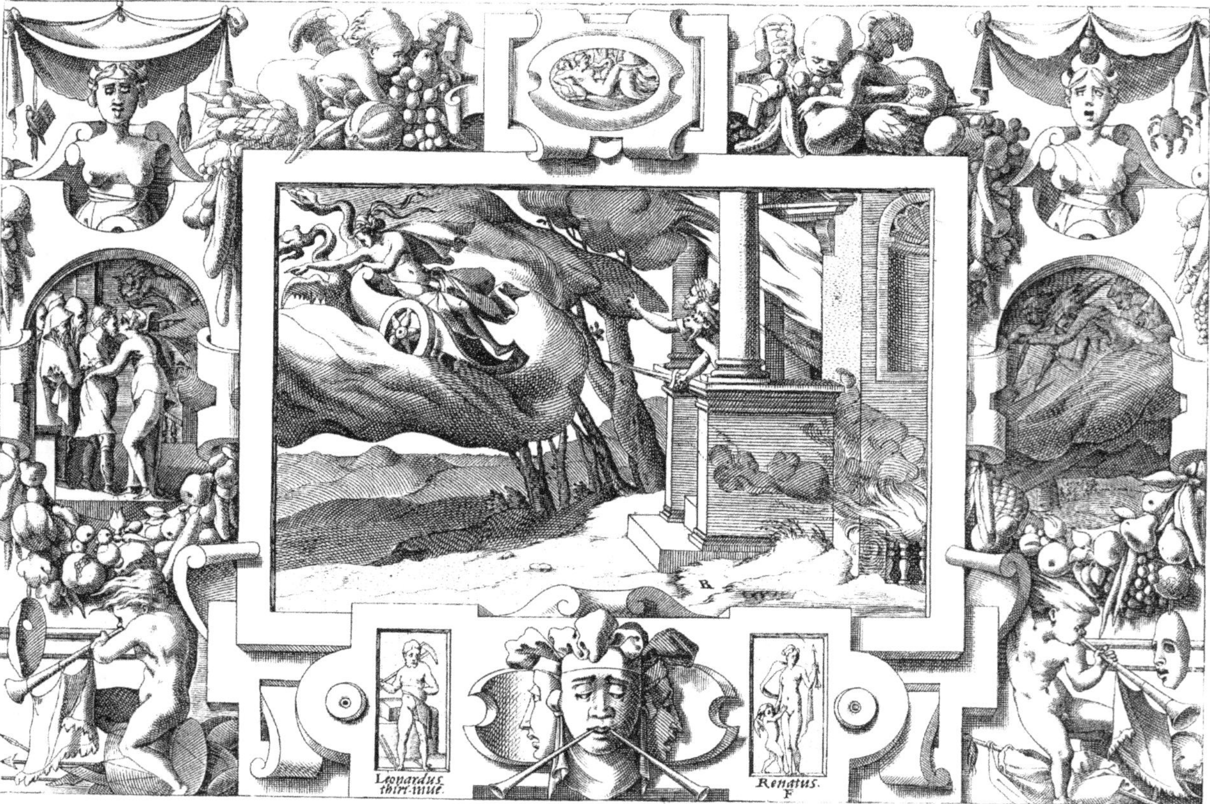

35. Medea calls on the gods and sees her chariot coming to her, René Boyvin 1563

36. Medea flees in a car pulled by dragons, René Boyvin (on object), 1563, The whole is framed by an ornamental list of putti and guirlandes.

37

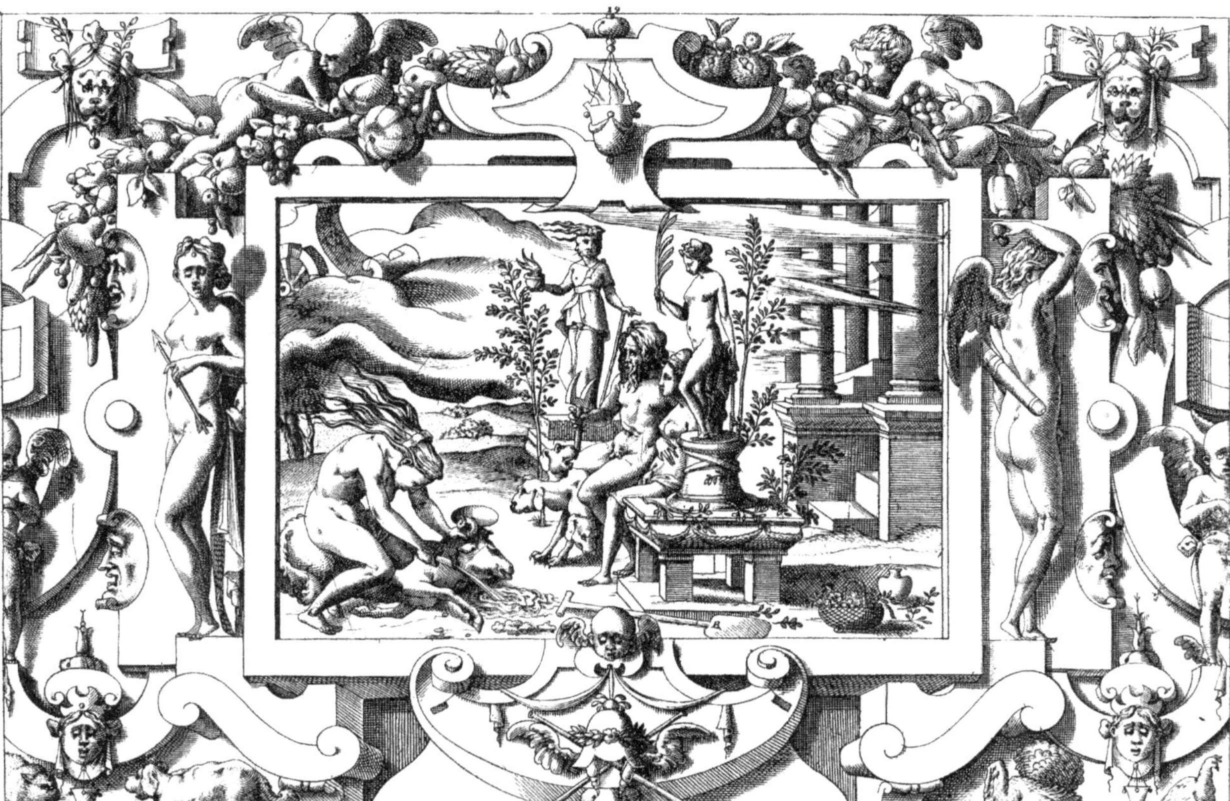

38

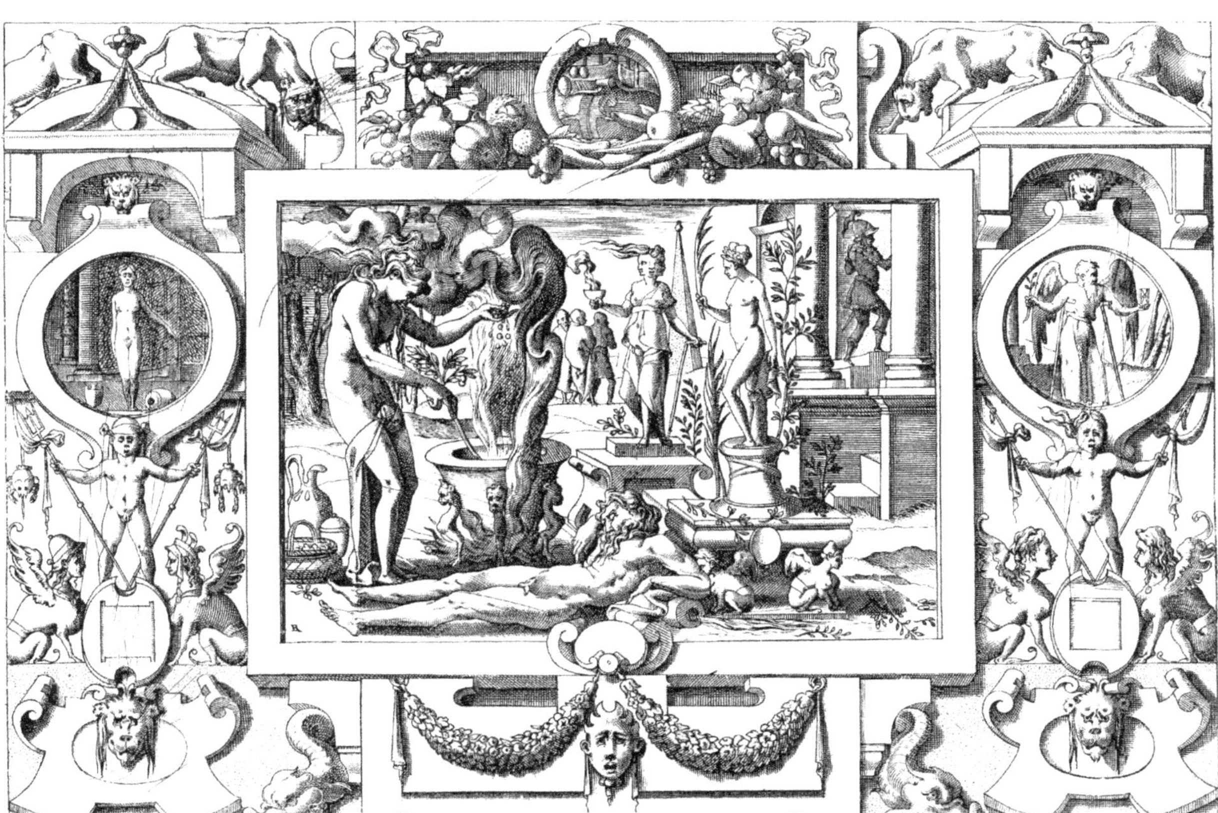

37. Medea sacrifices a ram for the altar of
Hecate and Hebe in front of Proserpina and
Pluto, René Boyvin (on object), 1563

38. Medea cooks magic herbs in a kettle for
Aeson, René Boyvin (on object), 1563

39

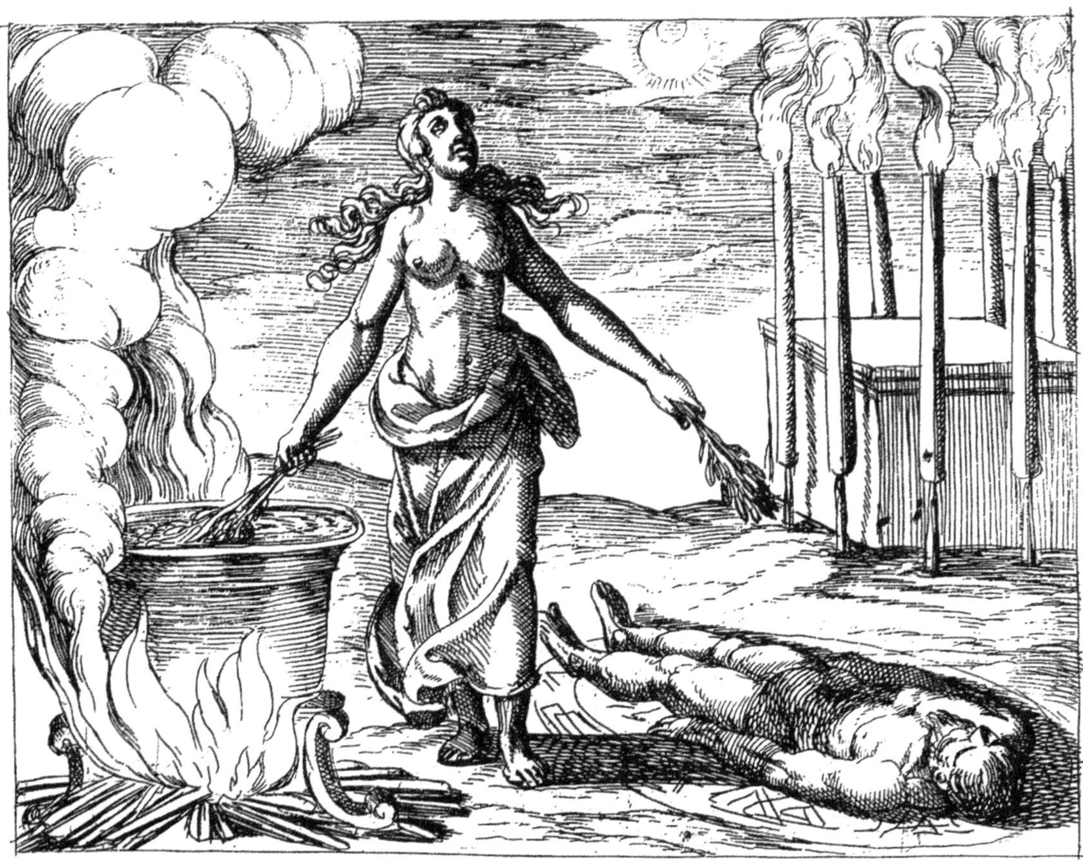

40

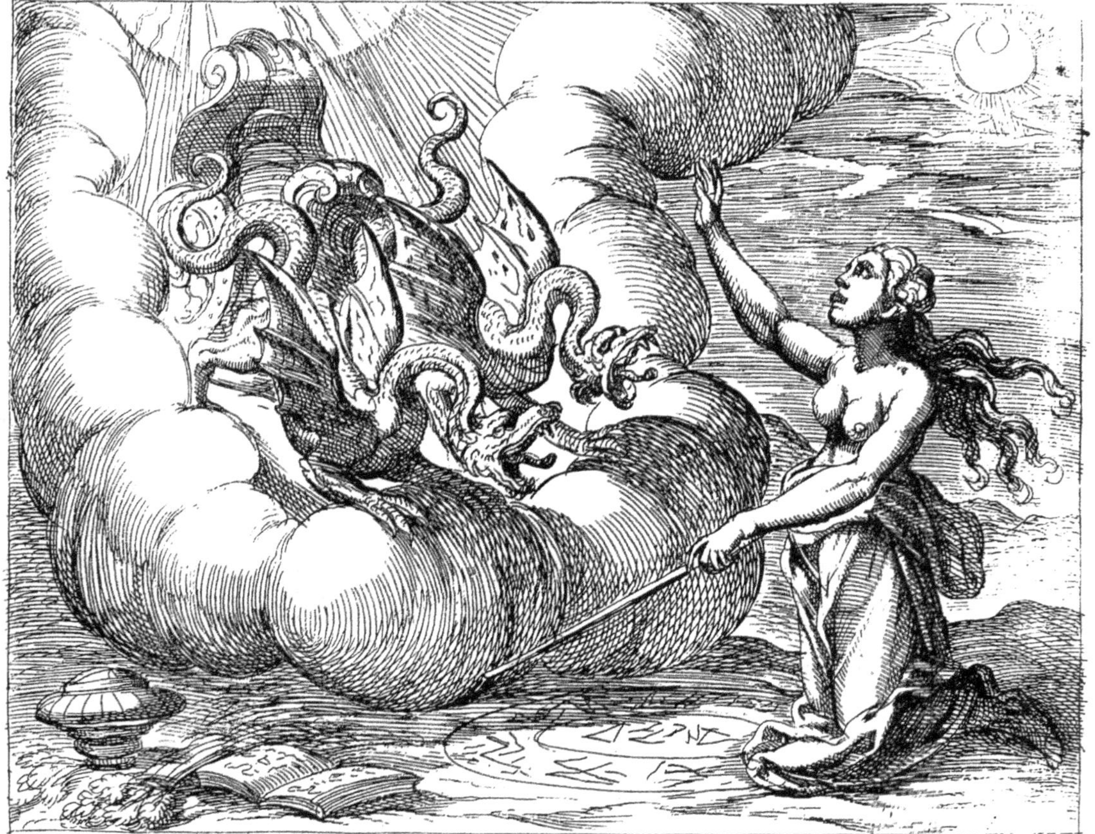

39. Medea restores Aeson's youth, Antonio
Tempesta, 1606

40. Medea conjures up her chariot, Antonio
Tempesta, 1606

41

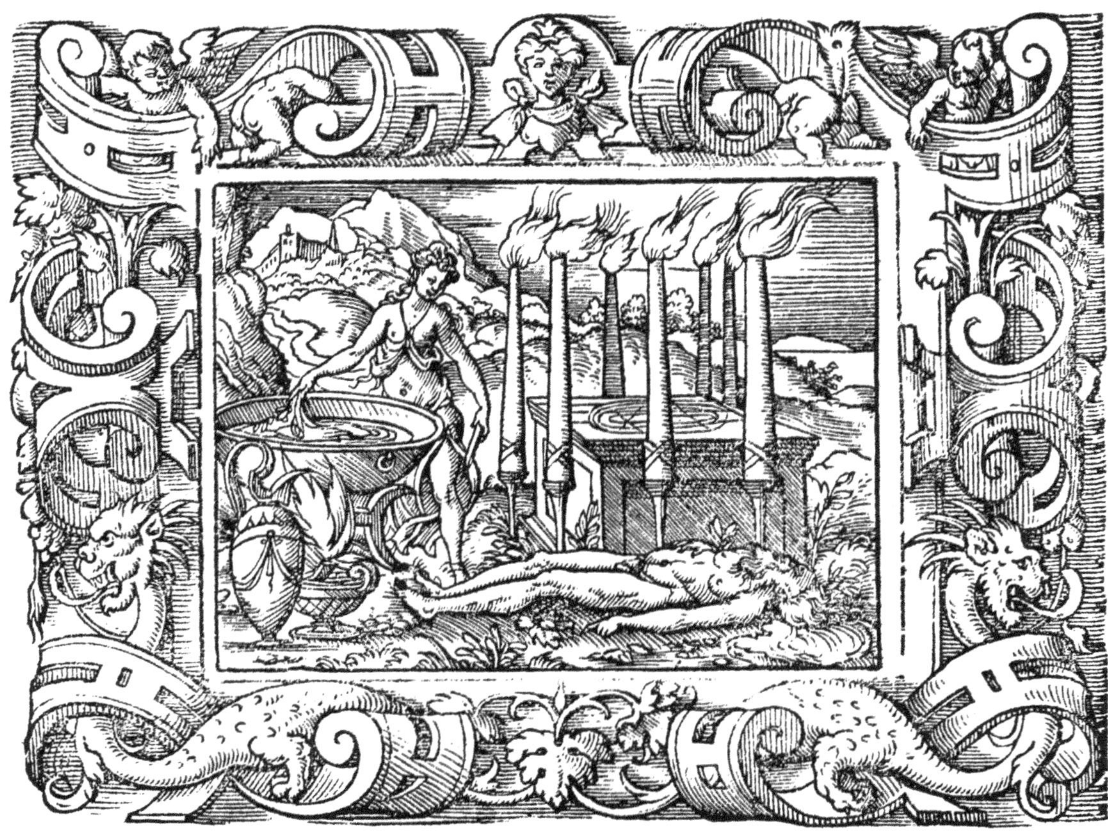

42

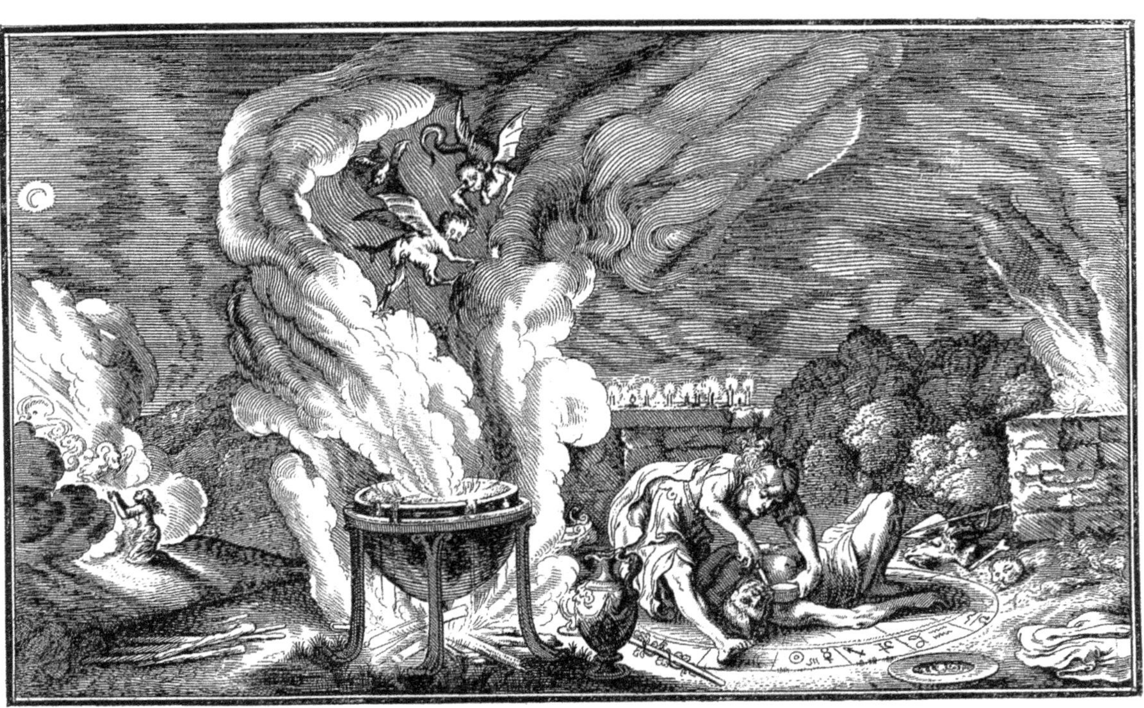

41. Medea restores Aeson's youth, Virgil Solis,
1569

42. Medea draining the blood of Aeson in
order to rejuvenate him with her special brew.
Engraving

43

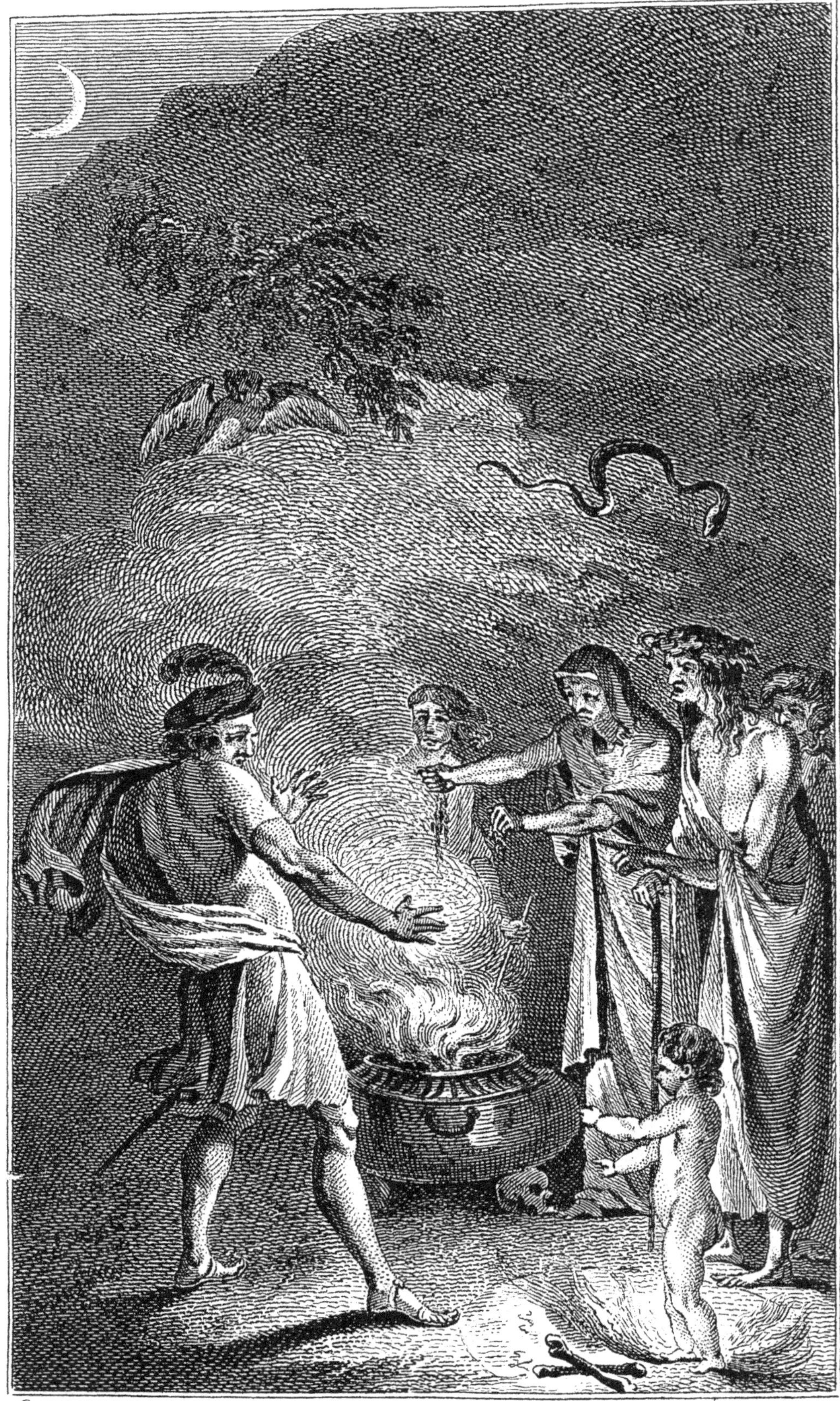

43. Macbeth consults the three witches;
Engraving by W. Byrne, 1773, after E. Edwards.,
Edwards, Edward, 1738–1806.

44.

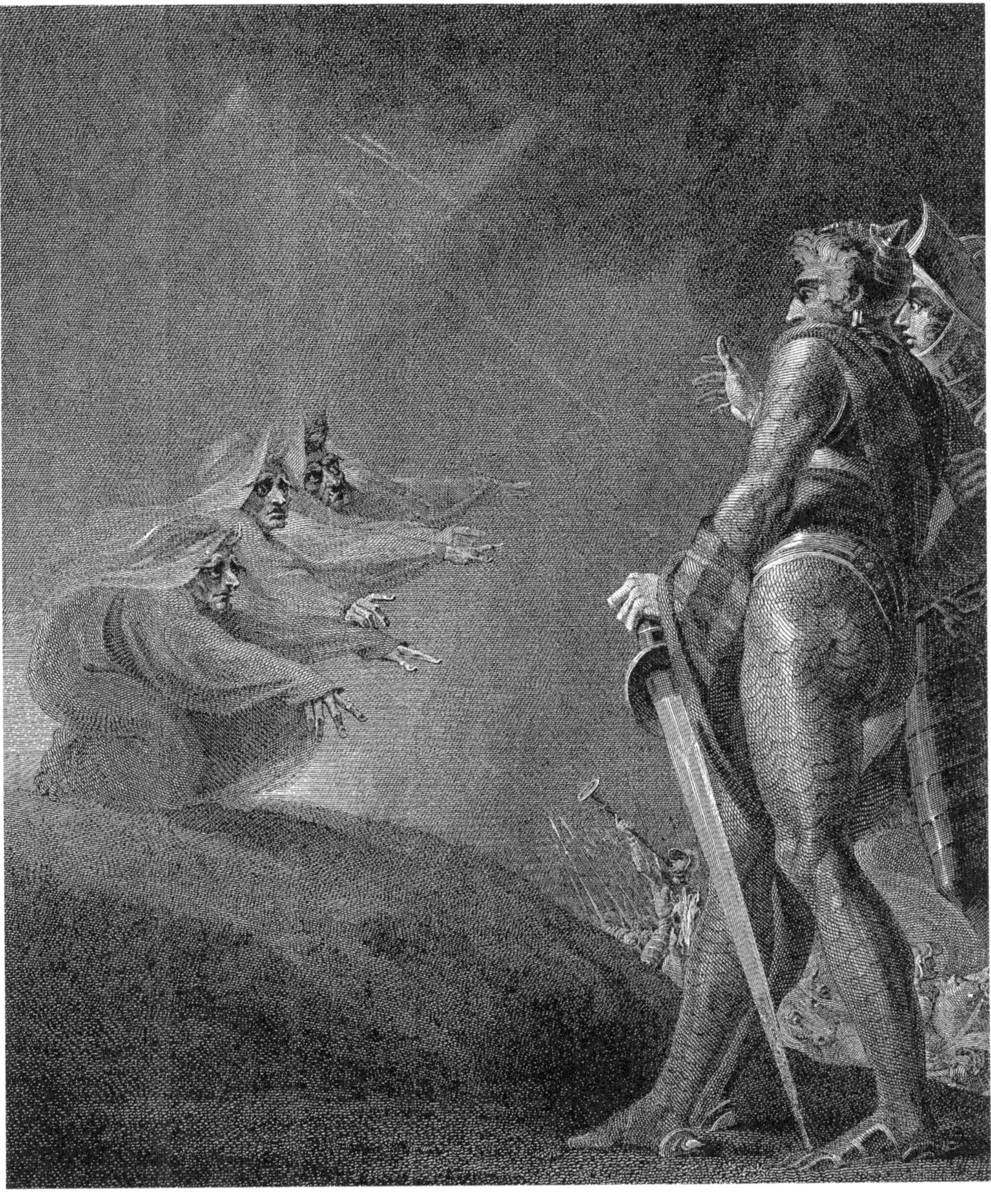

44. Macbeth and Banquo meet the three witches.
Engraving by W. Bromley after J.H. Füssli (Fuseli).
Fuseli, Henry, 1741–1825.

45

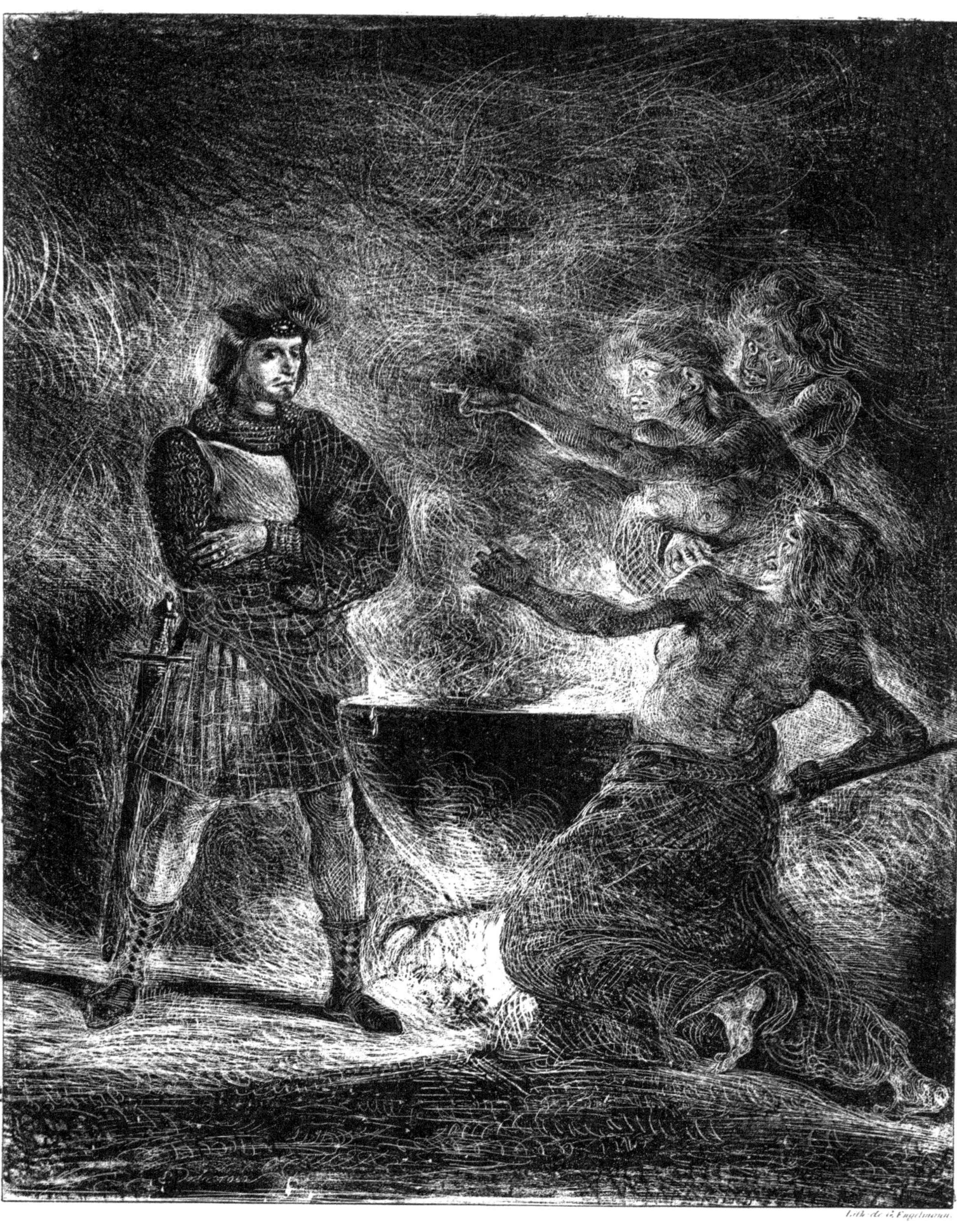

45. Macbeth Consulting the Witches, Eugène
Delacroix, 1825

46

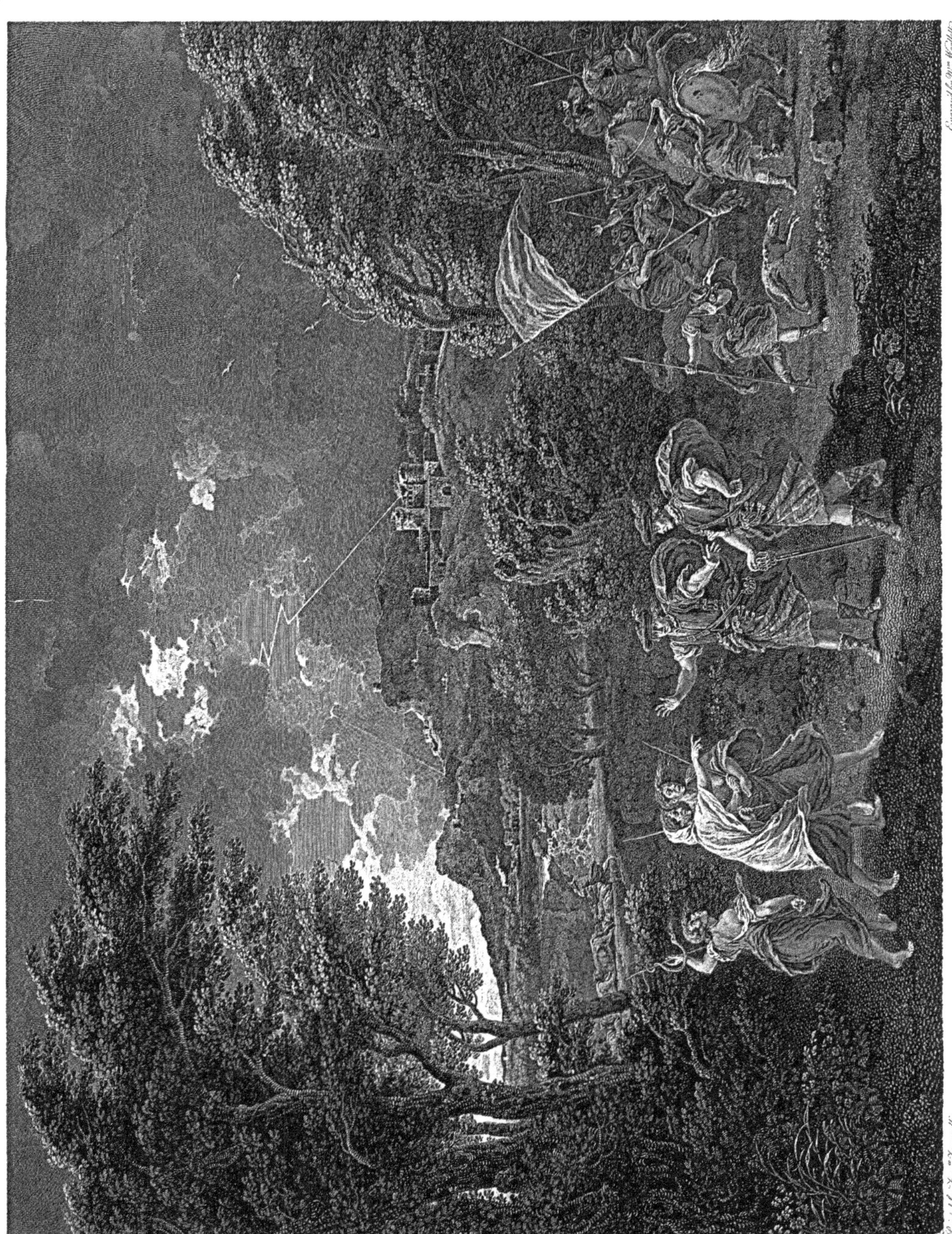

46. Macbeth and the Witches

47

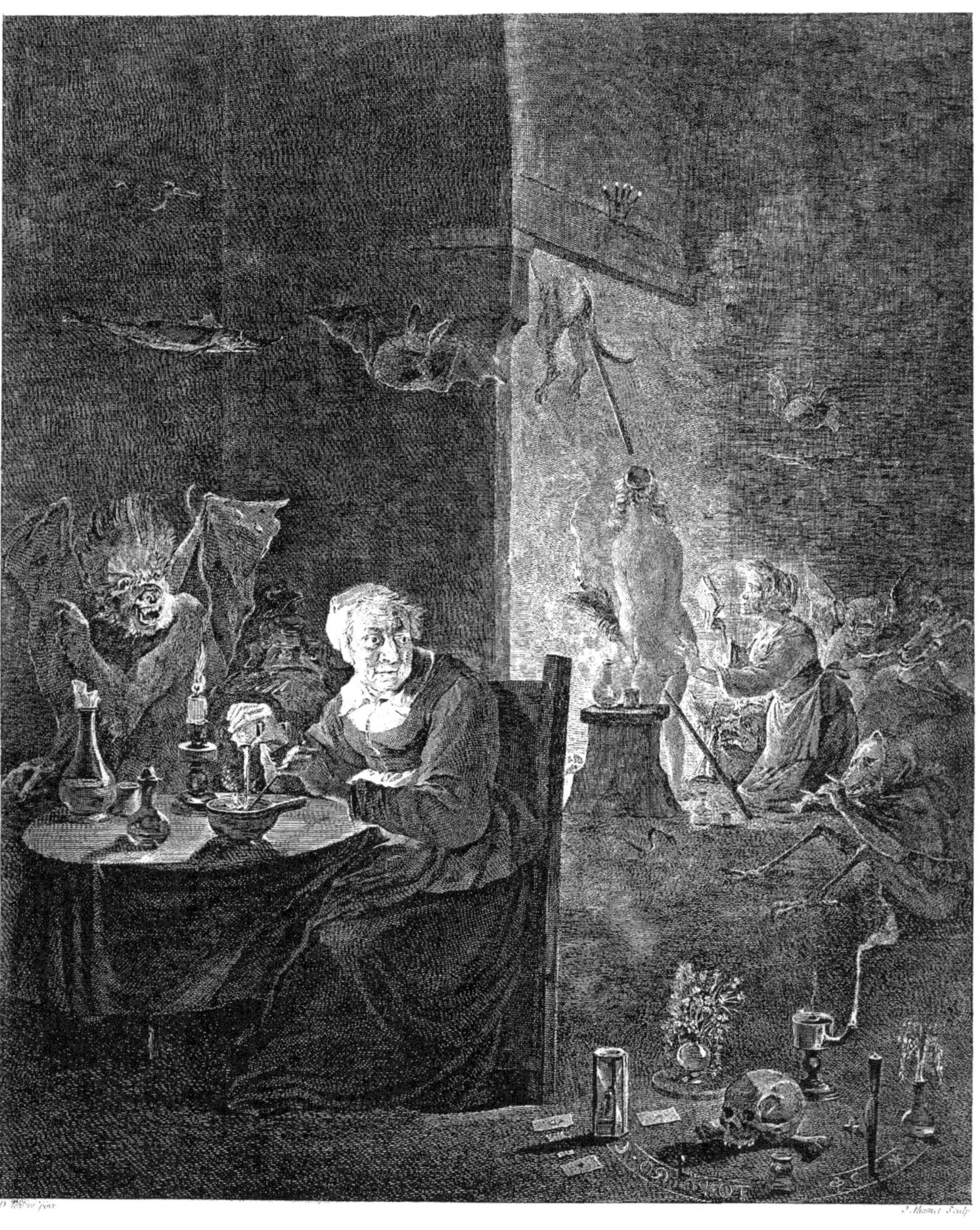

47. Witches' sabbath, Jacques Aliamet (on object), 1755

48

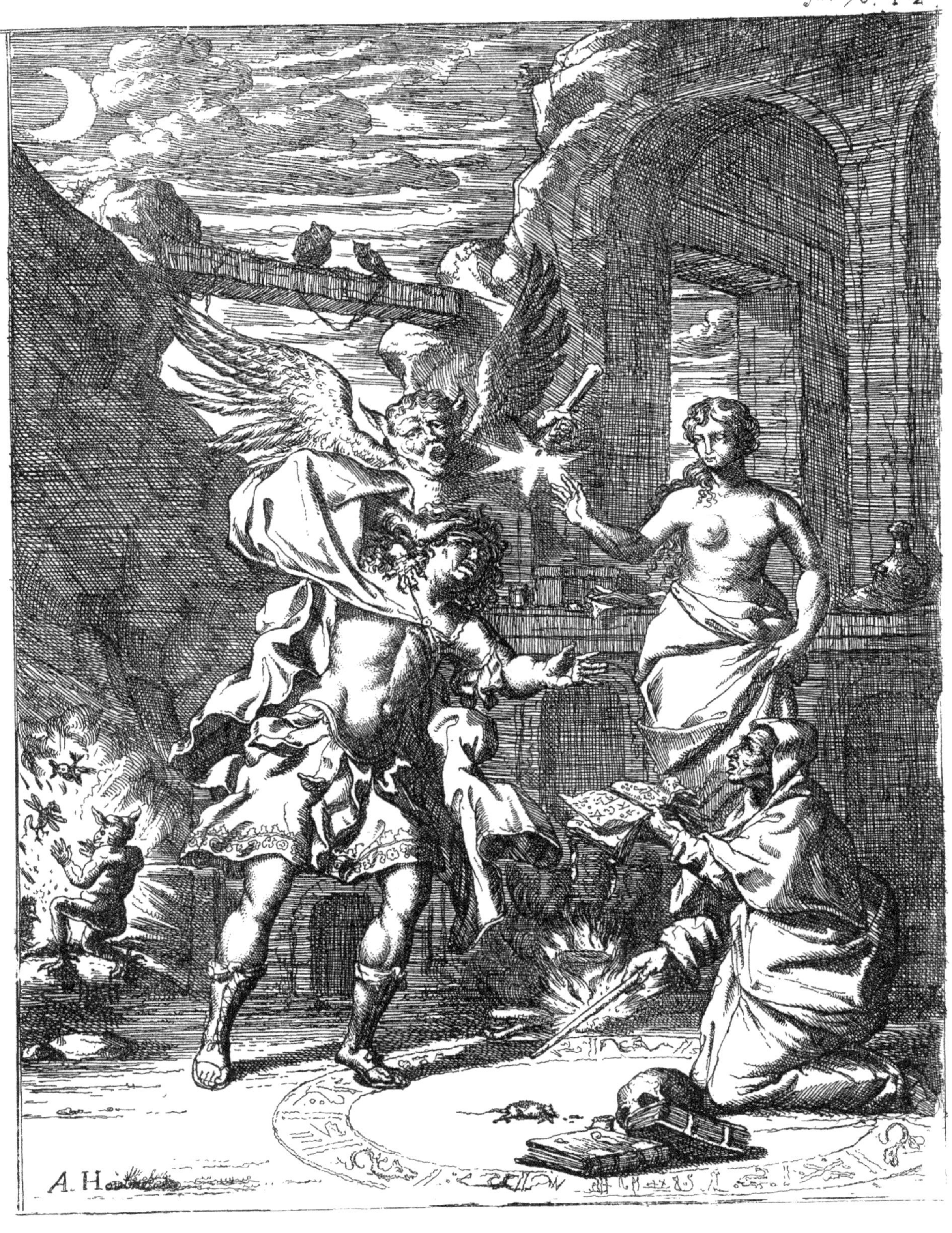

48. Warrior and a witch, Arnold Houbraken (on
object), 1681 – 1683

WITCHES & WIZARDS

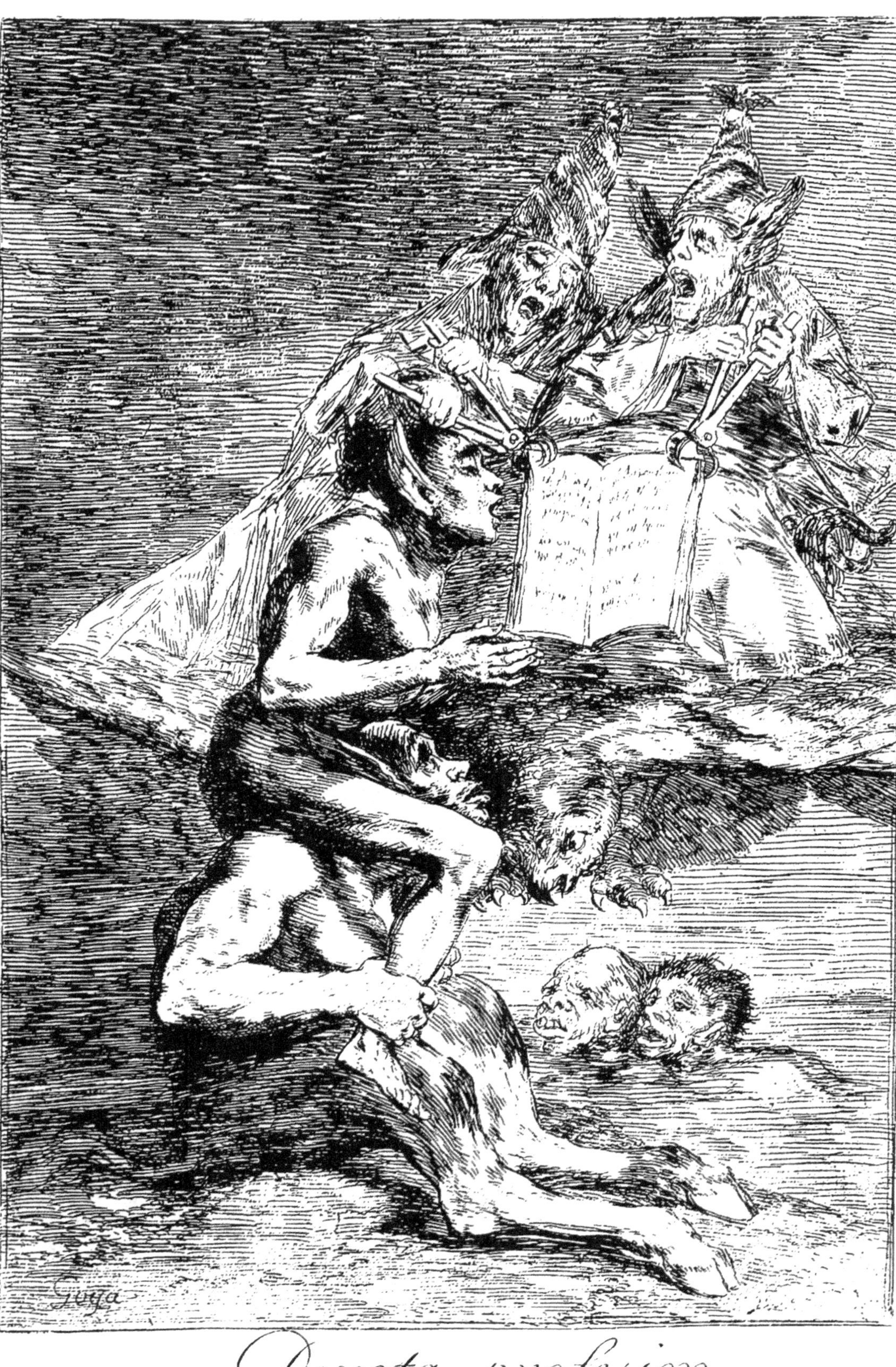

49. A naked witch carried on the shoulders of a
monster. Etching by F. Goya, 1796/1798

50

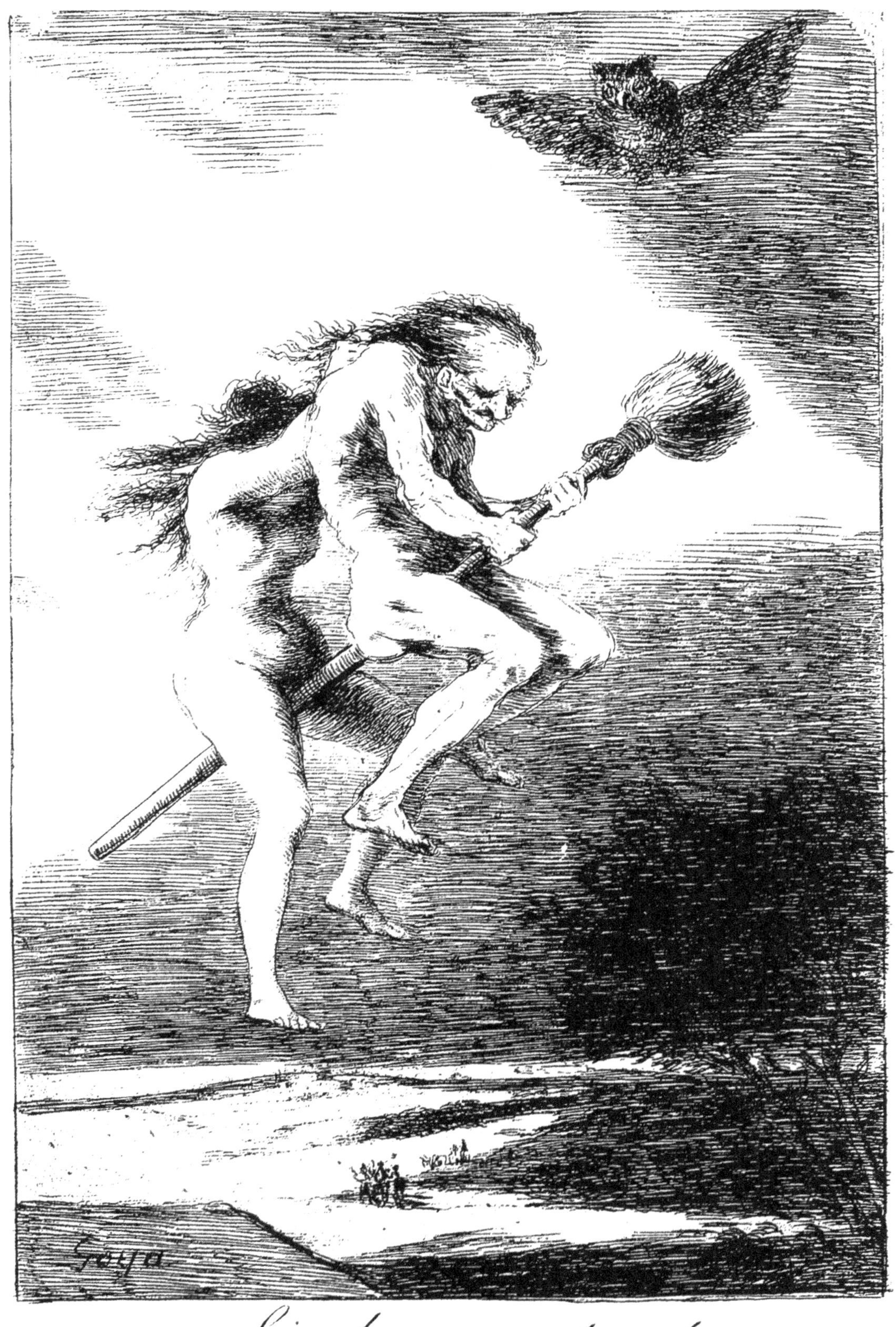

50. Two naked witches riding on a broomstick
accompanied by an owl. Etching by F. Goya,
1796/1798.

51

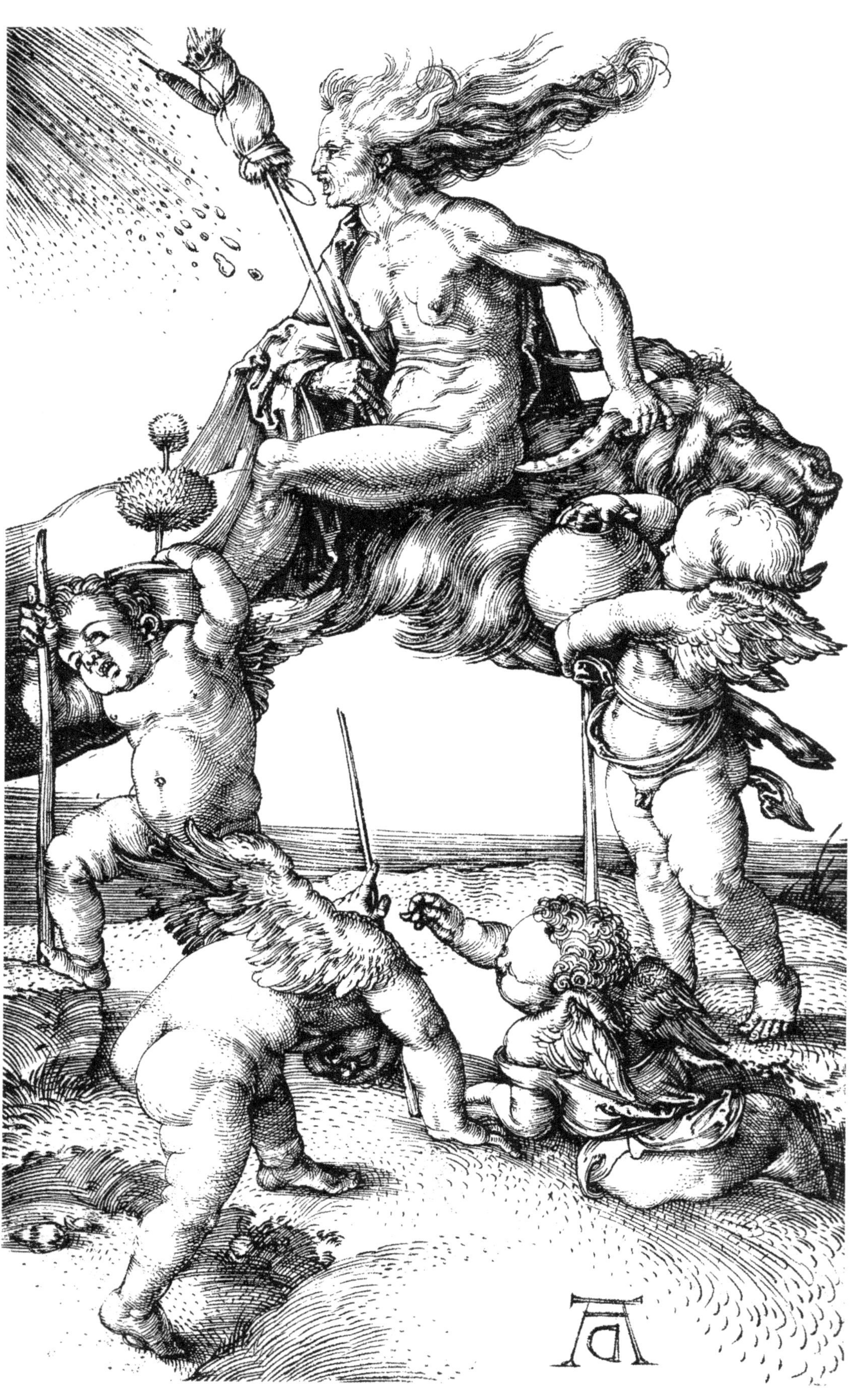

51. Witch Riding Backwards on a Goat, Albrecht
Durer

52

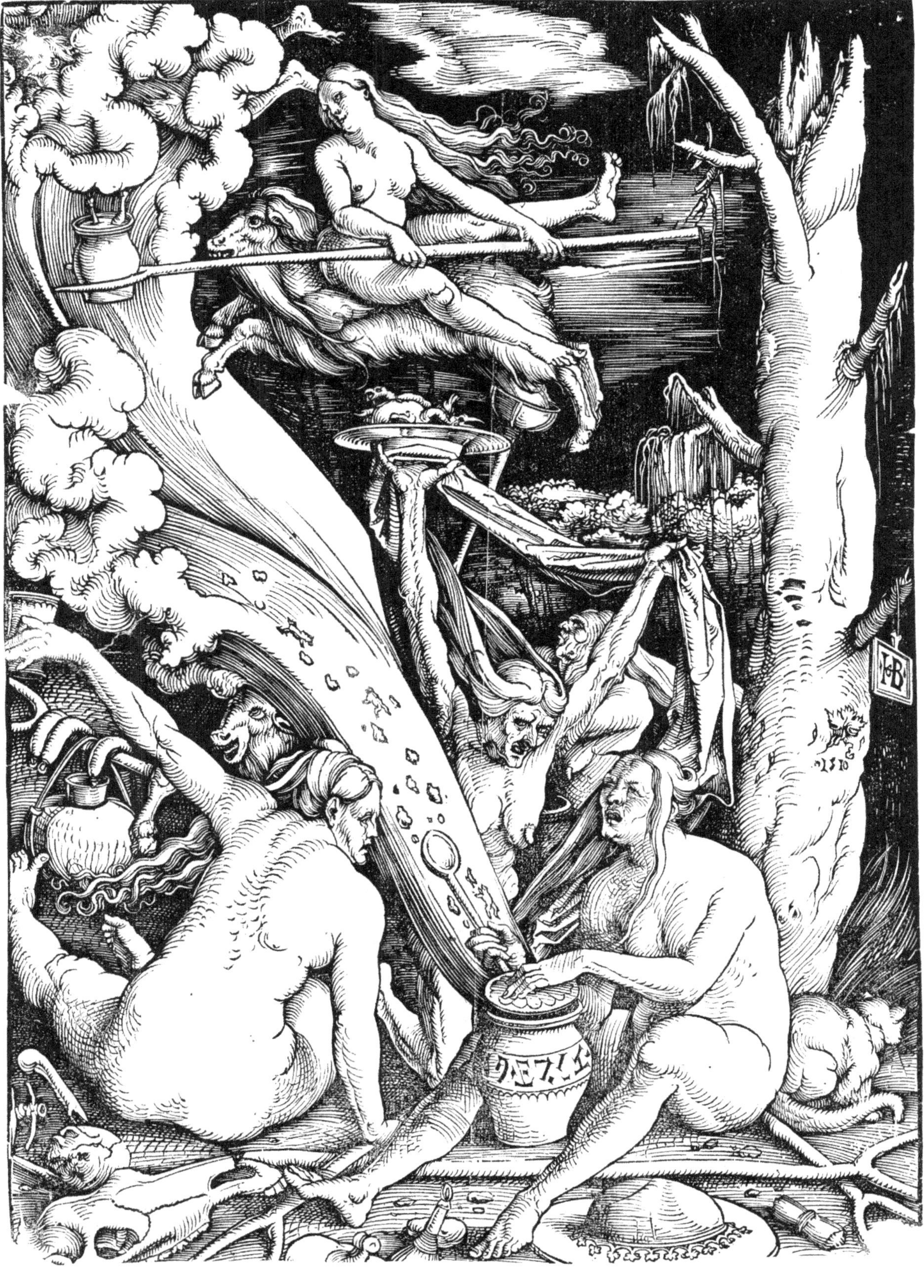

WITCHES & WIZARDS

52. The Witches Hans Baldung (called Hans
Baldung Grien) German, 1510

53

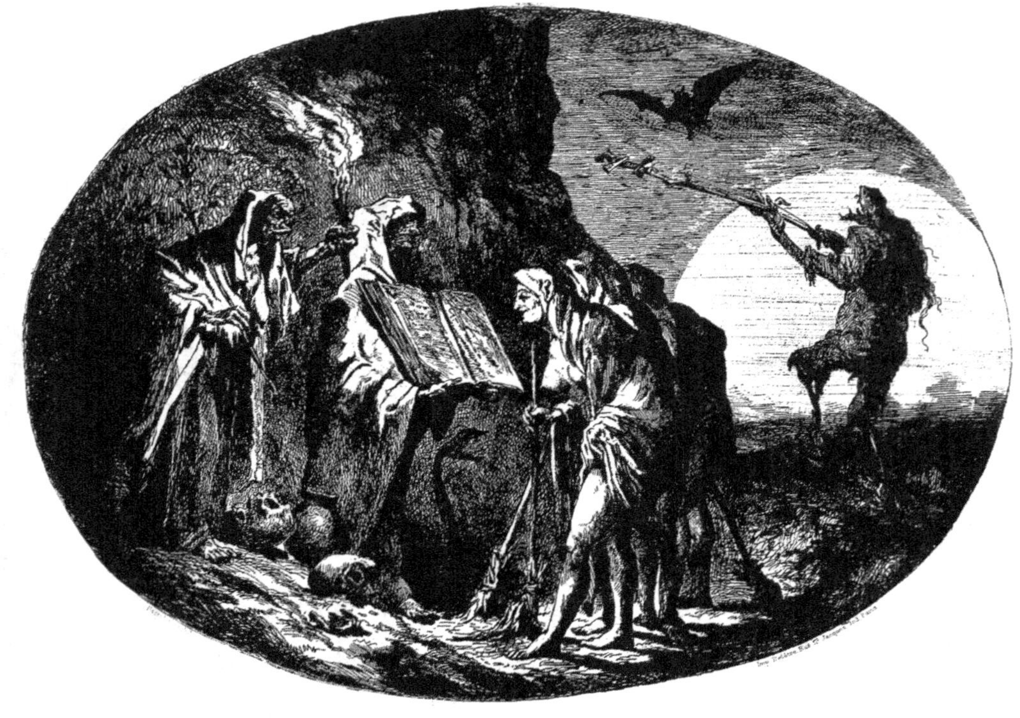

54

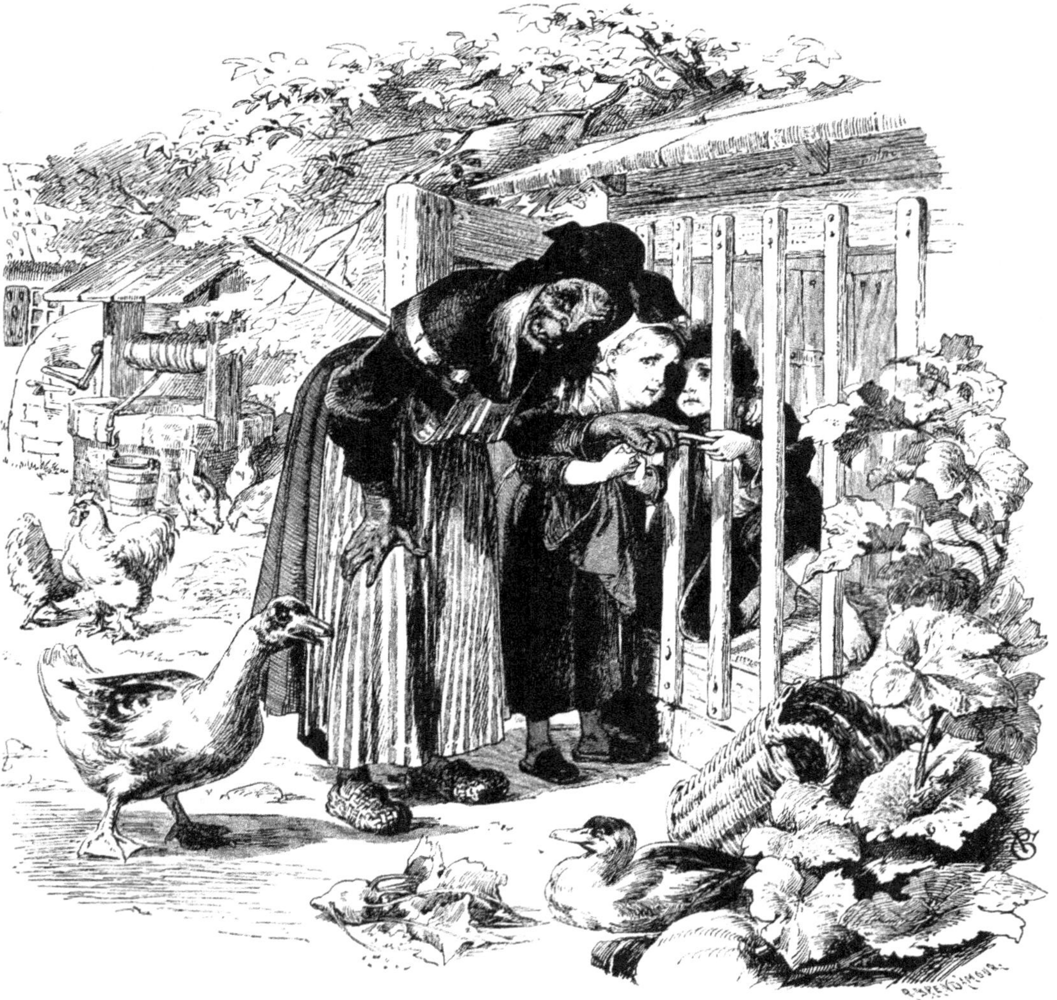

53. Witches meeting and performing spell.
Etching by J.A.A. Pastelot.   Pastelot, Jean
Amable Amédée, –1870.

54. The witch mistakes the chicken bone for
Hans' finger, 1912

55

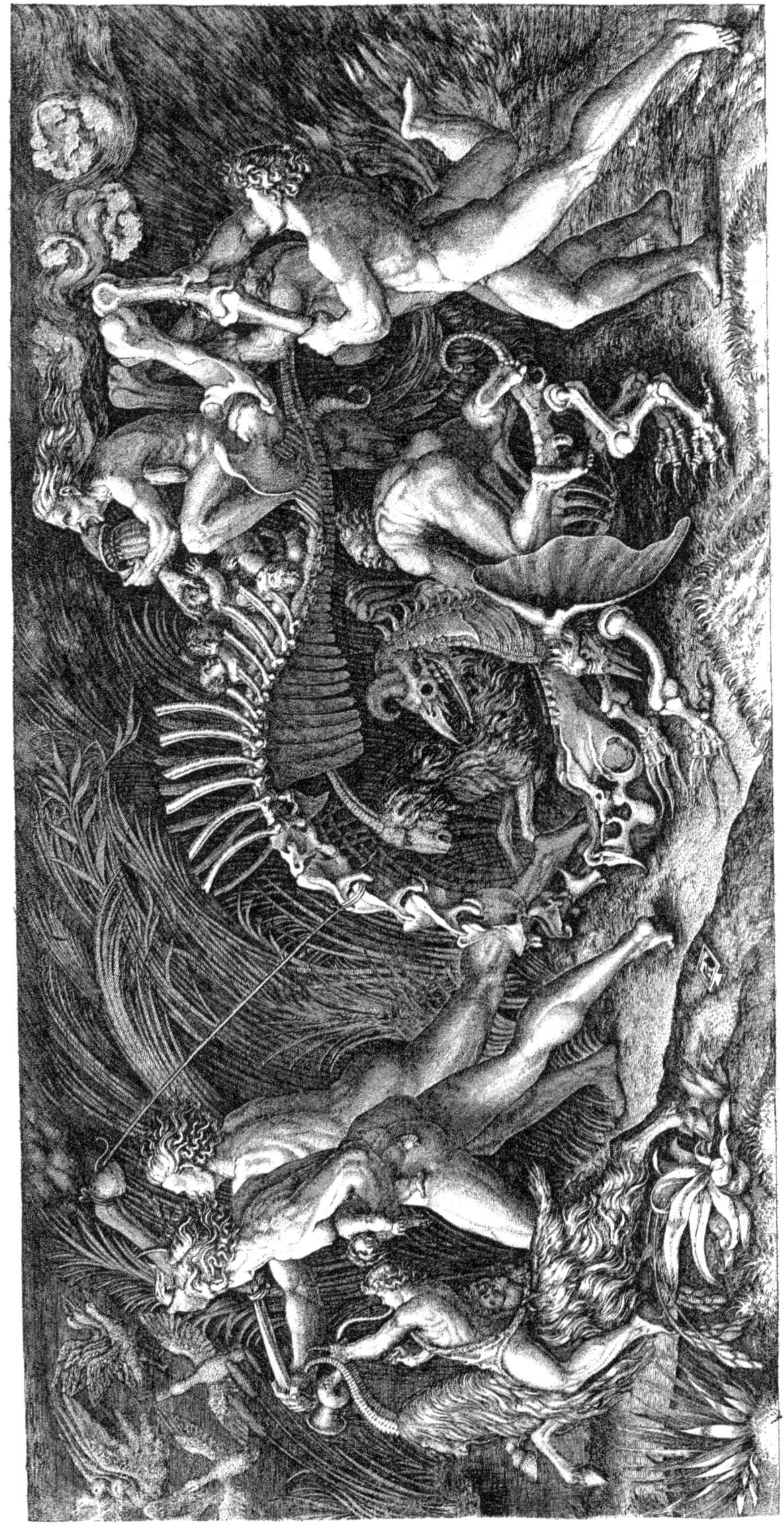

55. The Carcass by Agostino Veneziano, 1500
– 1536

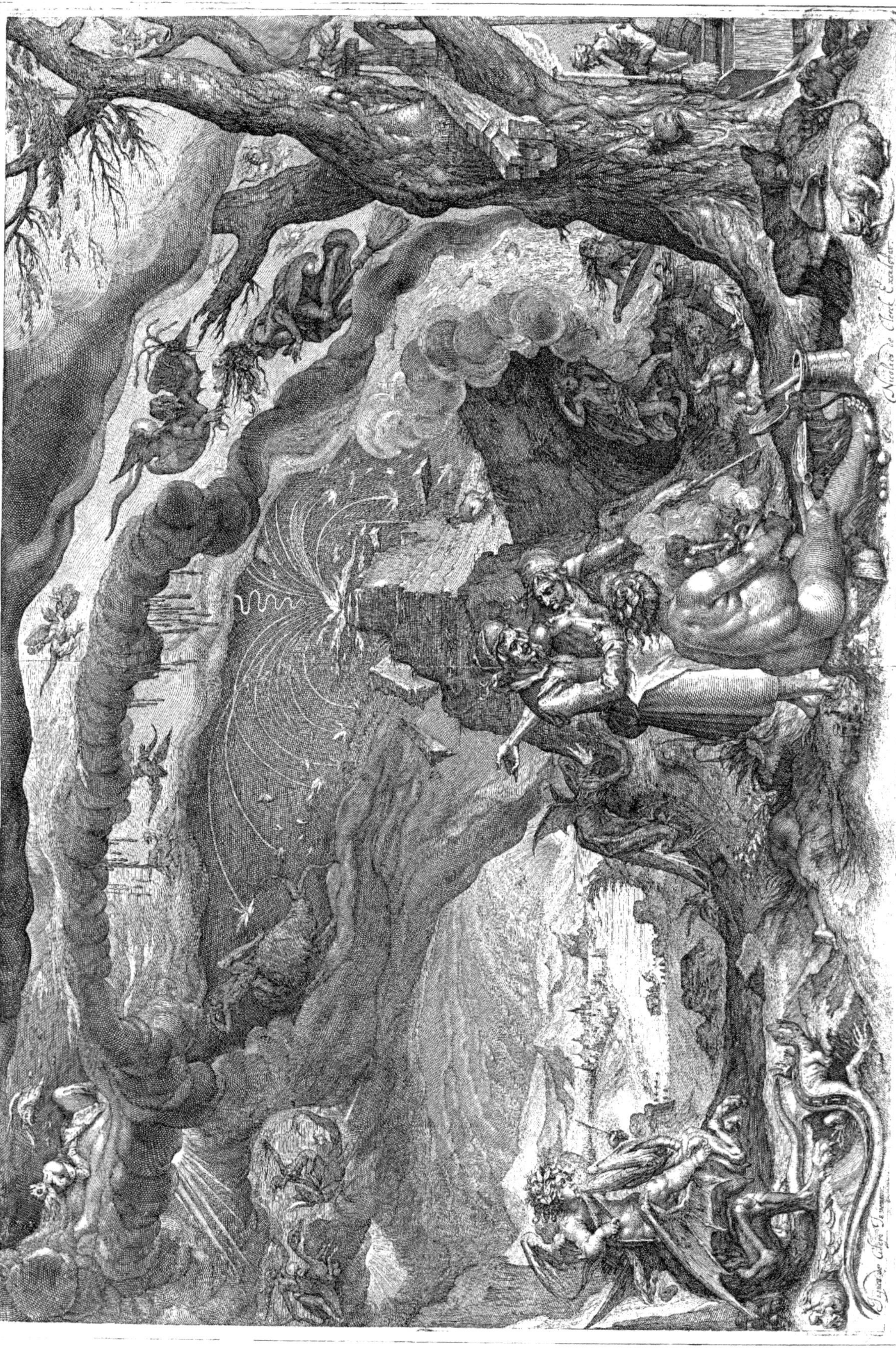

56. Witches' Sabbath, attributed to workshop of
Jacques de Gheyn (II), 1608 – 1612

57

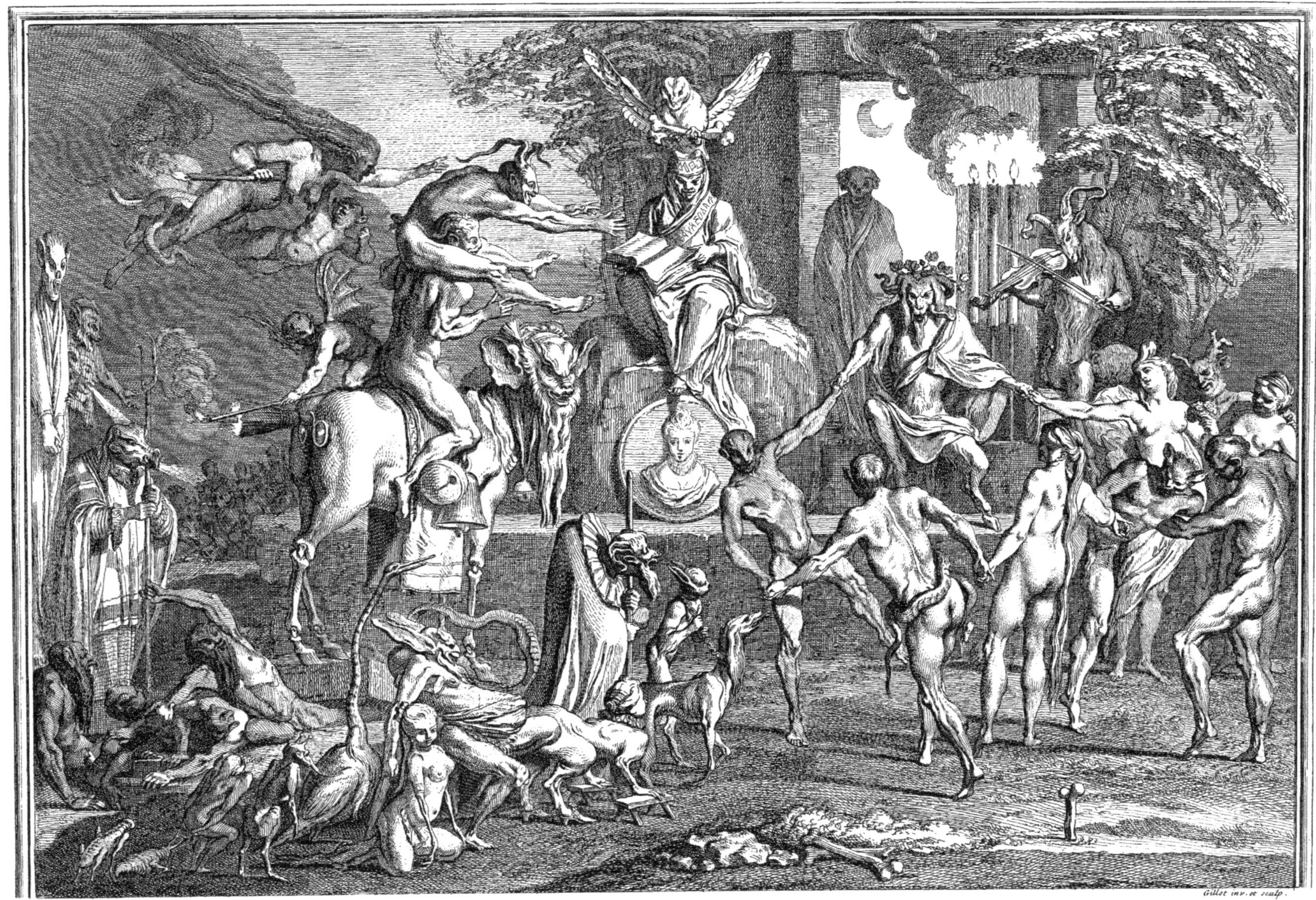

57. Witches' Sabbath, Claude Gillot (mentioned on object), 1683 – 1722

58

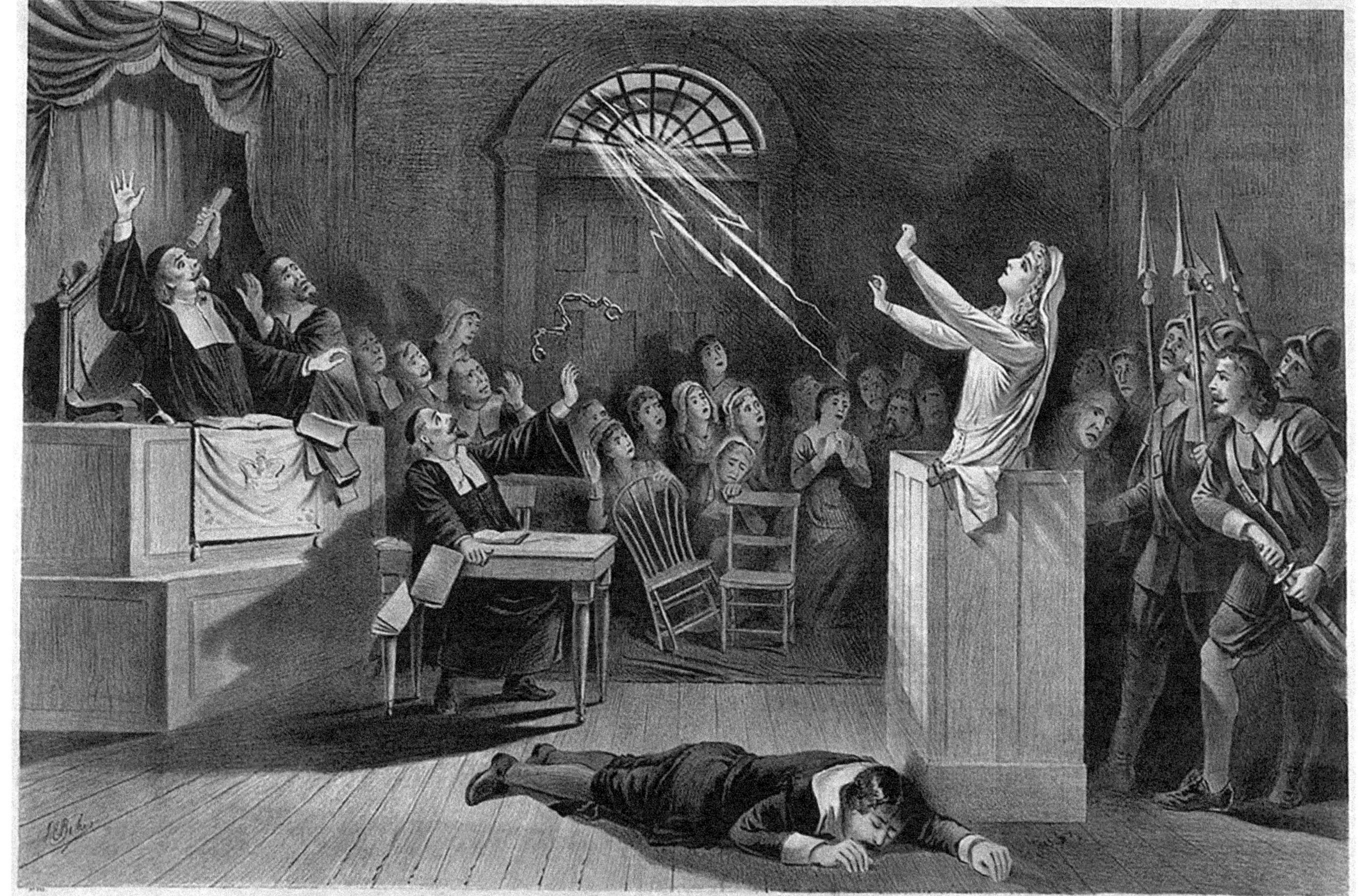

58. The Witch by Joseph E. Cena, 1892

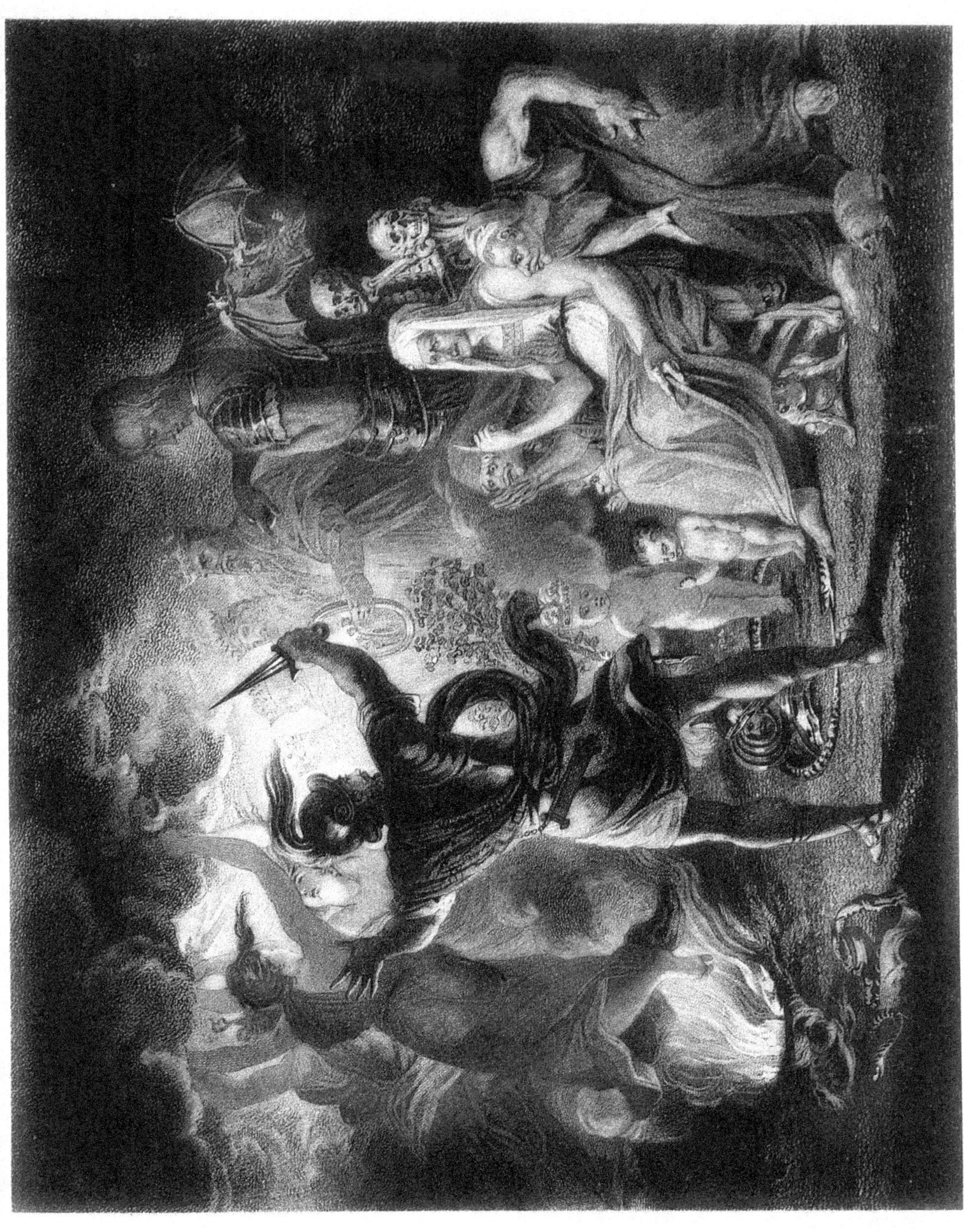

59. Macbeth seeing the three witches, with other
horrifying visions. Etching after J. Reynolds, ca.
1786–1790, after W. Shakespeare

60

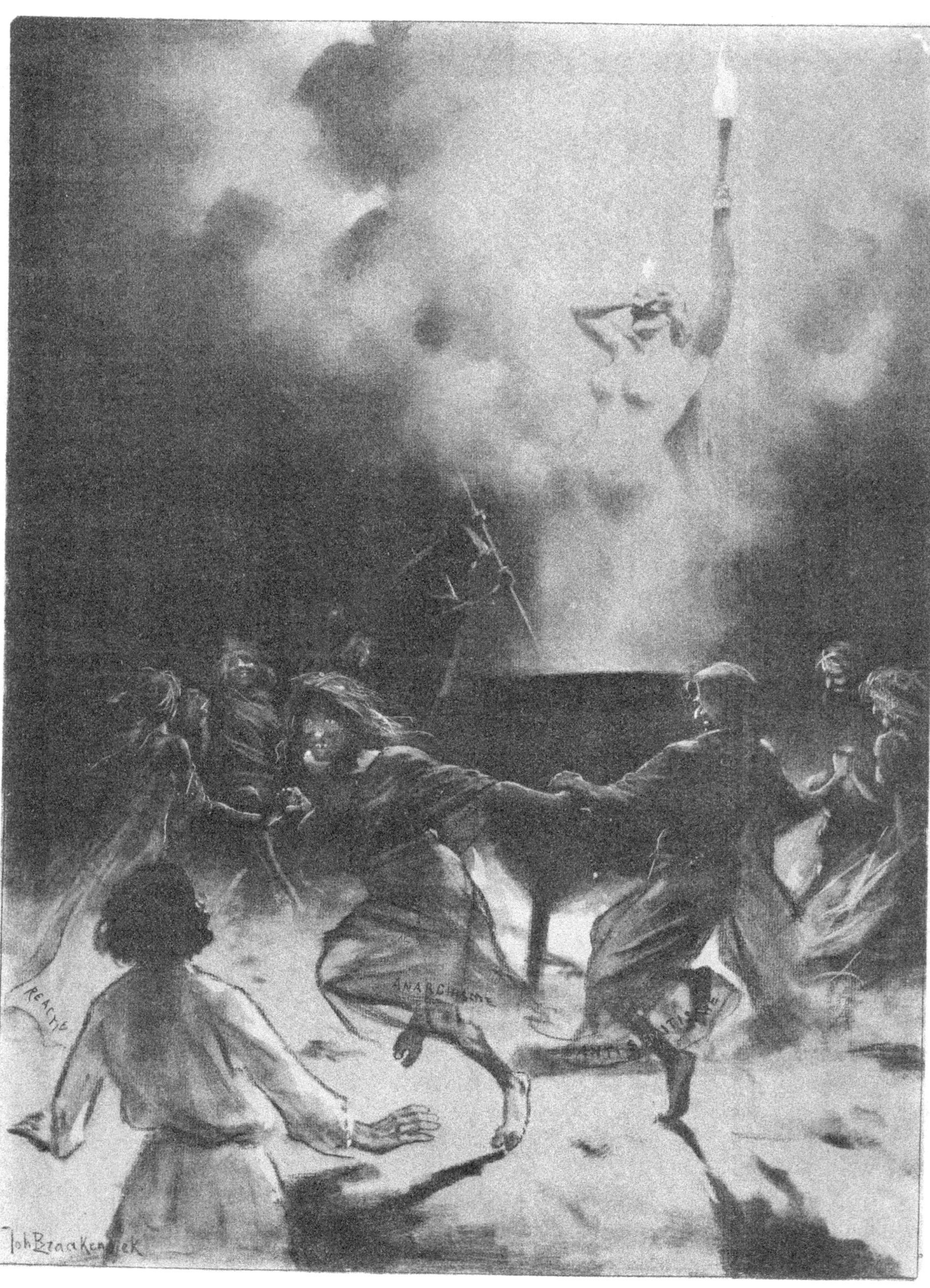

60. "De heksenketel in Rusland" (The Witches'
Cauldron in Russia), Johan Braakensiek, 1905

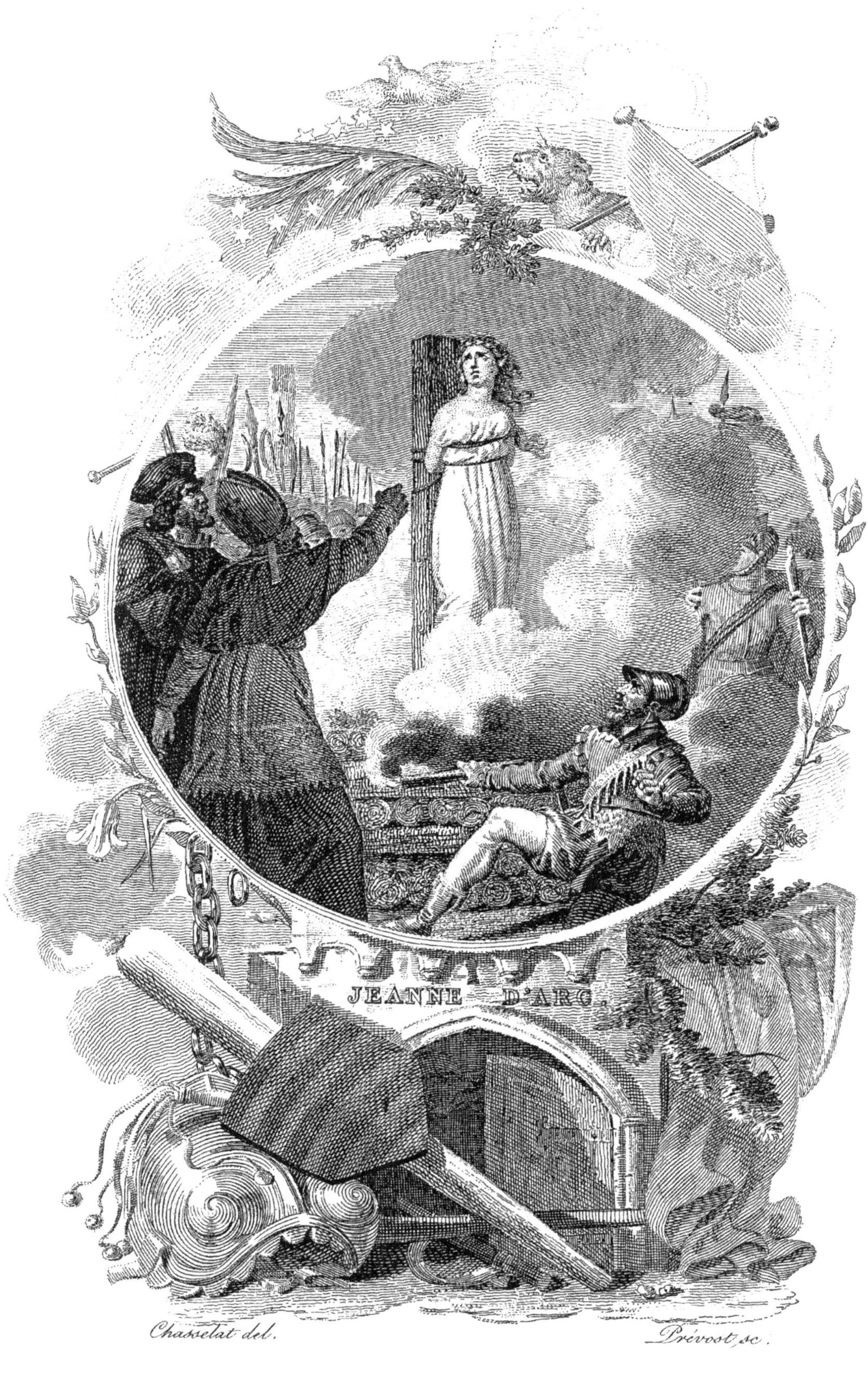

61. Jeanne D'Arc, Charles–Abraham Chasselat
(1782-1843)

62

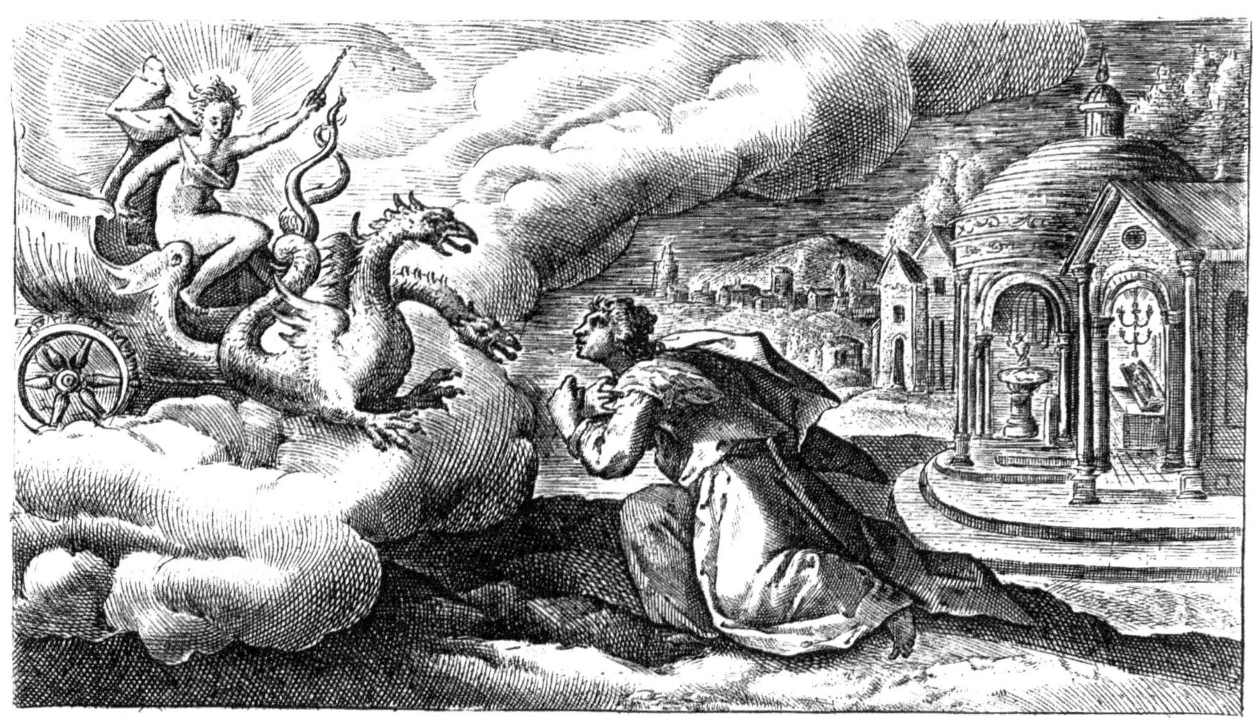

63

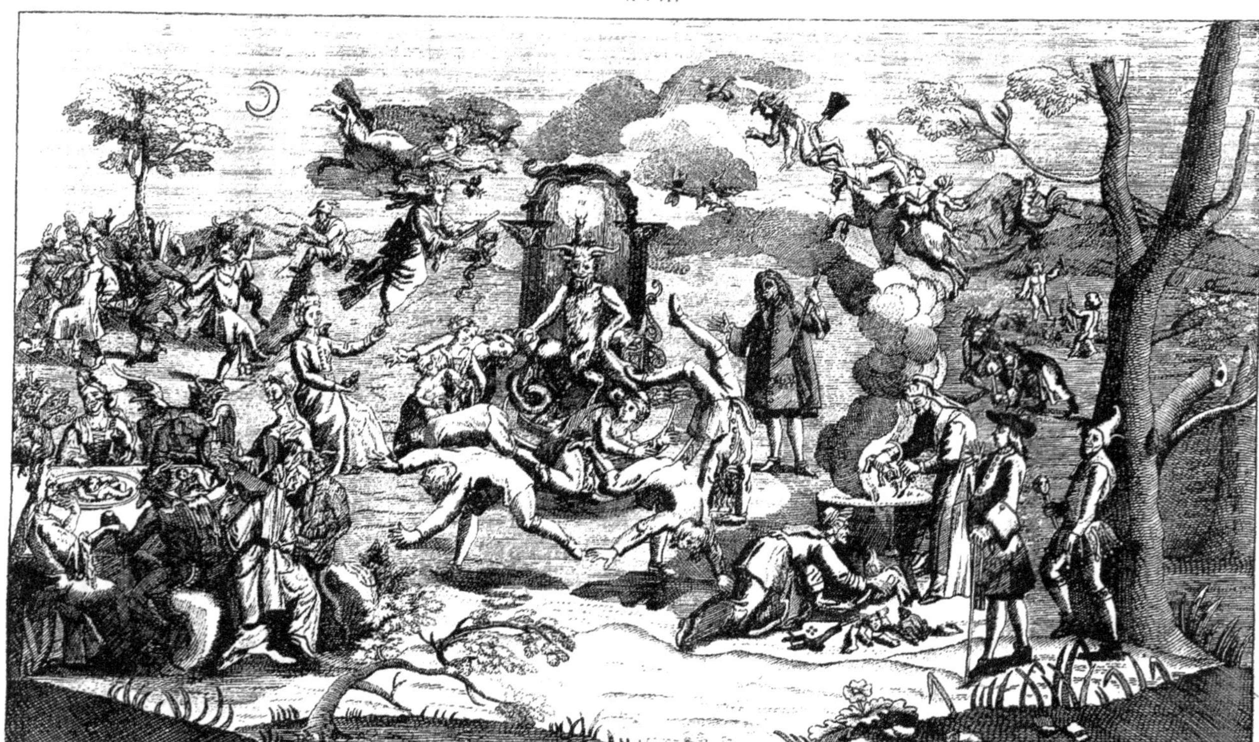

62. Medea prays to Hecate, Crispain of the Passe (I), 1602 – 1607

63. A witches' sabbath. Spranger

64

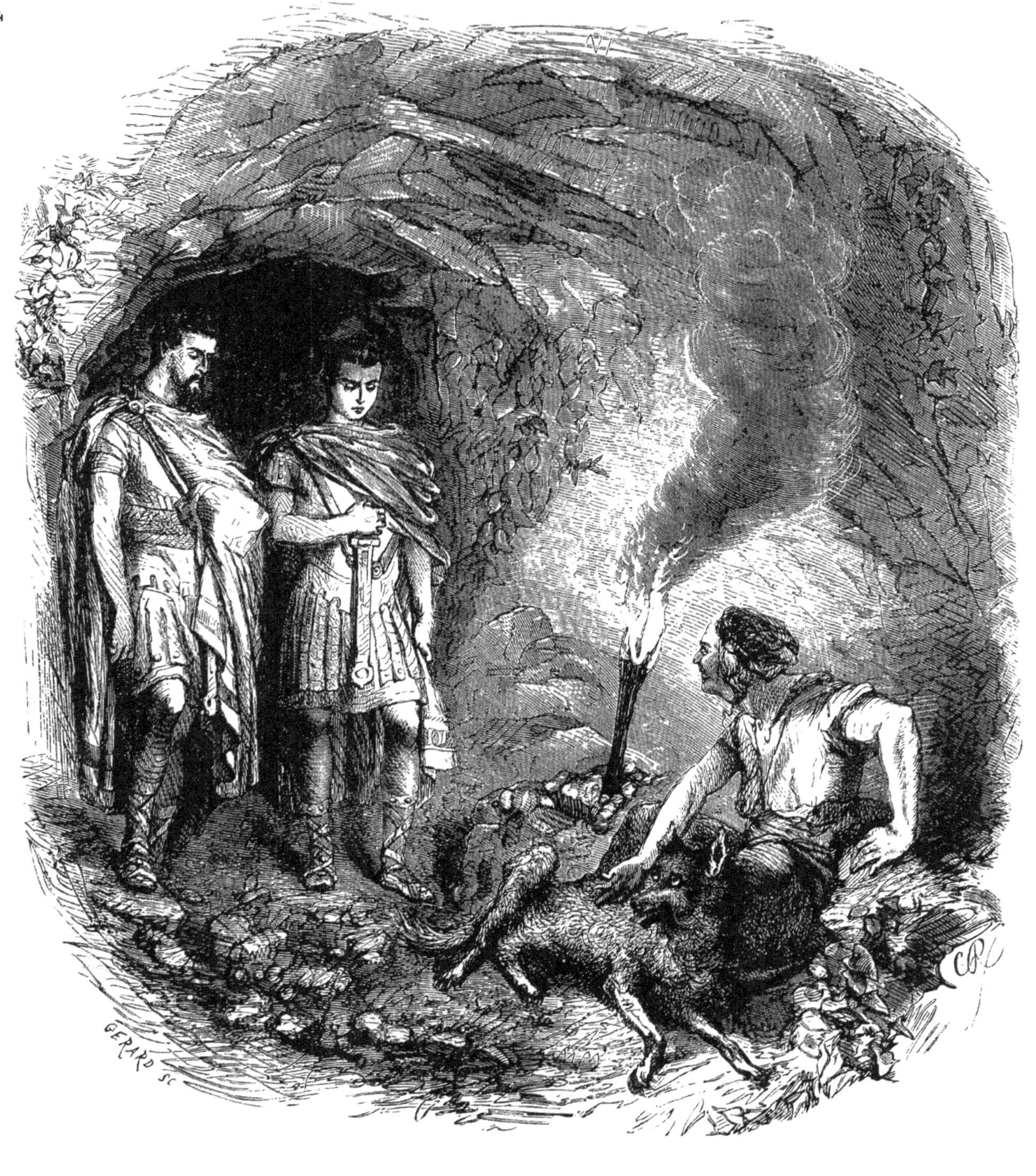

64. Two soldiers with a witch in a cave, Théodore
Gérard (manned on object), 1839 – 1895

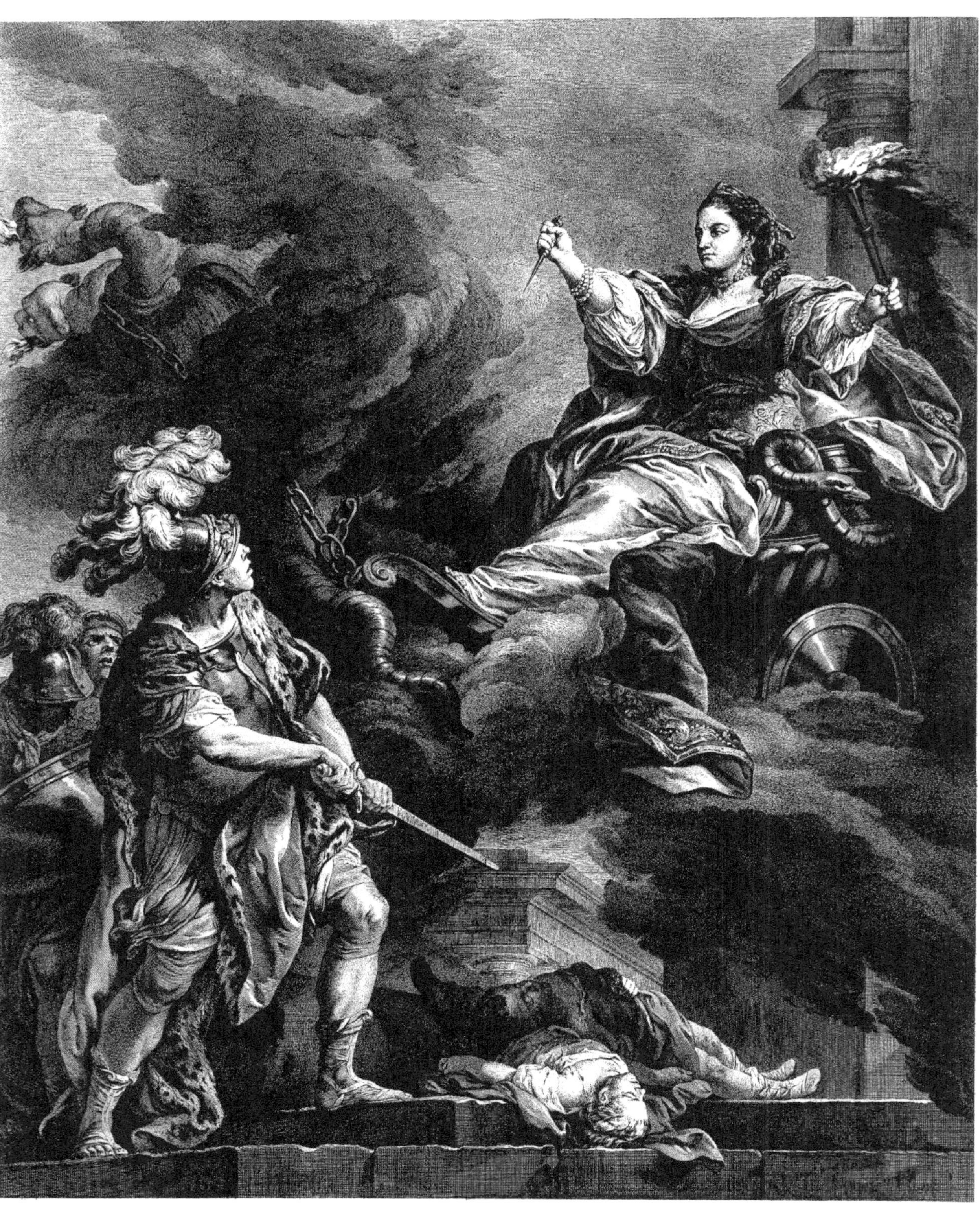

65. Portrait of Claire Clairon in the role of Medea,
Laurent Cars (on object), 1764

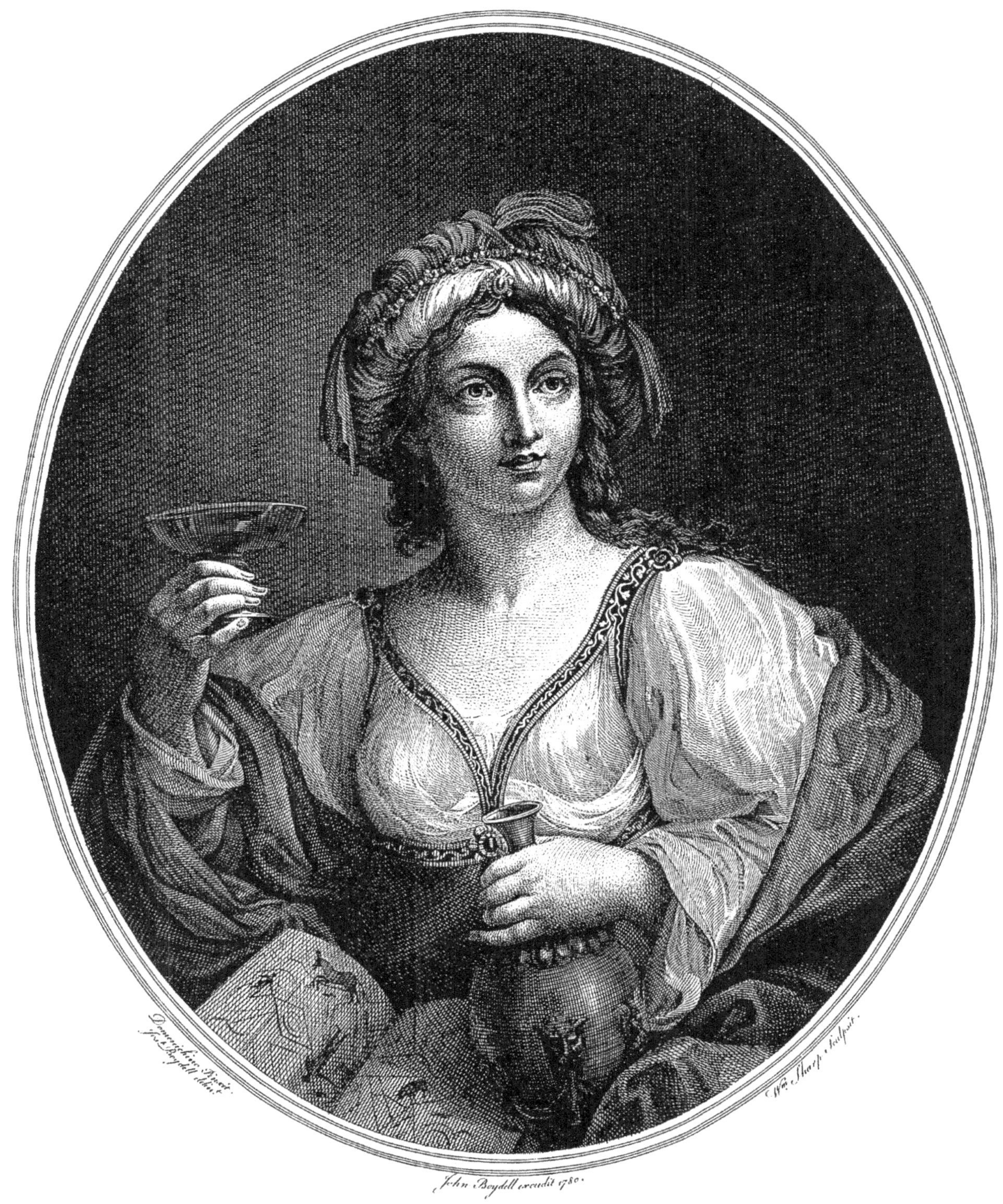
Domenichino Pinx.
Jos. Boydell delin.
Wm. Sharp Sculpsit.
John Boydell excudit 1780.
CIRCE.
From the Original Picture in the Possession of Mr. Moreland.
Size of the Picture............ 2.4 by 3.2 high.
Published Sepr. 29th 1780, by J. Boydell, in Cheapside,—London.

67

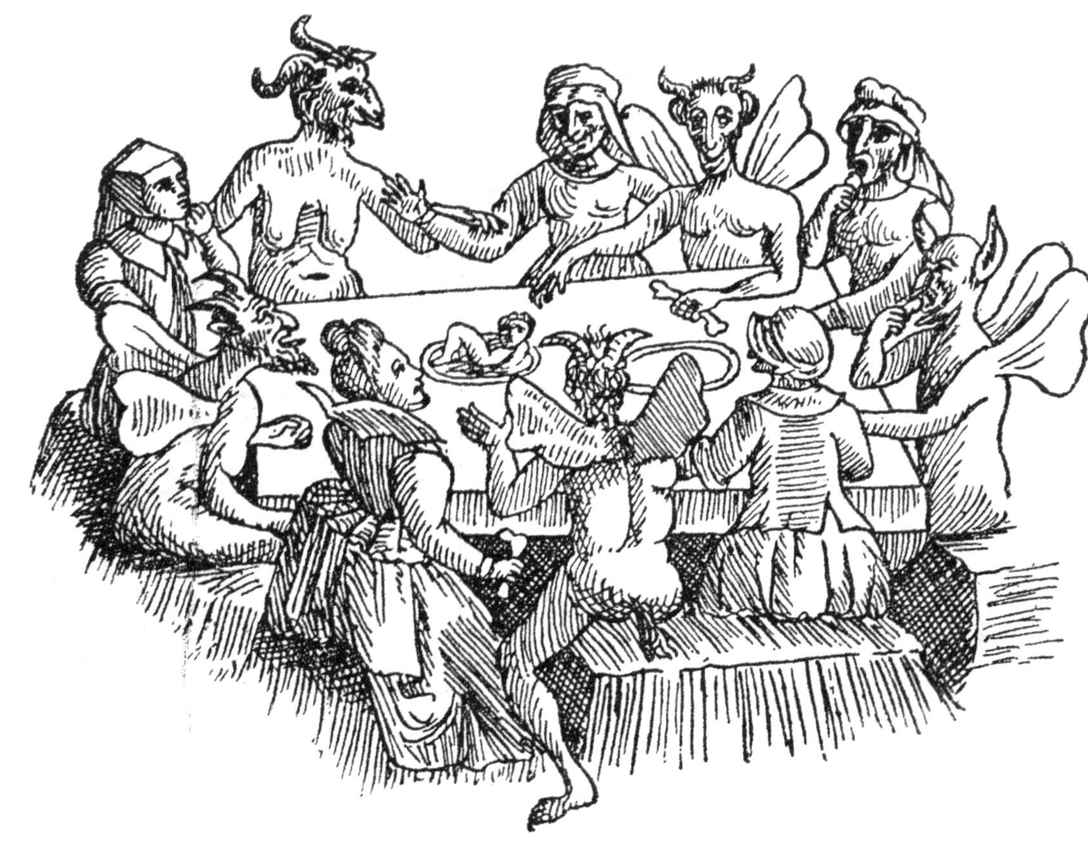

68

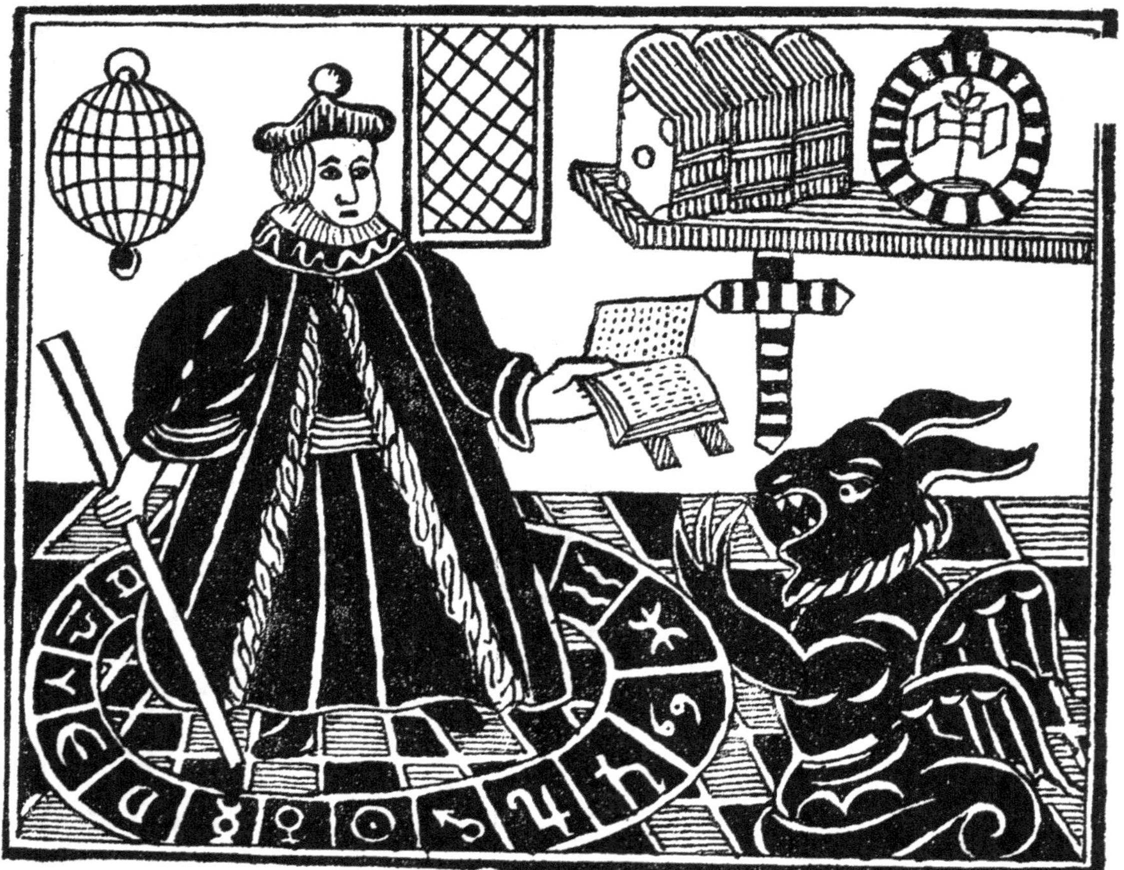

67. The Devil in Britain and America II, 1896   68. The Devil in Britain and America, 1896

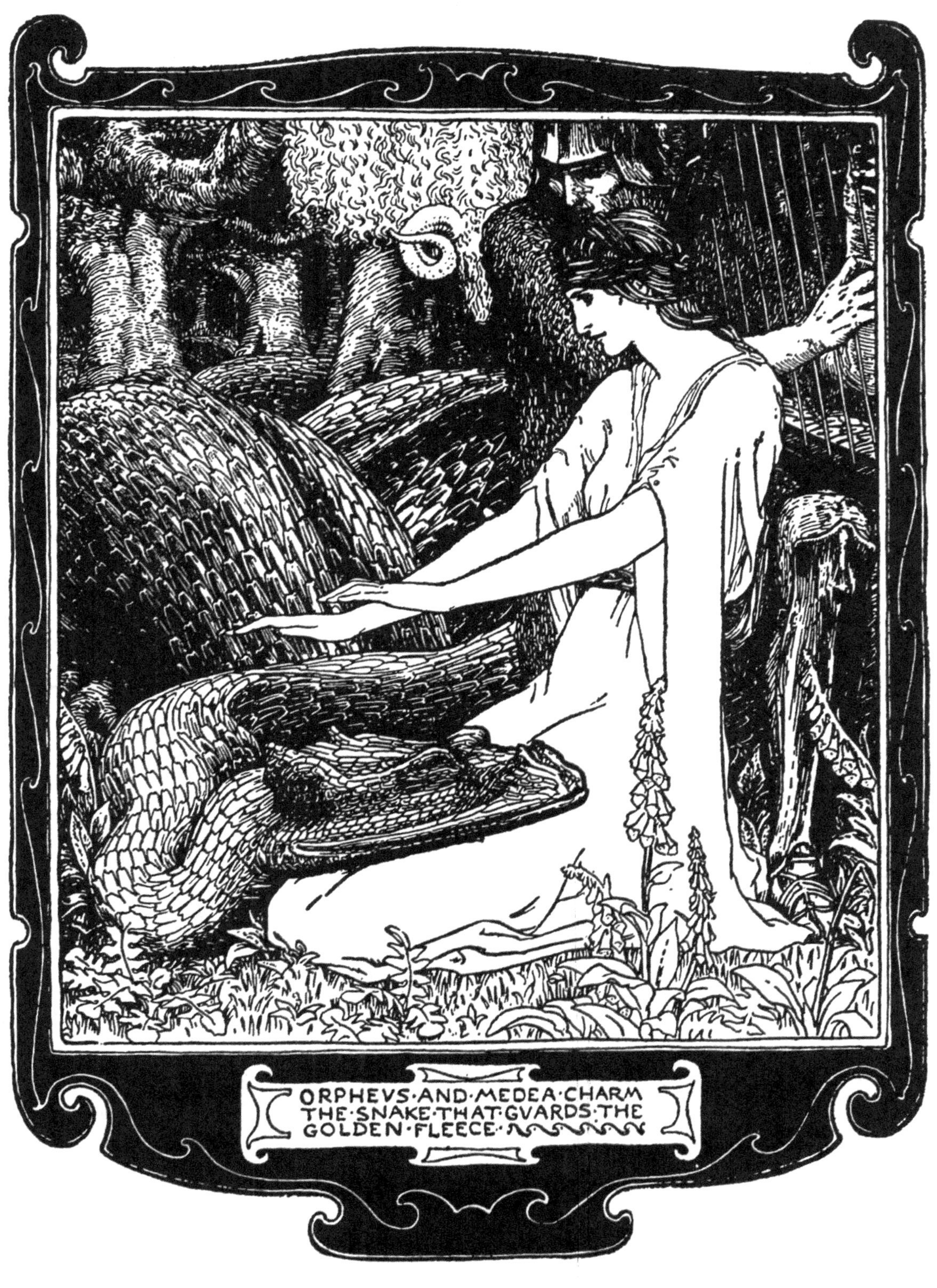

WITCHES & WIZARDS

69. Medea The Book of Wonder Voyages by
Joseph Jacobs and J.D Batten, 1896

70

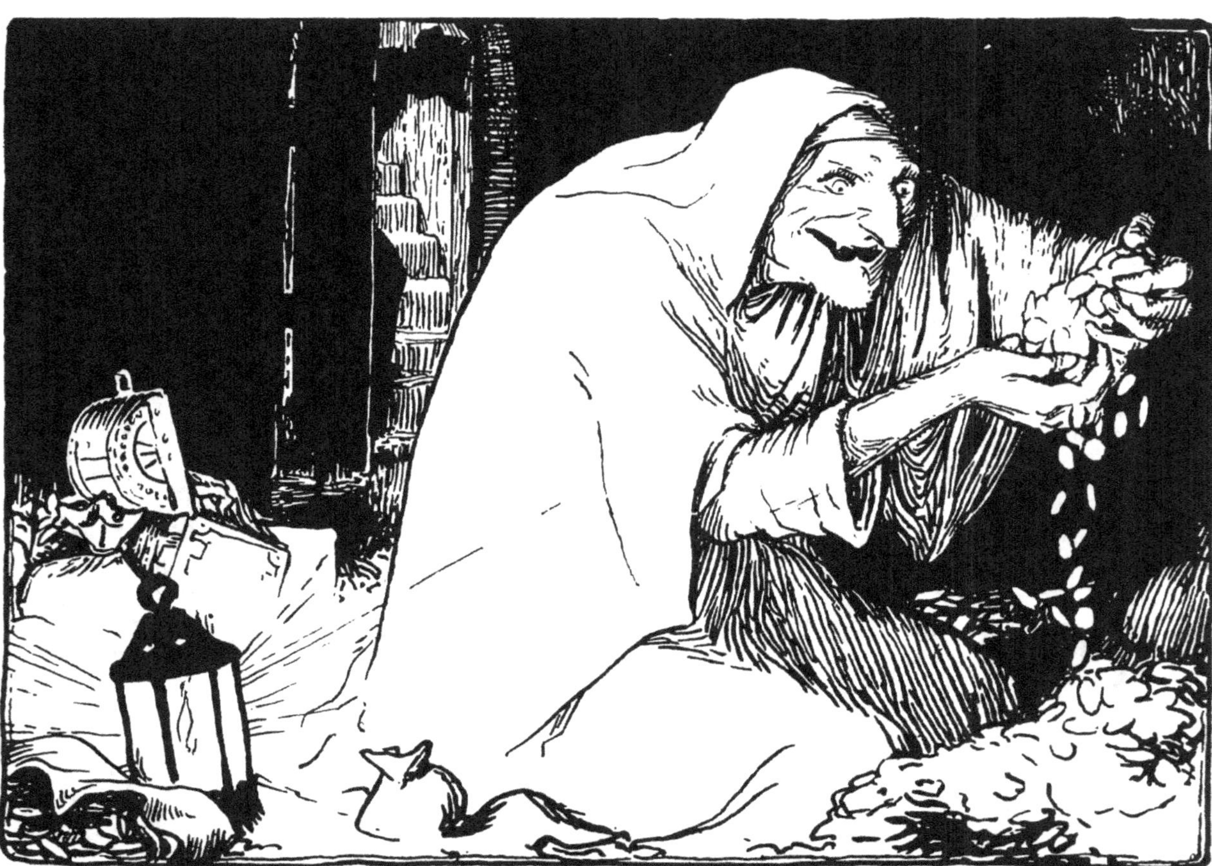

71

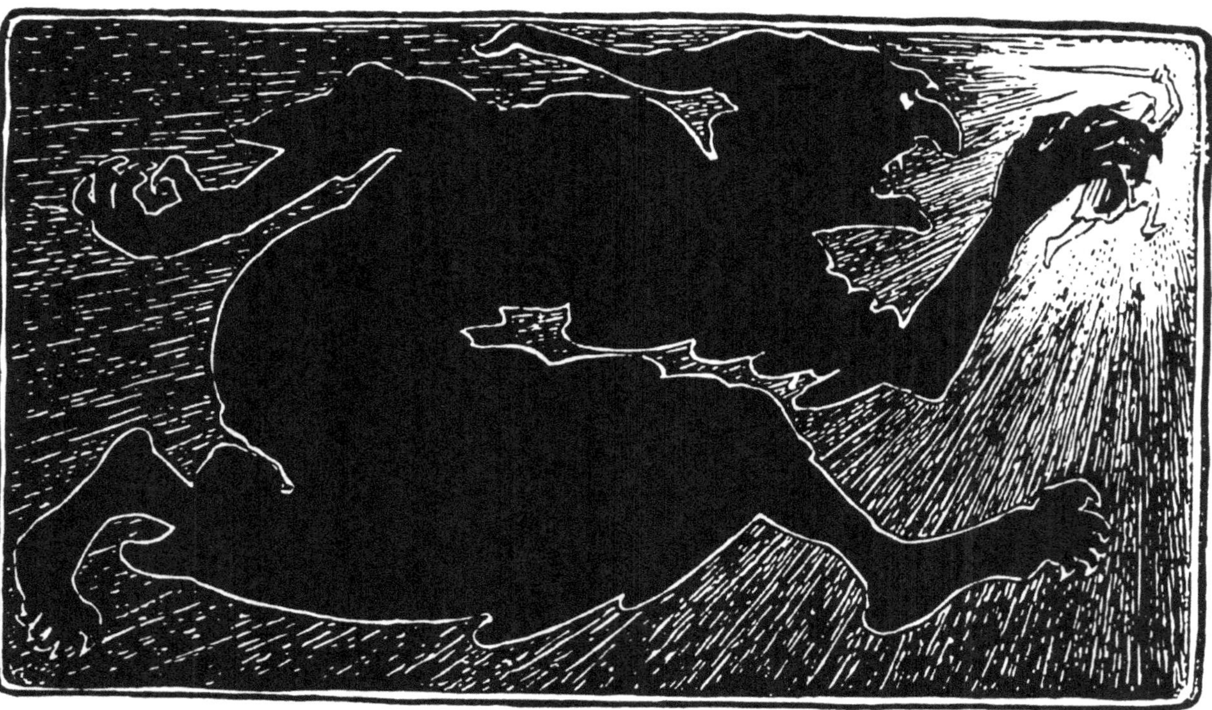

70. Witch II from More Celtic Fairytales by Joseph Jacobs and J.D Batten, 1895

71. Witch from More Celtic Fairytales by Joseph Jacobs and J.D Batten, 1896

72

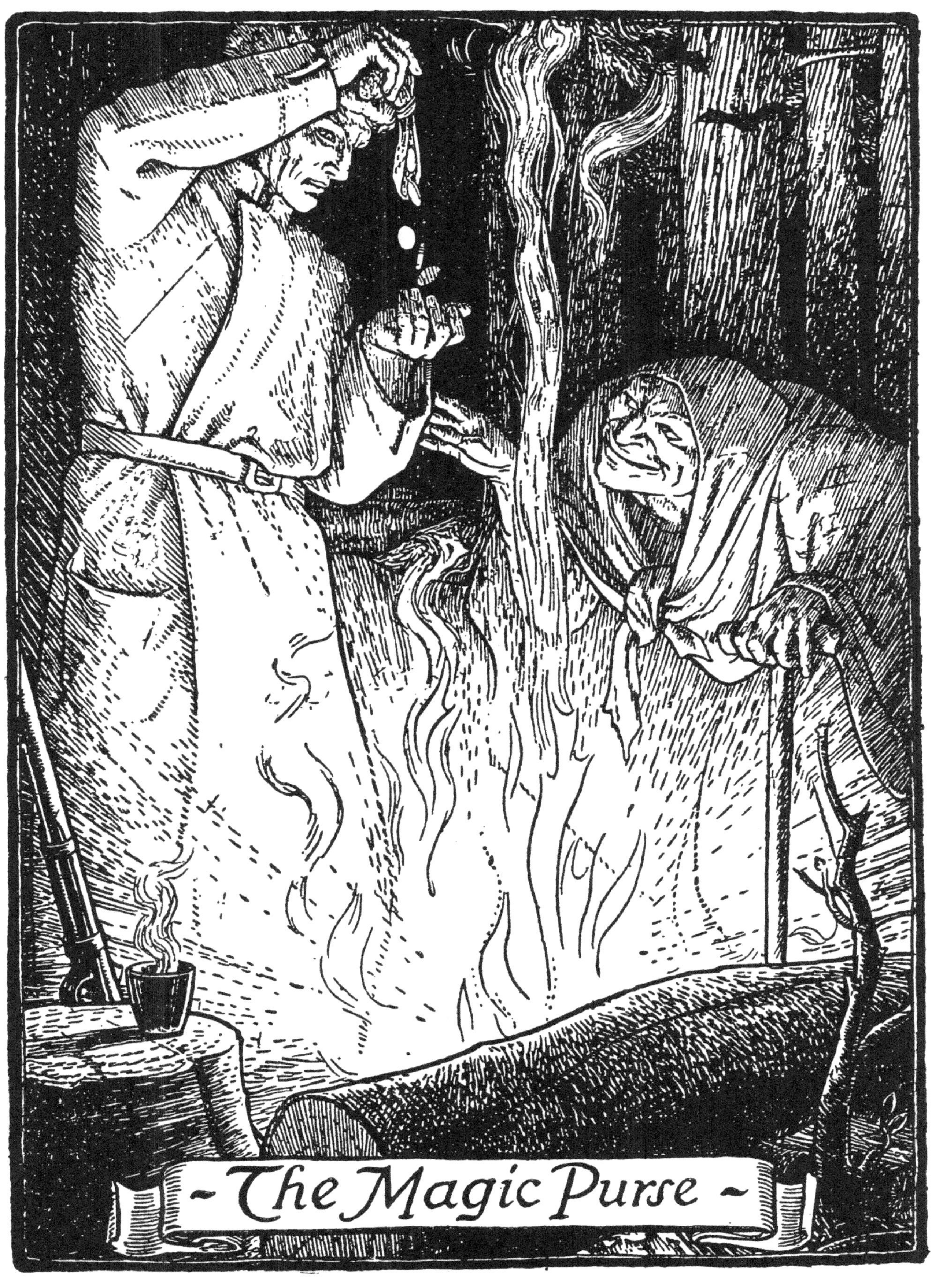

72. Witch 1 from Europa's fairy book, by Joseph
Jacobs, 1854–1916, John Dickson, Batten, 1860–
1932, (1916)

73

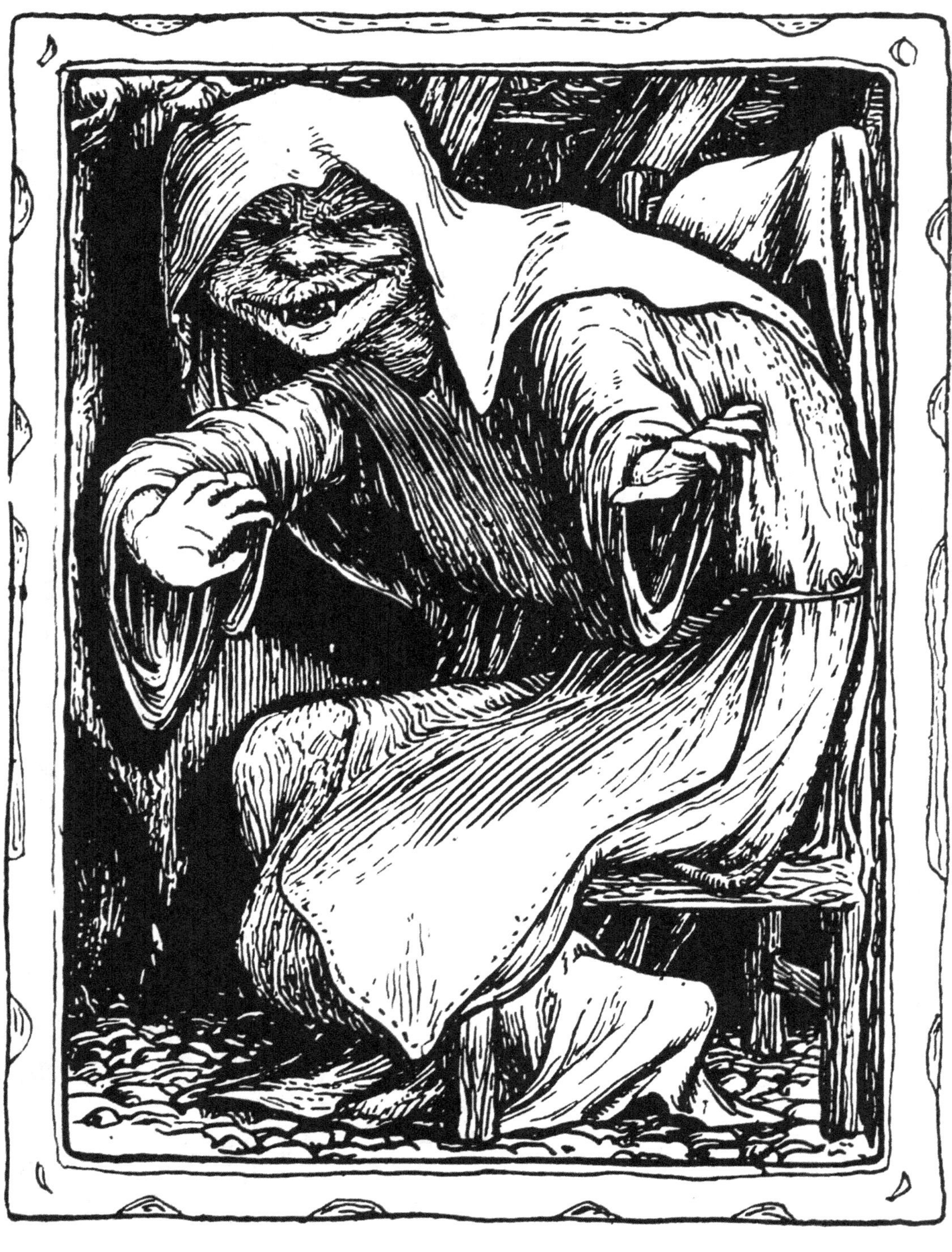

73. Old Hag / Witch from More Celtic Fairytales by
Joseph Jacobs and J.D Batten, 1895

74

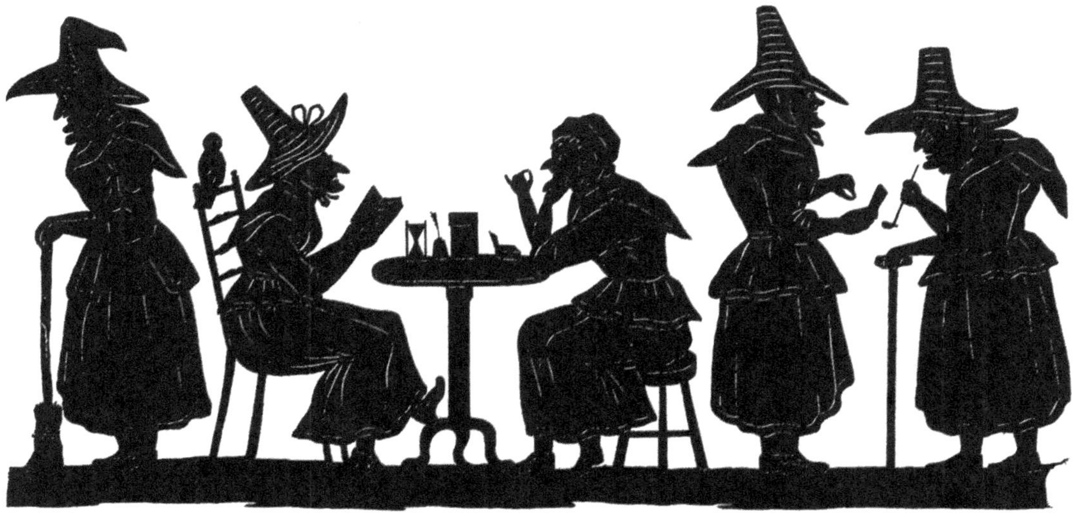

75

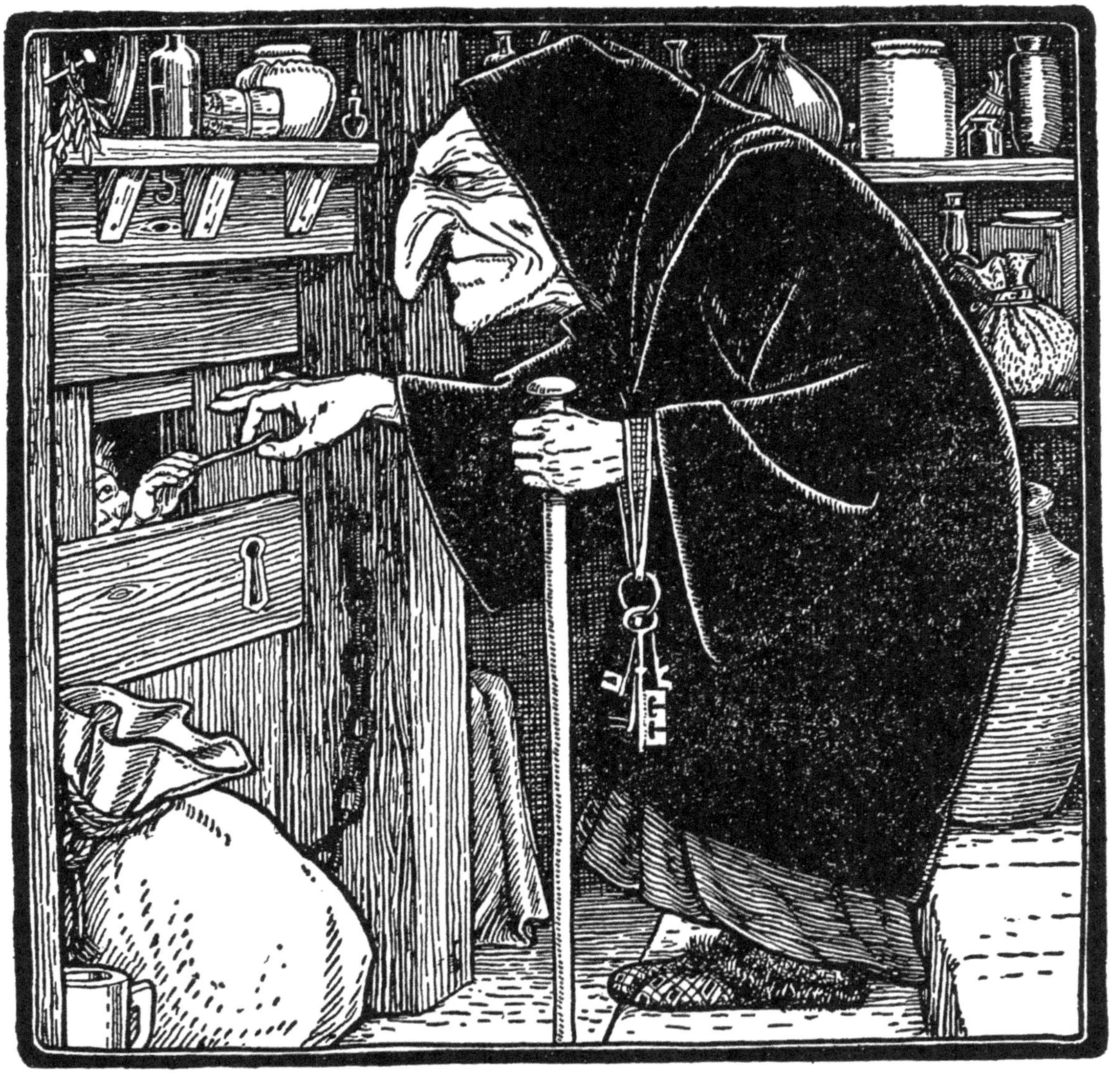

The Witch

74. Witches– five silhouetted figures. Aquatint by
M. Dubourg after B.A. Townshend, 1815

75. Witch 2 from Europa's fairy book, by Joseph
Jacobs, 1854–1916, John Dickson, Batten, 1860–
1932, (1916)

76

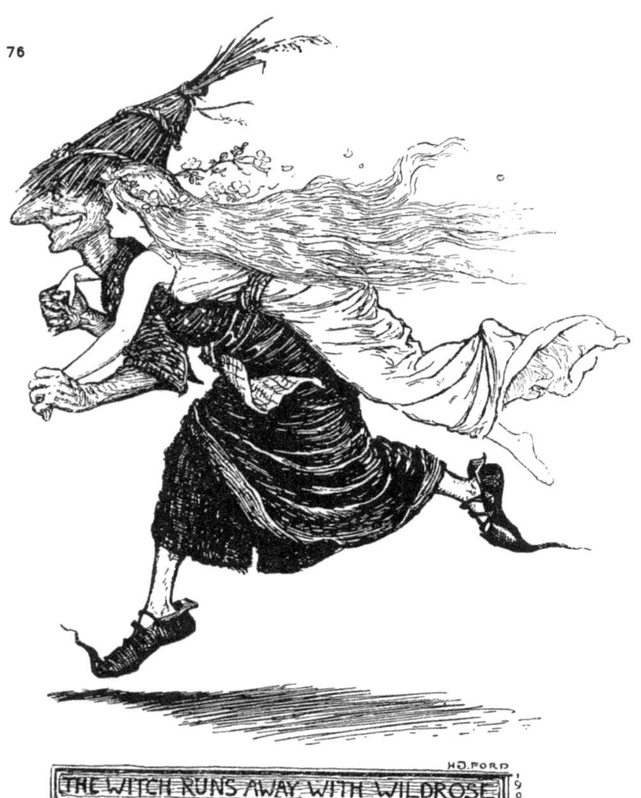

77

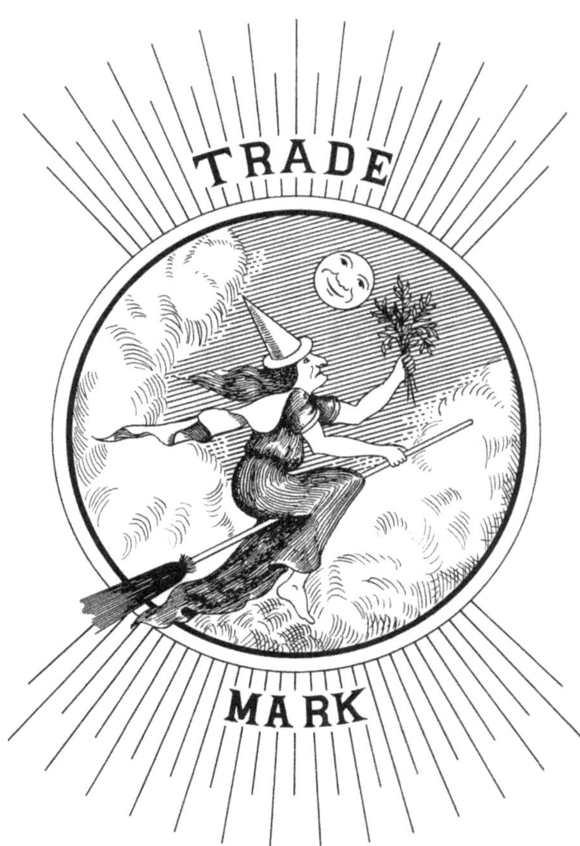

78

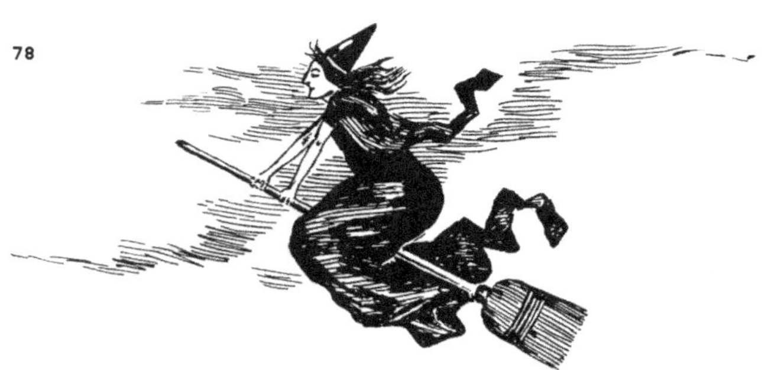

79

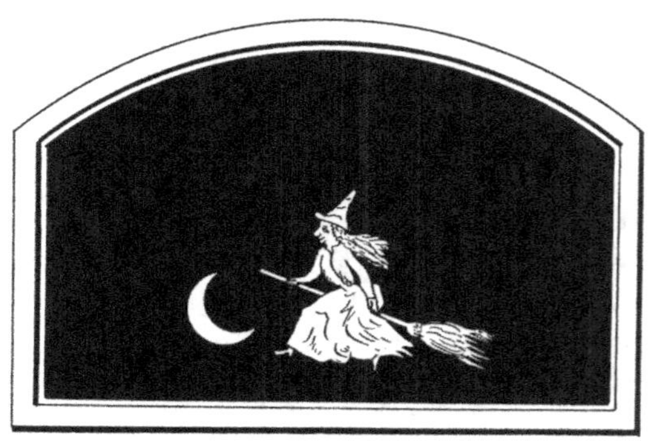

80

WITCH

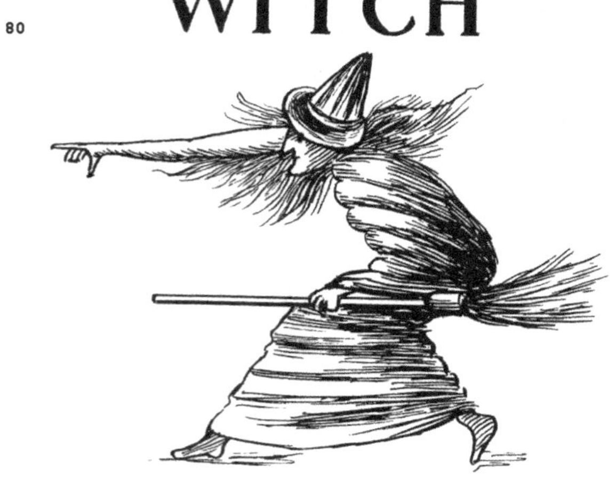

81

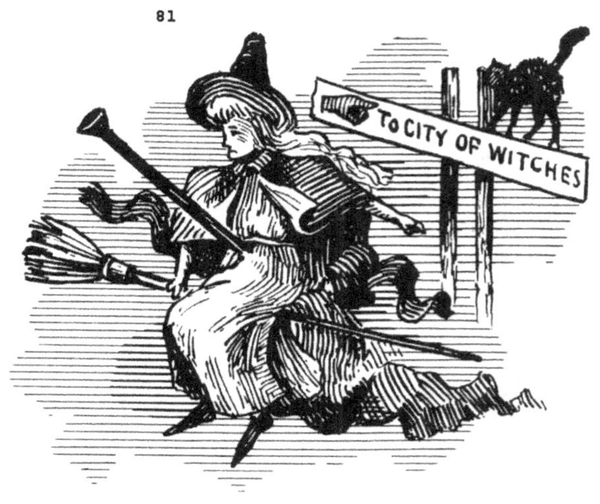

76–87. Various Witch Themed Trademarks

82

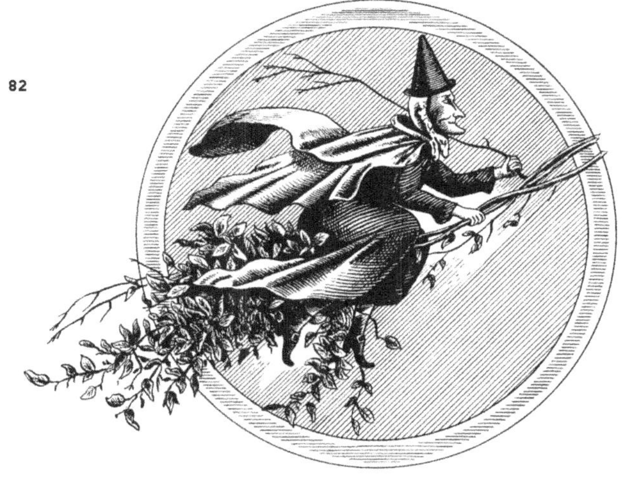

83

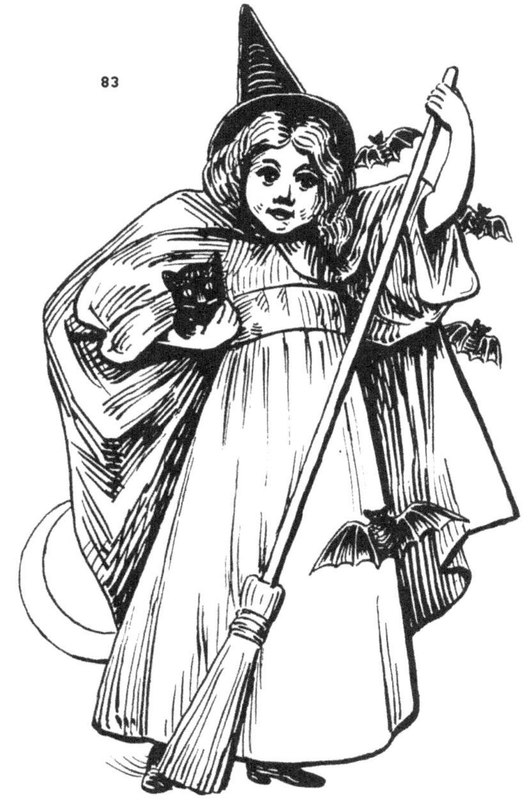

84

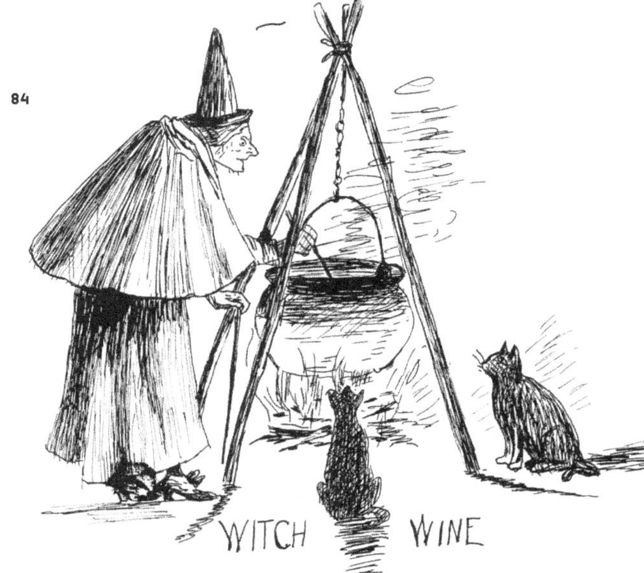

85

86

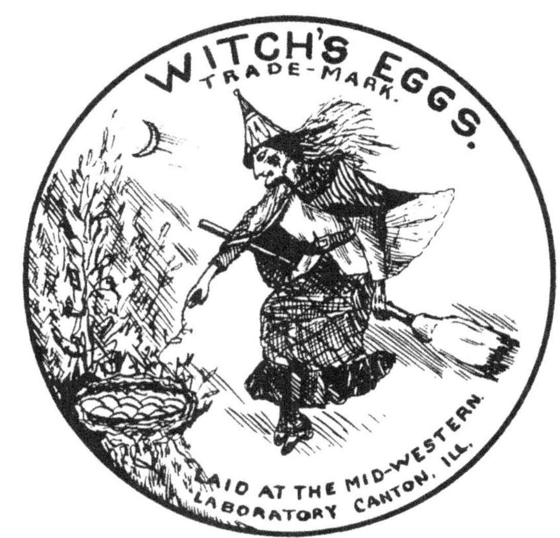

87

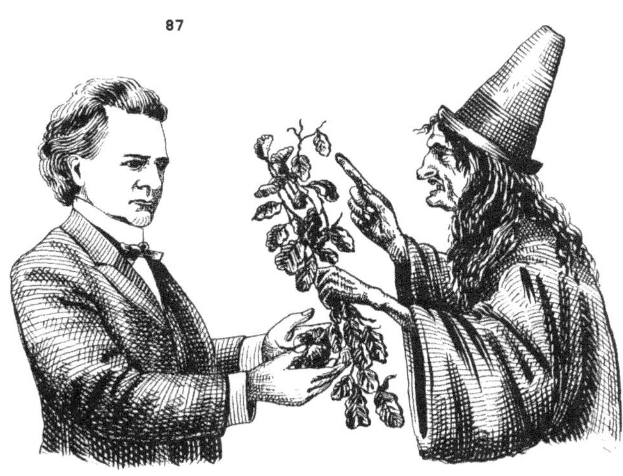

88

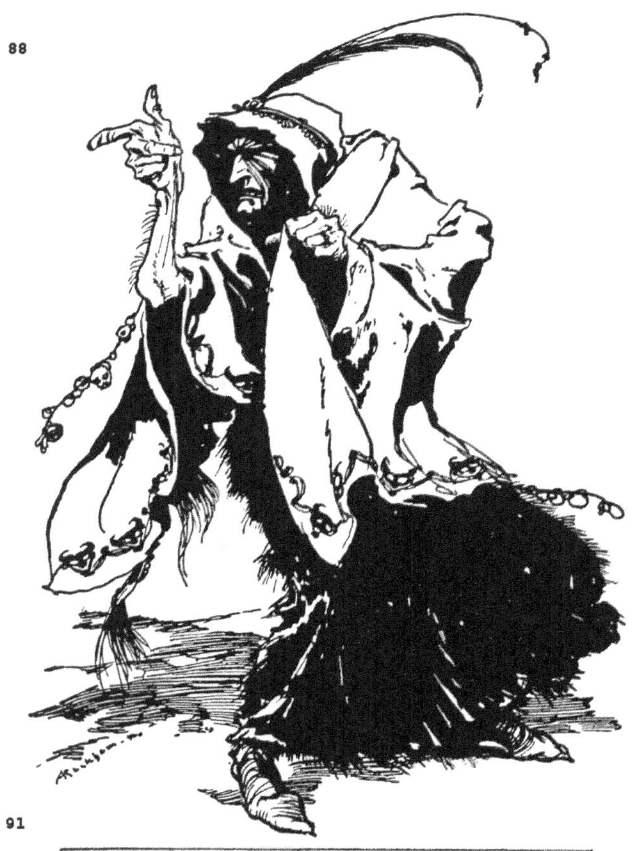

89

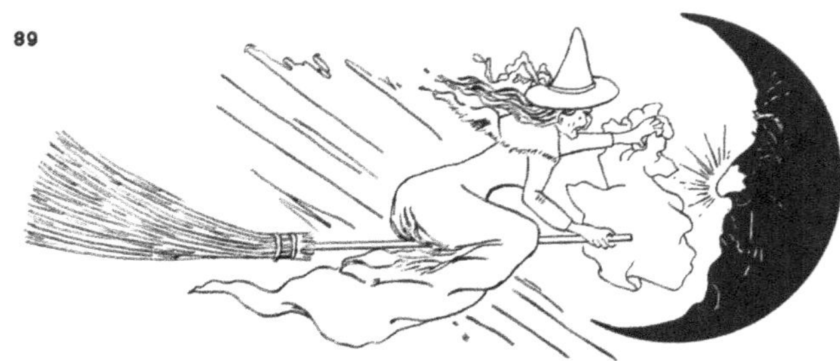

90

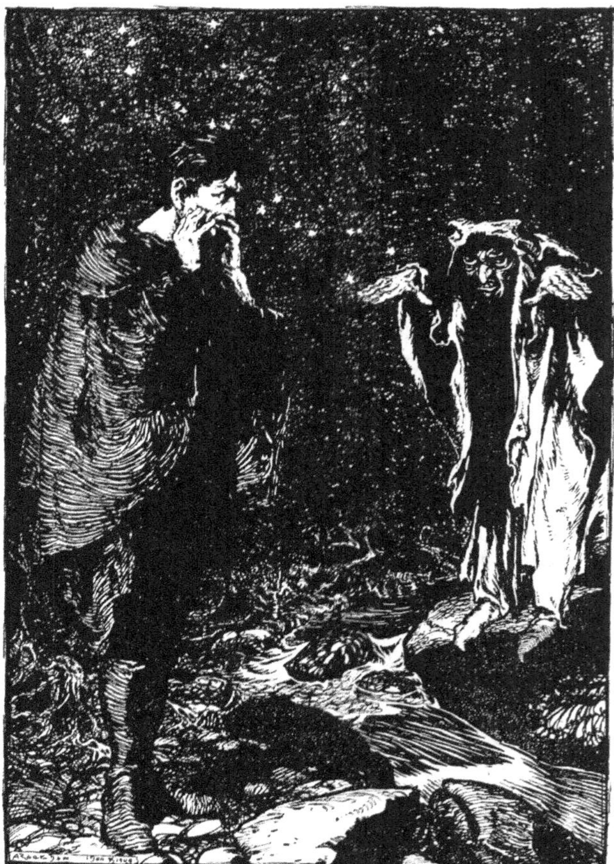

91

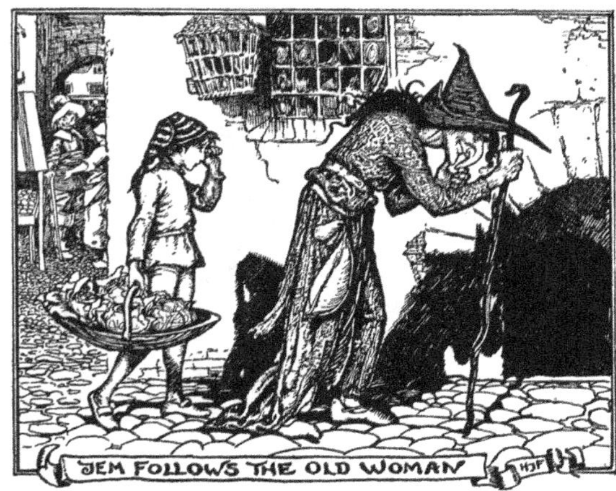

92

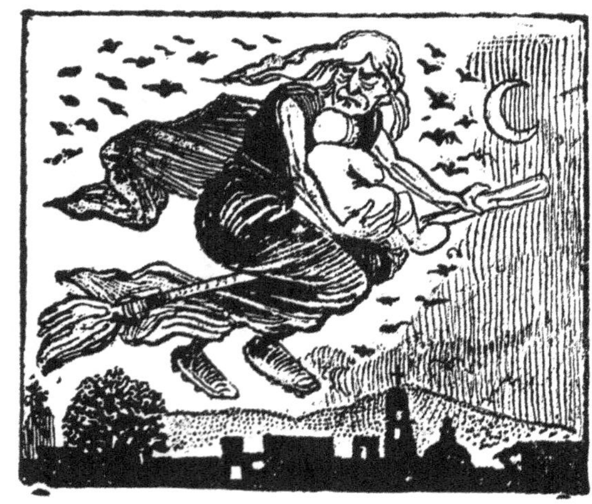

93

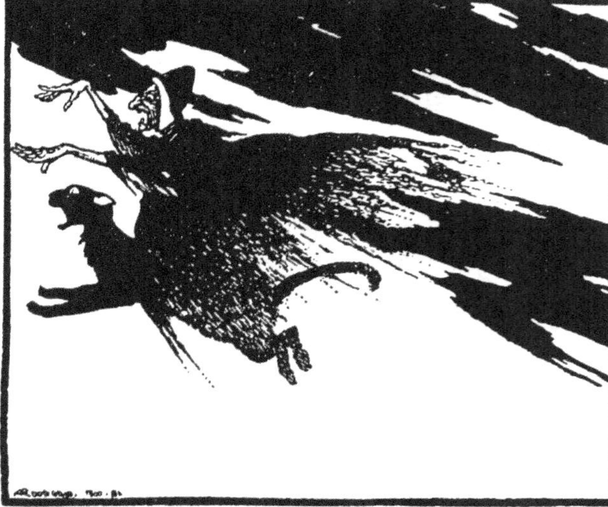

88–97. Various illustrations of witches. See
image index for complete description.

94

95 >

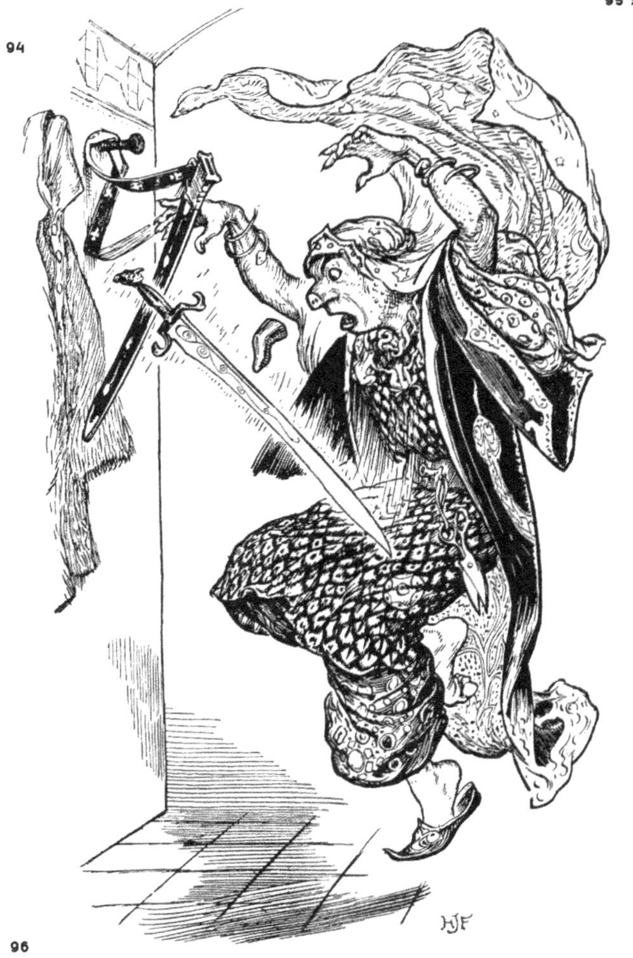

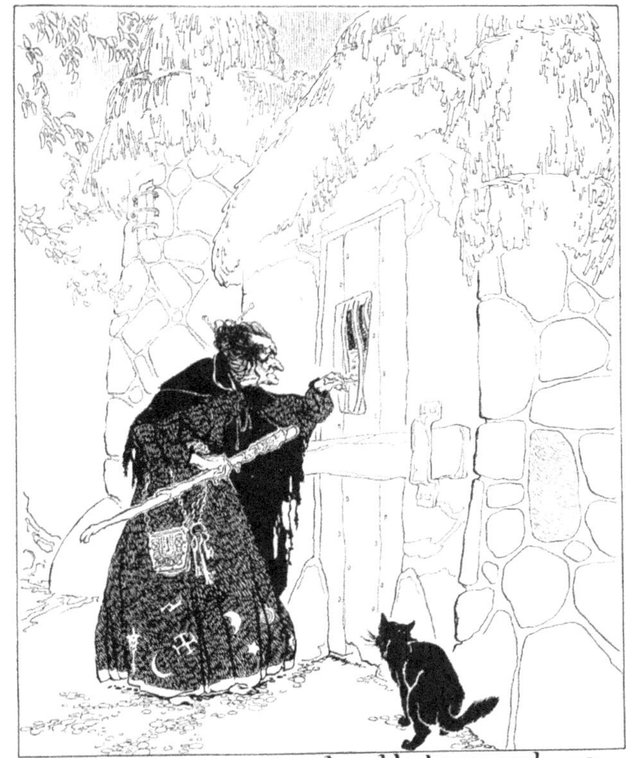

HANSEL put out a knuckle-bone and the old woman, whose eyes were dim, thought it was his finger

96

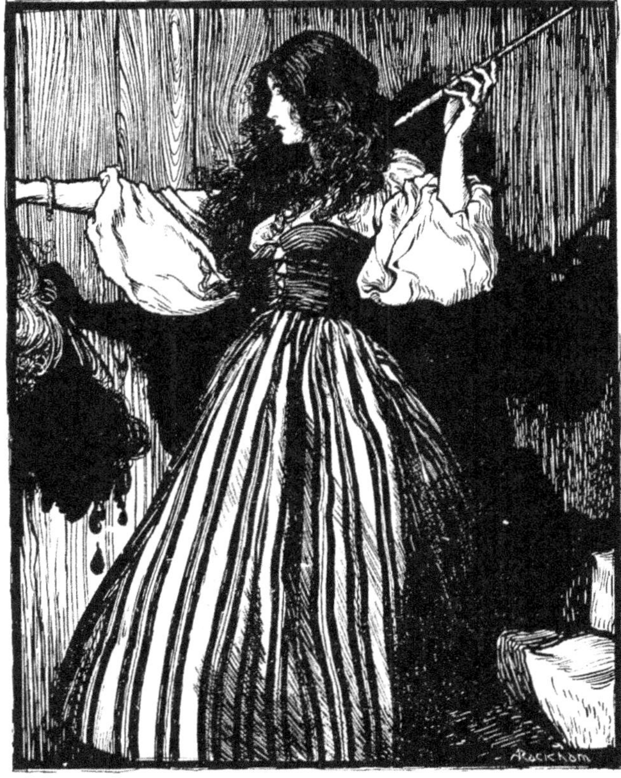

97

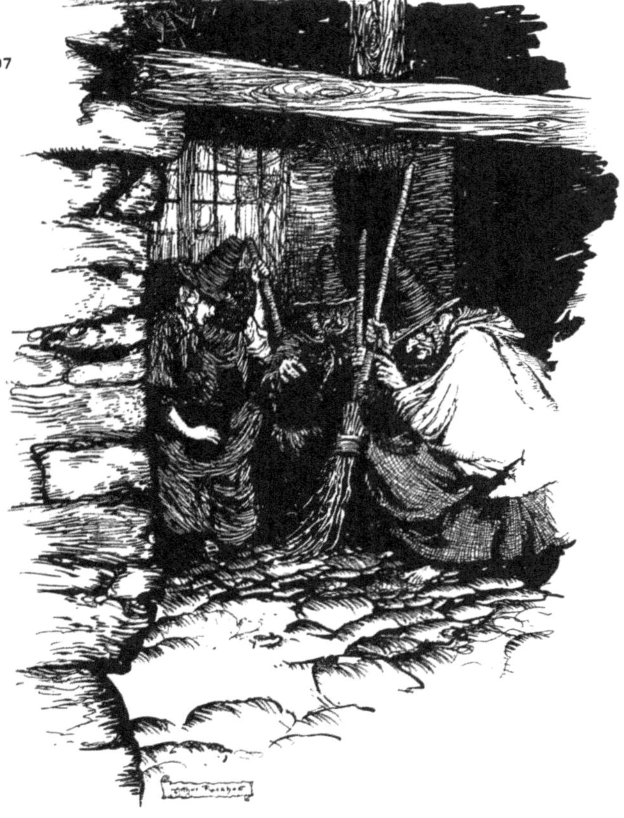

AND THERE WERE GOSSIPS SITTING THERE
BY ONE, BY TWO, BY THREE . . . .

98

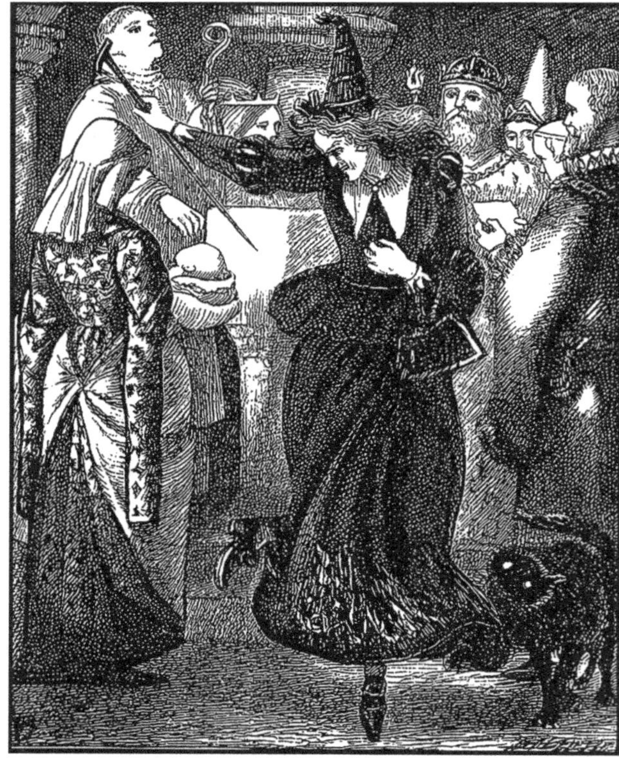

99

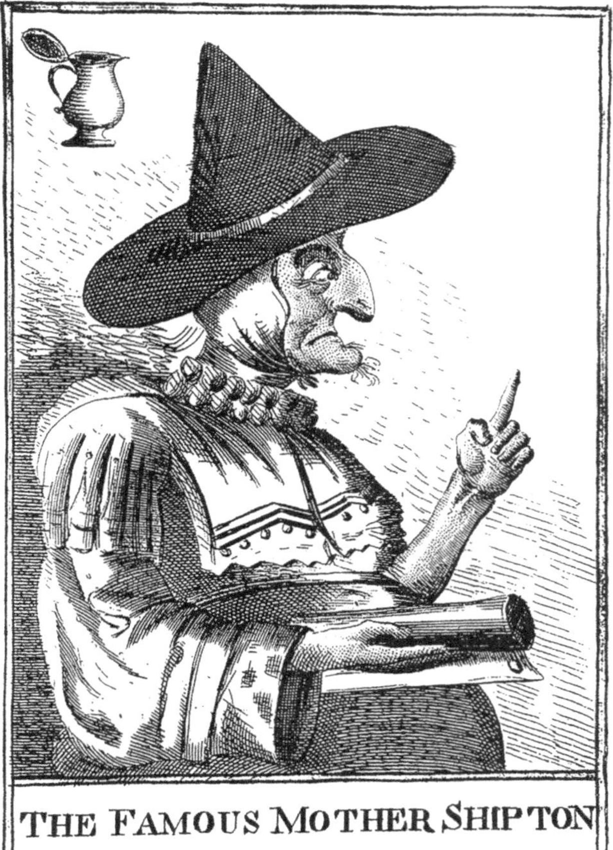

100

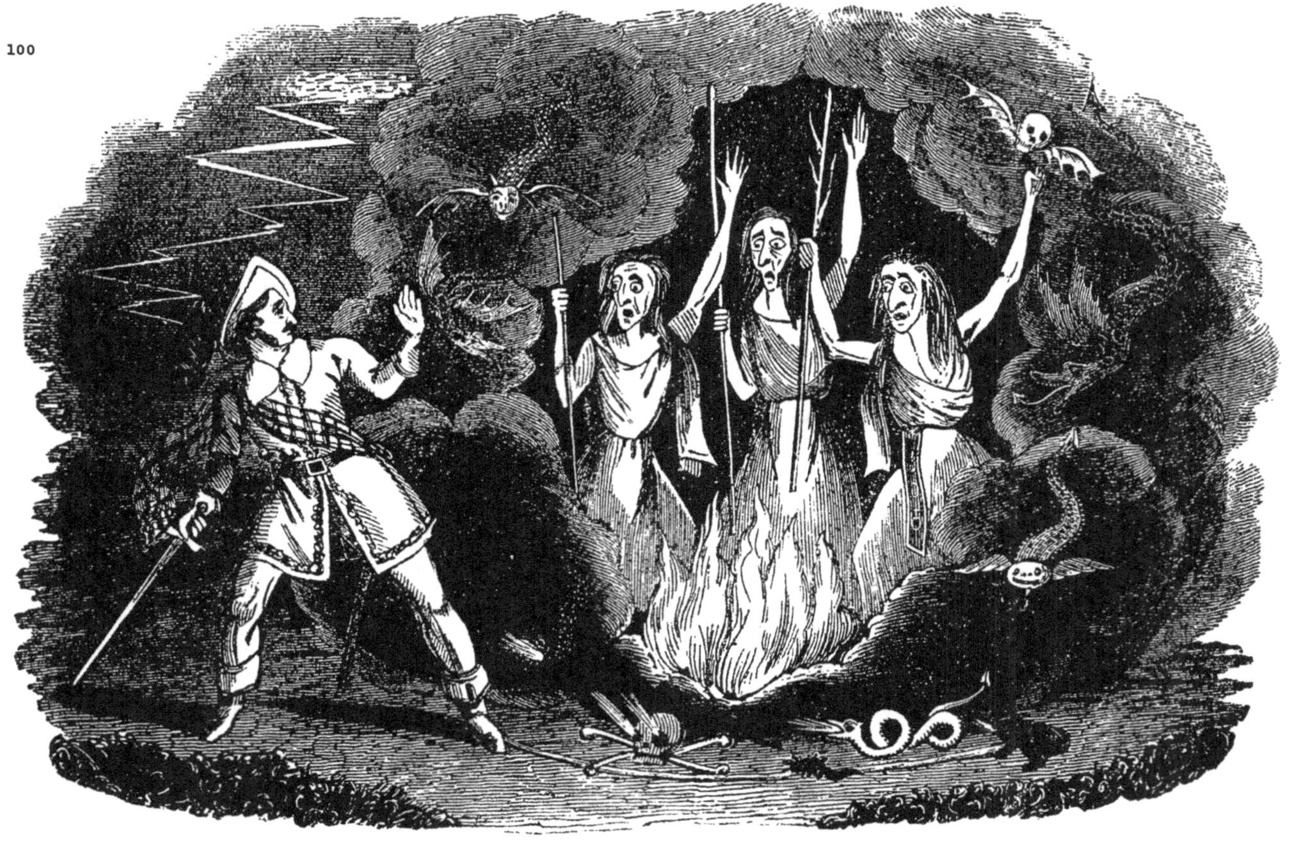

98. Dealings with the fairies, George MacDonald, illustrated by Arthur Hughes 1867

99. The Famous Mother Shipton, artist and date unknown – Source

100. Macbeth meets the three witches; scene from Shakespeare's 'Macbeth'. Wood engraving, 19th century

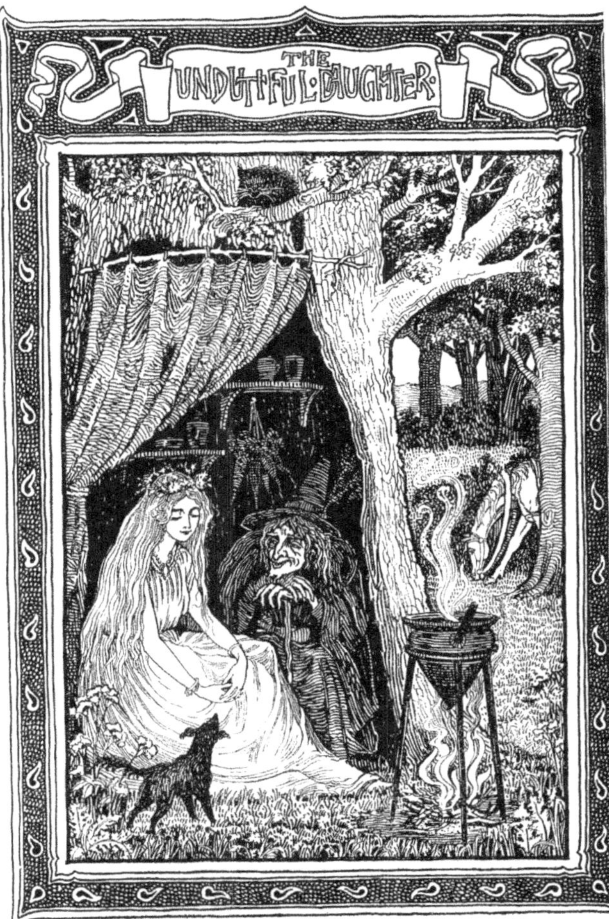

101

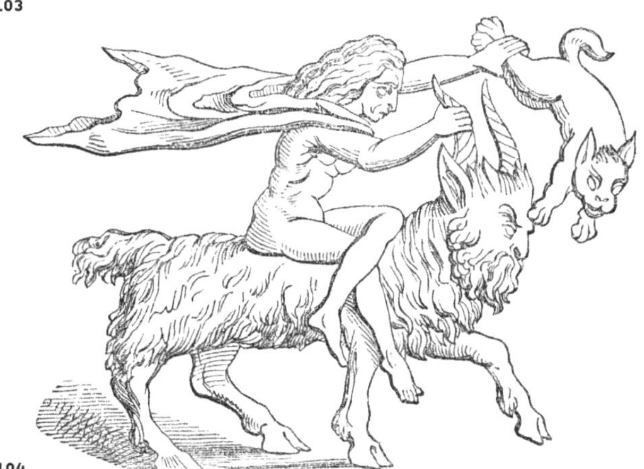

103

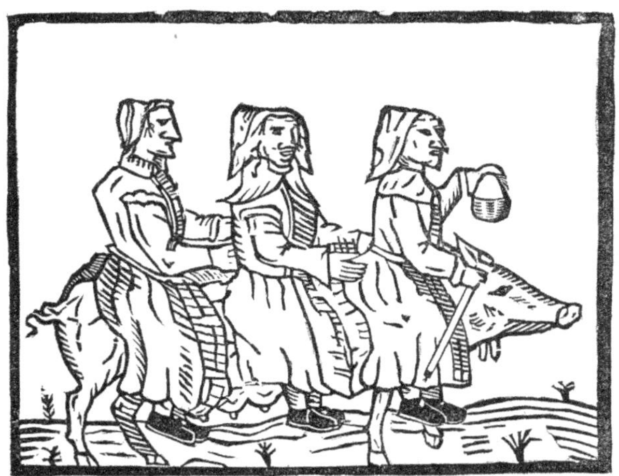

104

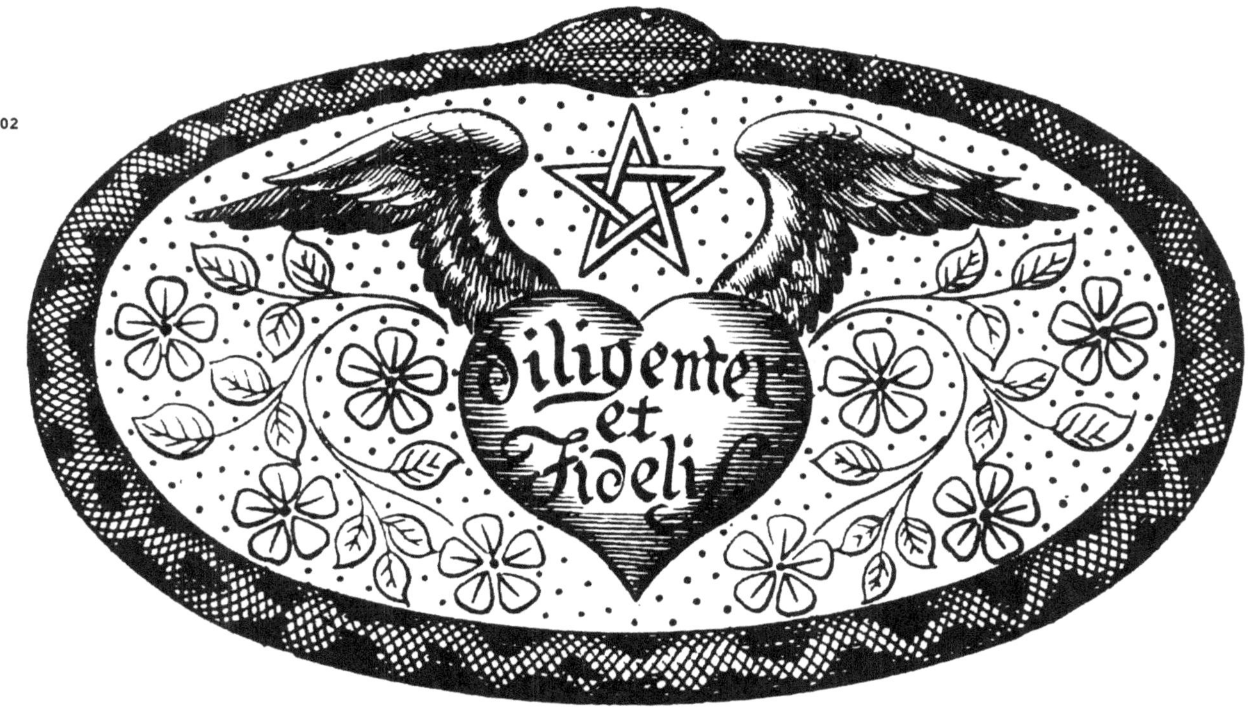

102

101. The Undutiful Daughter, from Old English Fairy Tales

102. Emblem from Ex-Libris of Wonders of an Invisible World

103. A witch riding a horned beast

104. The Witches of Northhamptonshire

105

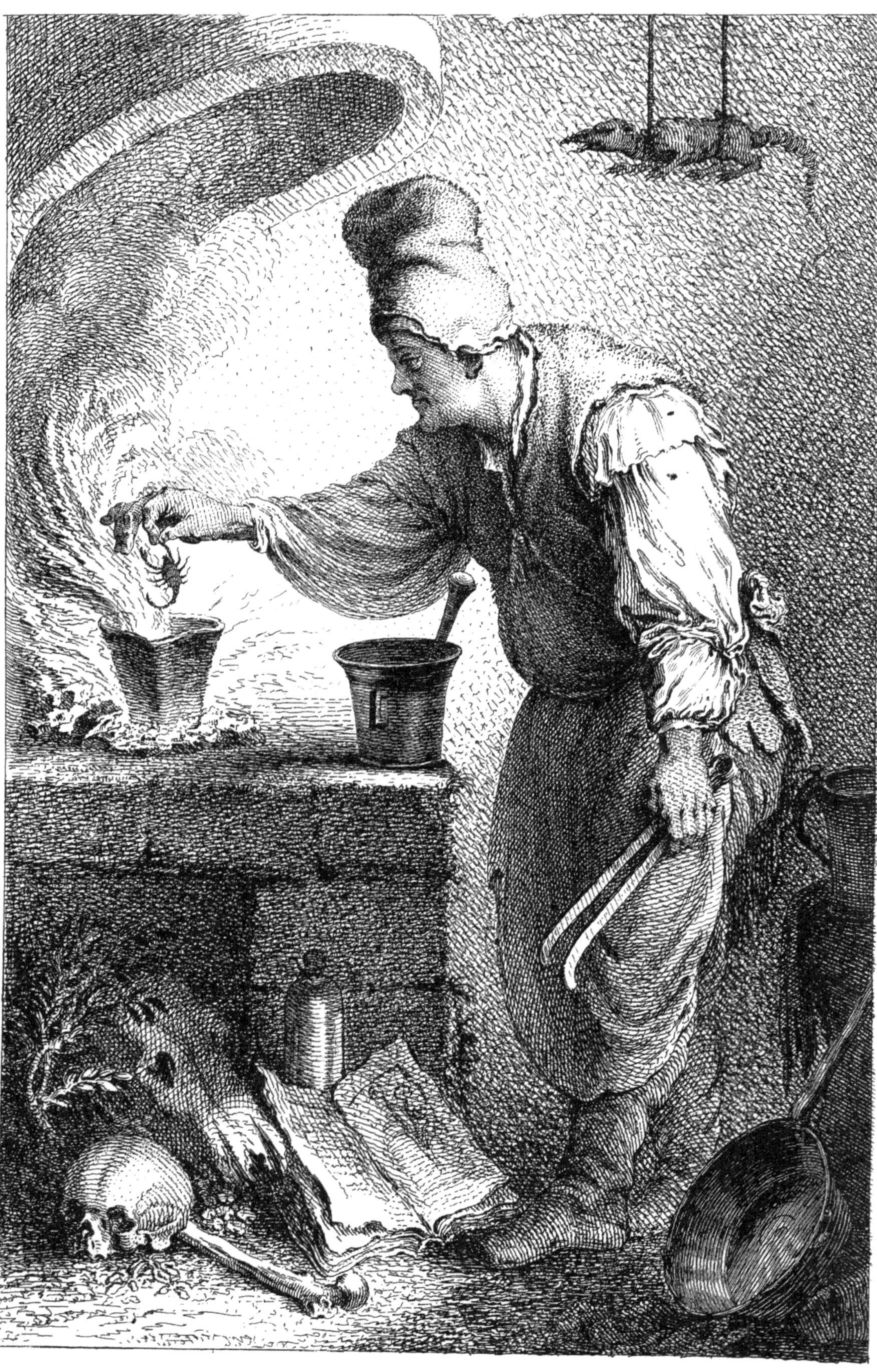

105. Woman at stove holds a scorpion over a
pan, Ferdinand Landerer, 1740 – 1795, Possibly
a witch in her kitchen

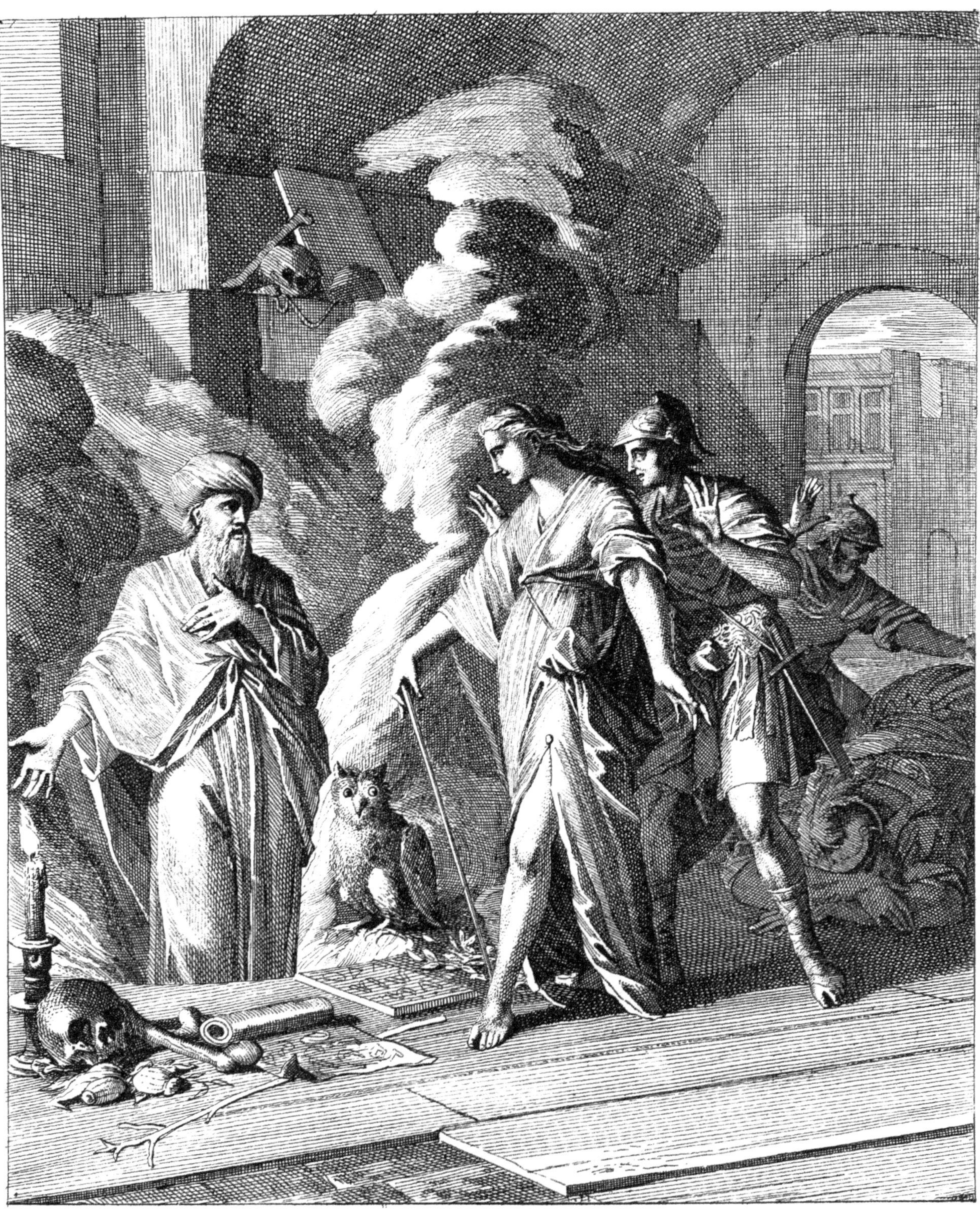

106. Samuel appears to Saul at the witch of
Endor, Caspar Luyken, 1708

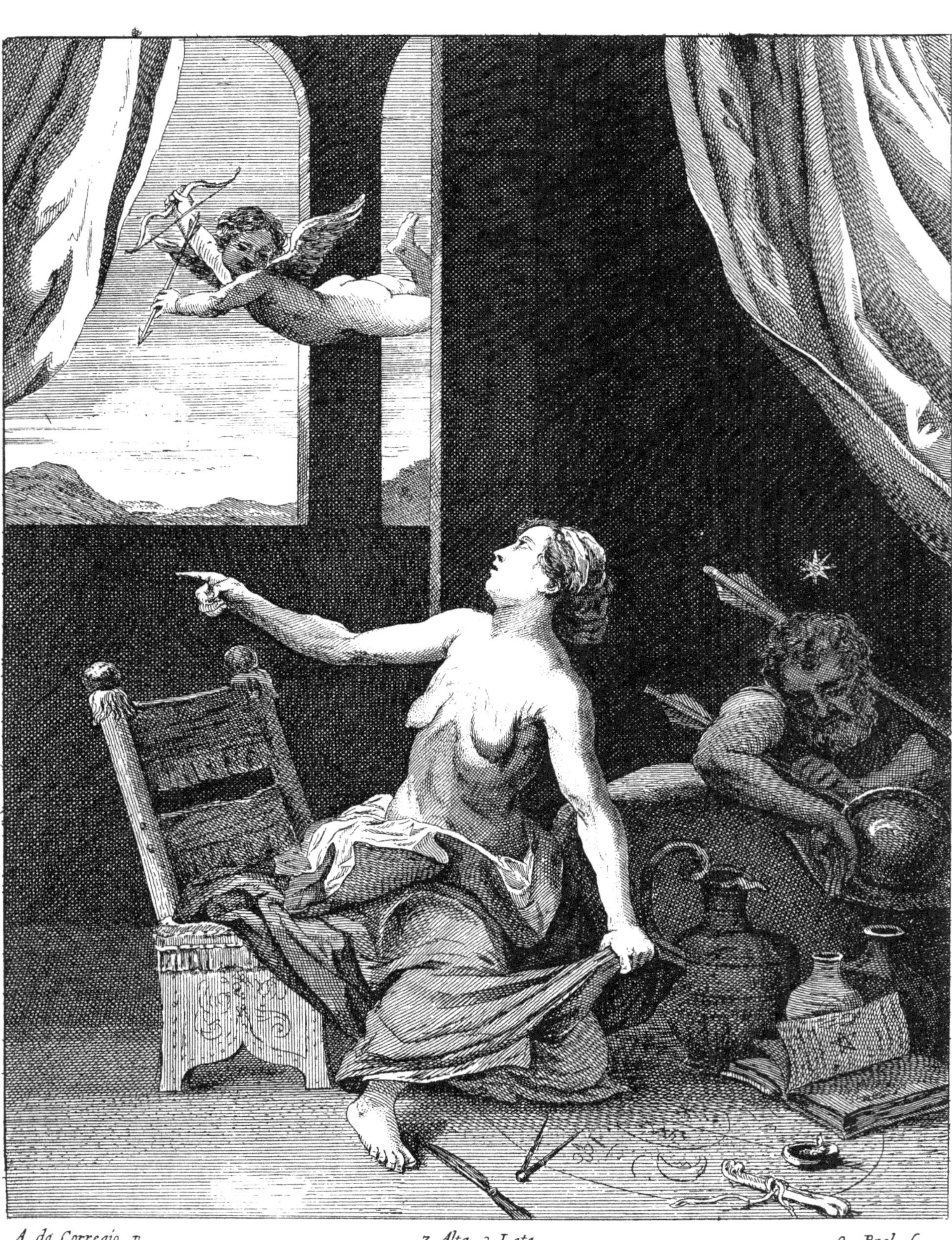

107. Amor with a sorceress and a sleeping
soldier, Quirin Boel (on object), 1660

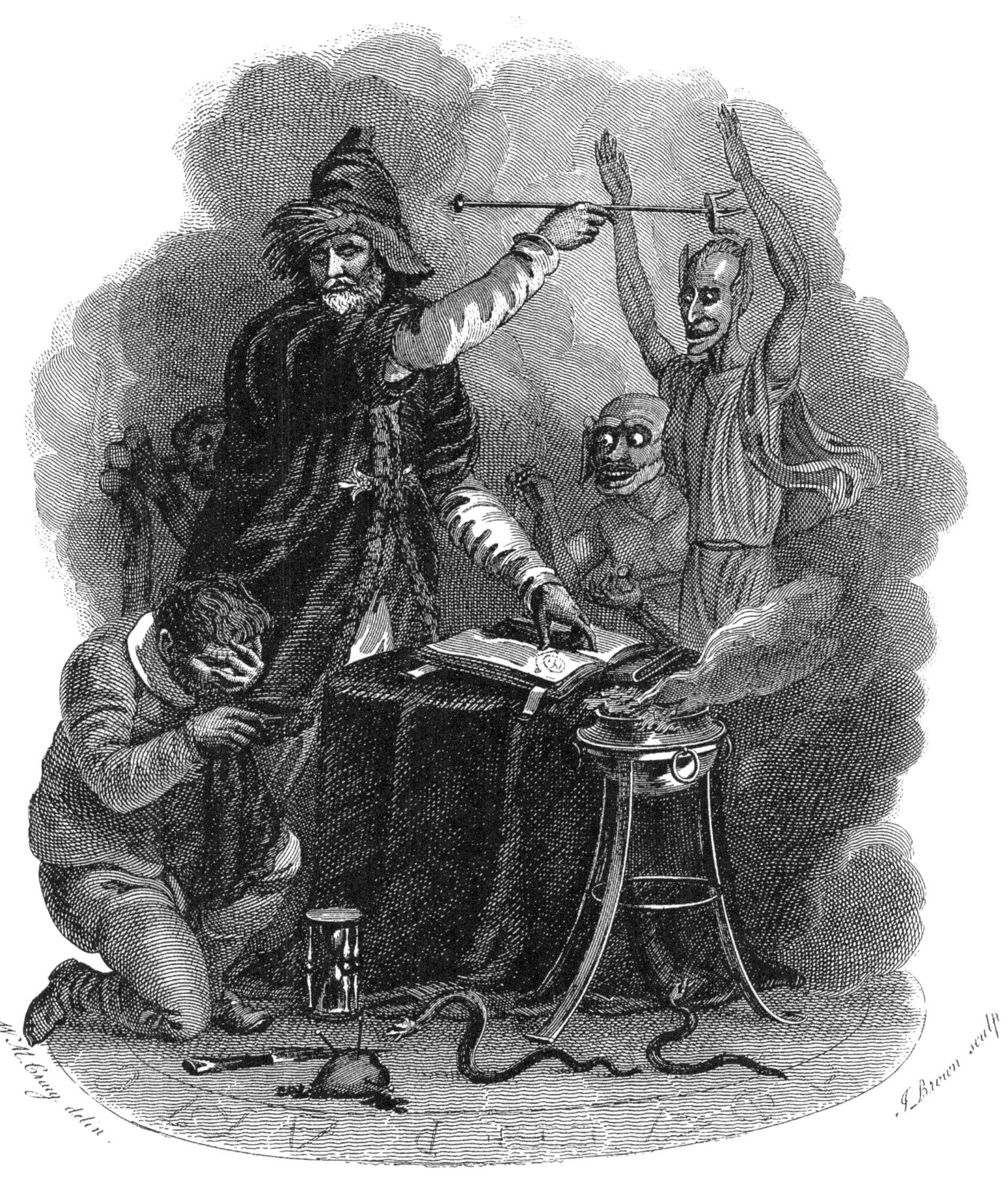

108. A conjurer casting spells with his wand
and fire surrounded by demons within the magic
circle. Engraving by J. Brown 1813.

109

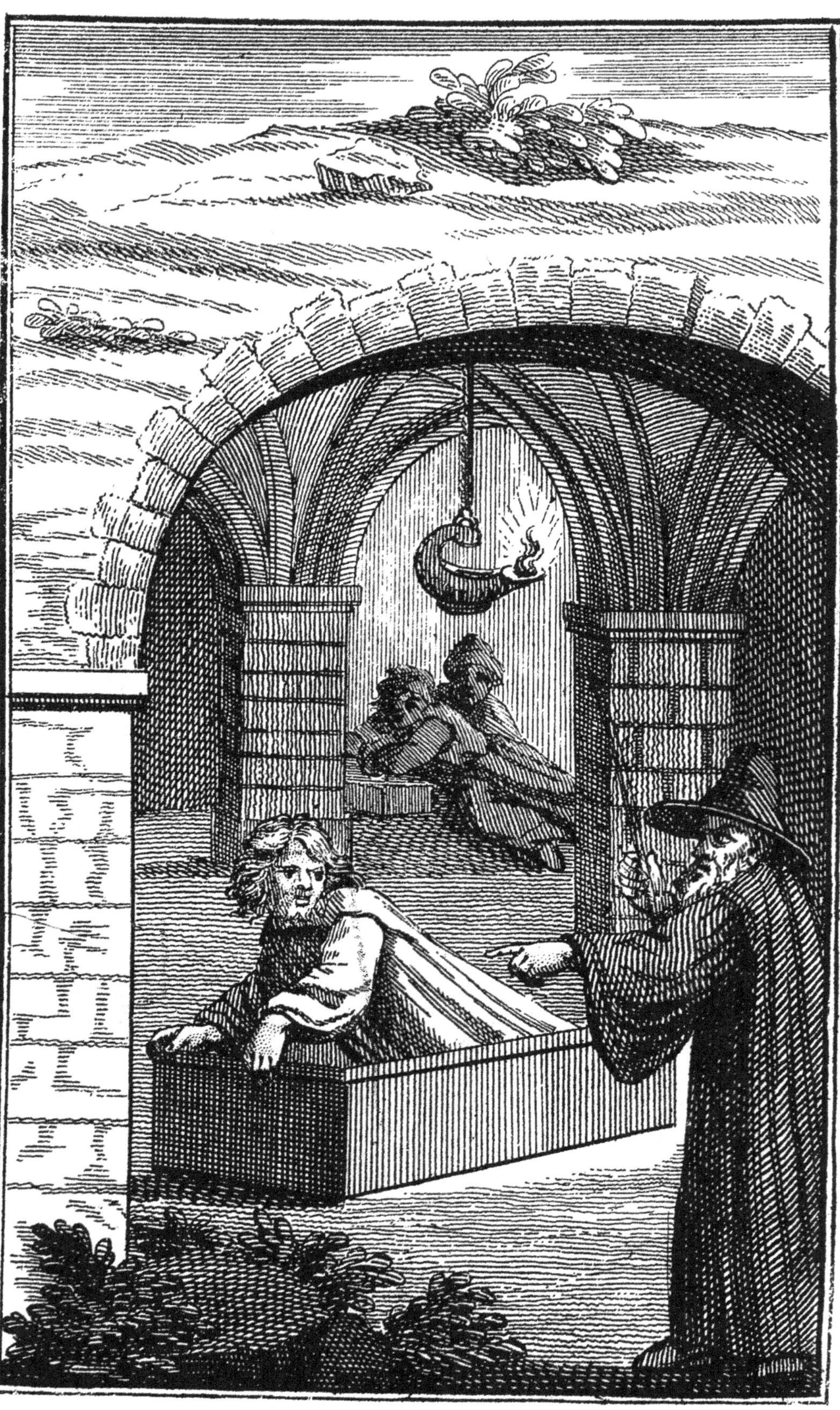

109. A wizard conjuring a man from his grave.
Etching.

110

Cholera
Influenza
O. Seitz
Des Todes schwarze Küche.
Für die "Jugend" gezeichnet von O. Seitz

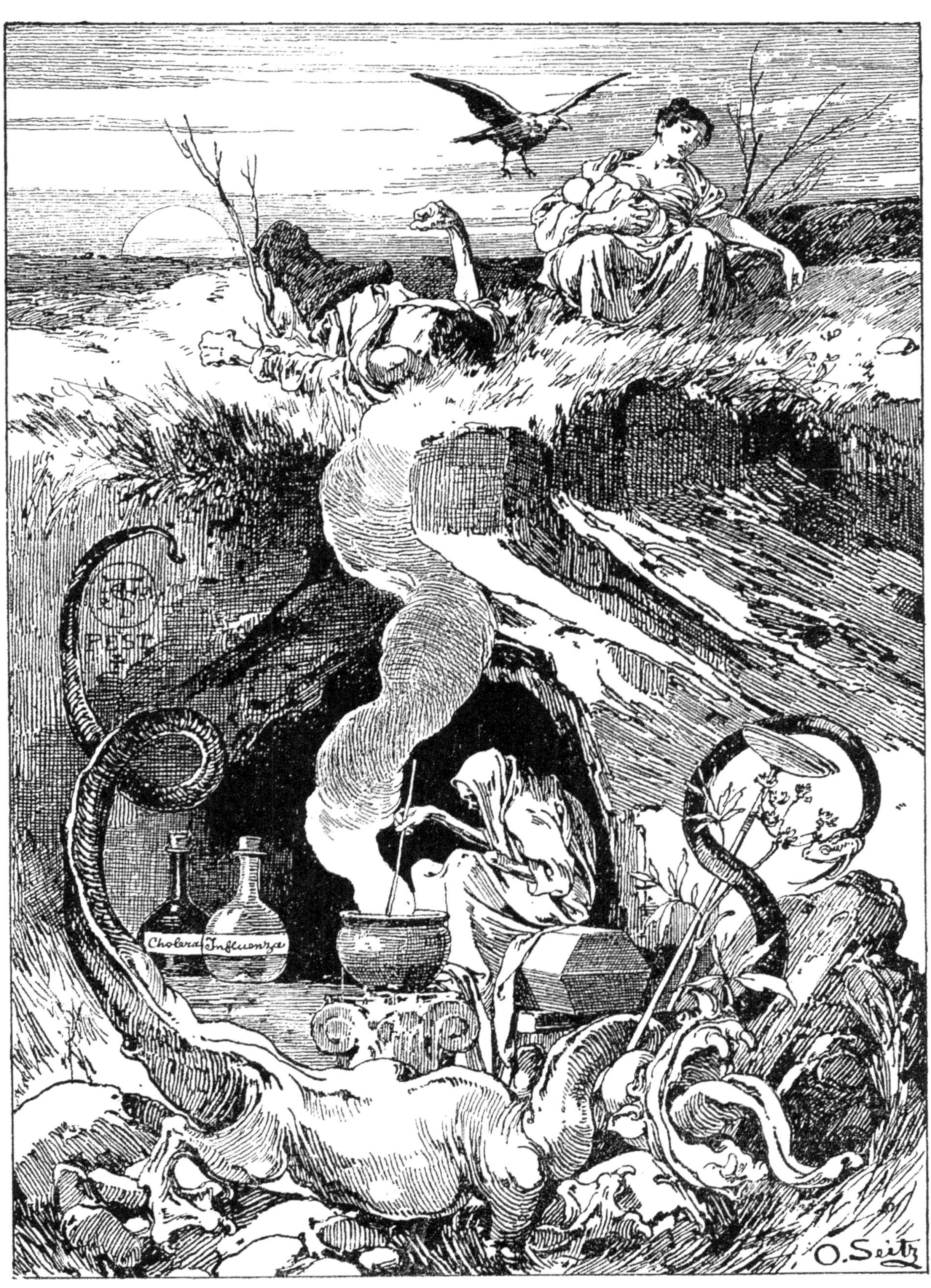

111

LOQUEBAR IN CONSPECTU REGUM.
La Couronne De Maistre Iean Brusle.
LOQUEBAR IN CONSPECTU REGUM · SICUT ODOR AGRI PLENI
GILLION.
LUCIEN EN B. HUM:
DIABLE BOSSU.
FAUSTA AUGURIA
RENVERSEMENT
FESTIN NUPTIAL.
Lecteur ne perdez aucun trait
De ce Prêcheur grand Parasite:
Chaque Embleme en est un Portrait,
Son Tribunal est la Marmite.
Guil: Du Vivier fe:

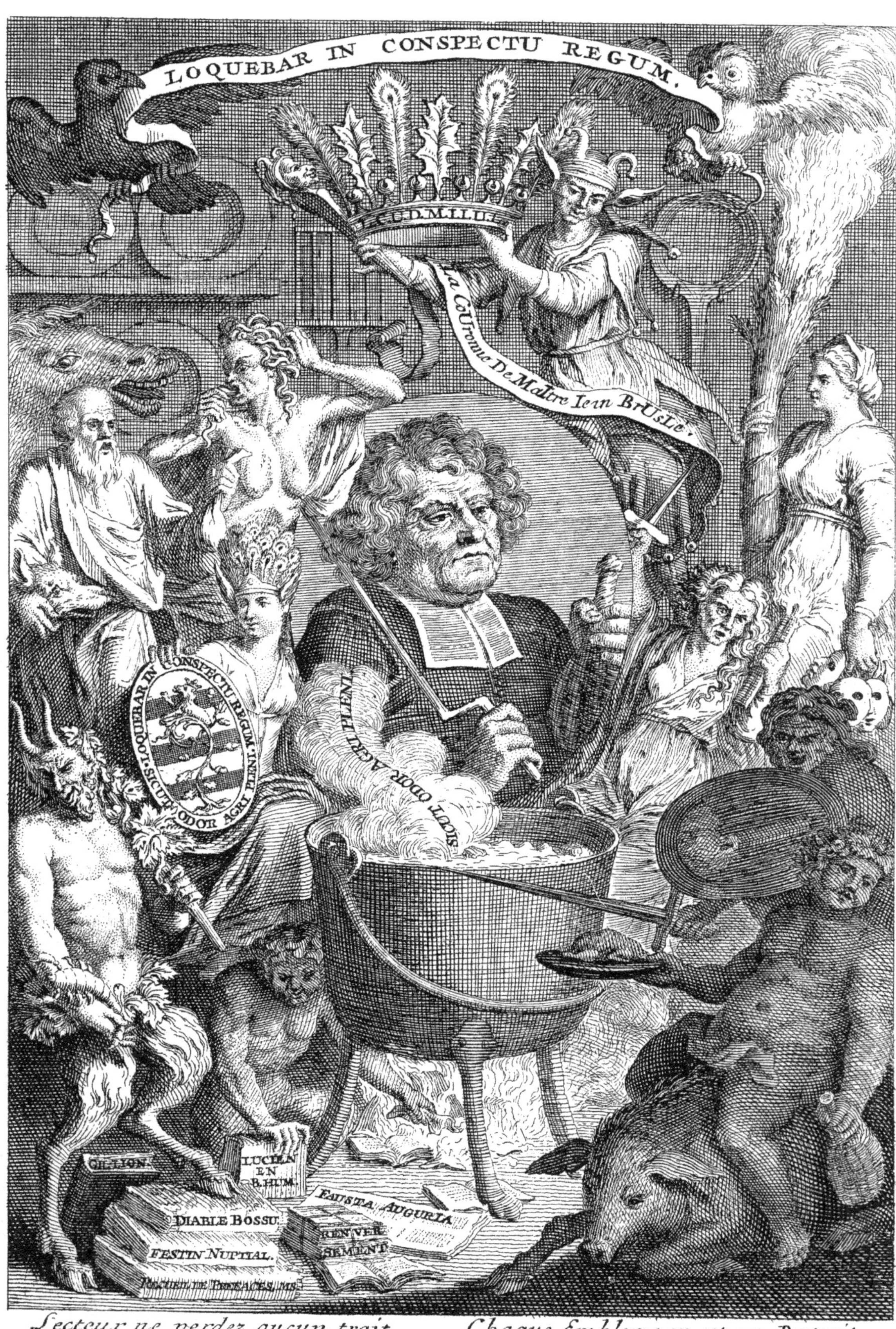

112

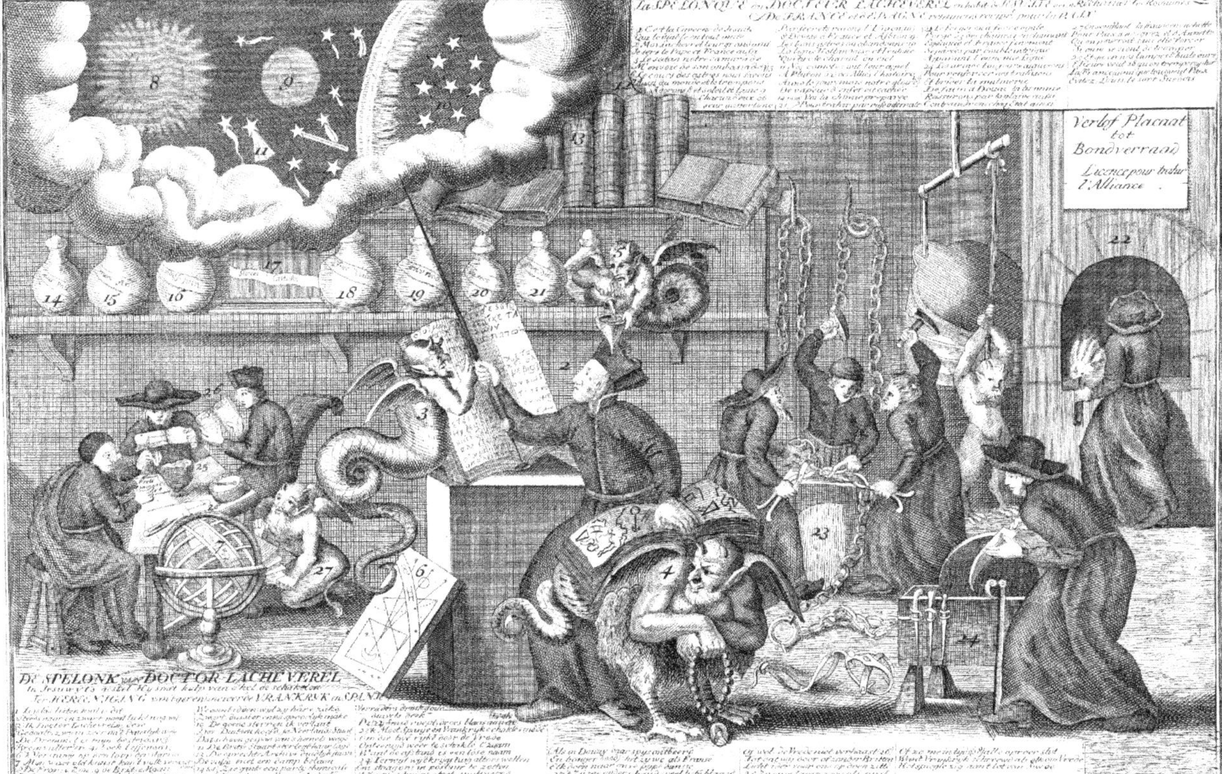

113

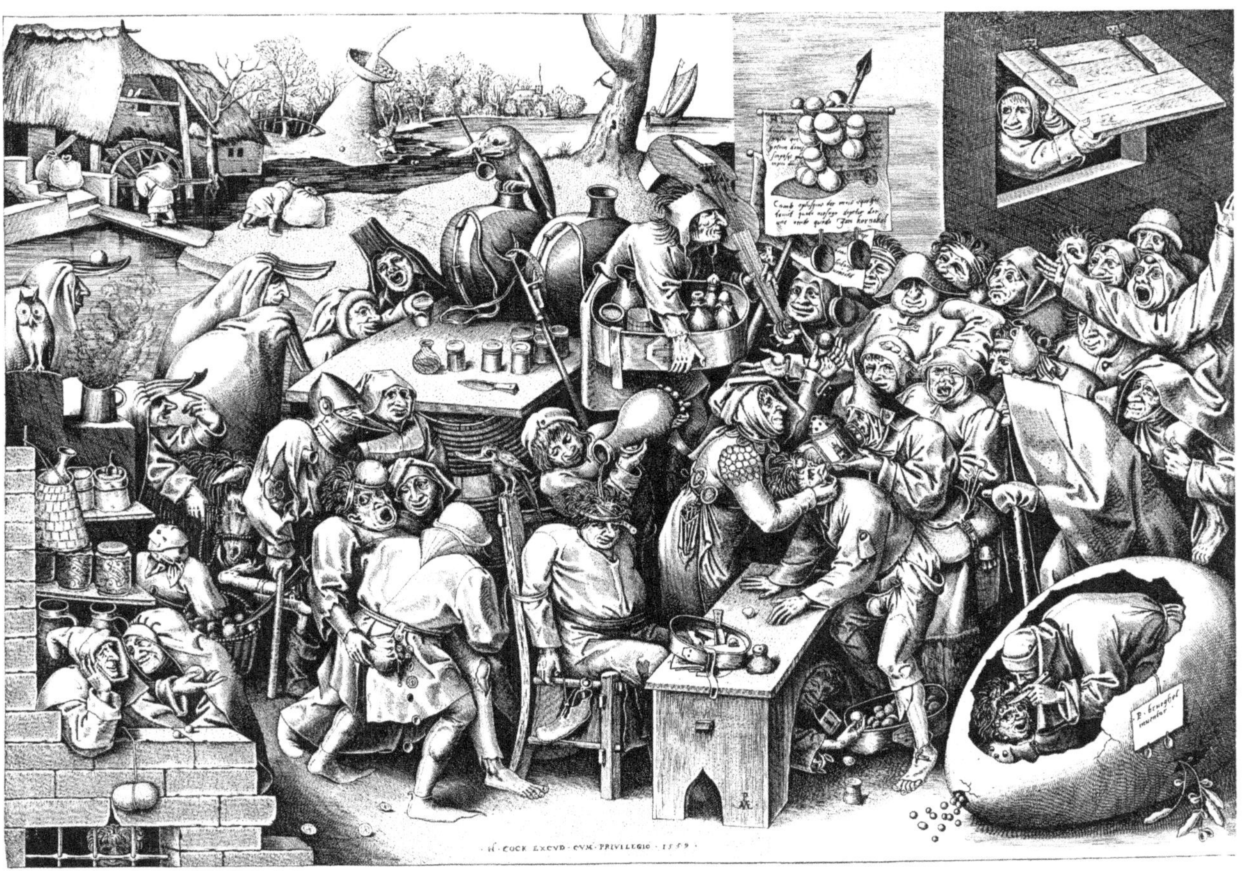

112. Spotlight on Henry Sacheverell, 1713,
attributed to Paul van Somer (II), 1689

113. Keisnijder or the witch of Mallegem by Pieter
van der Heyden, 1559

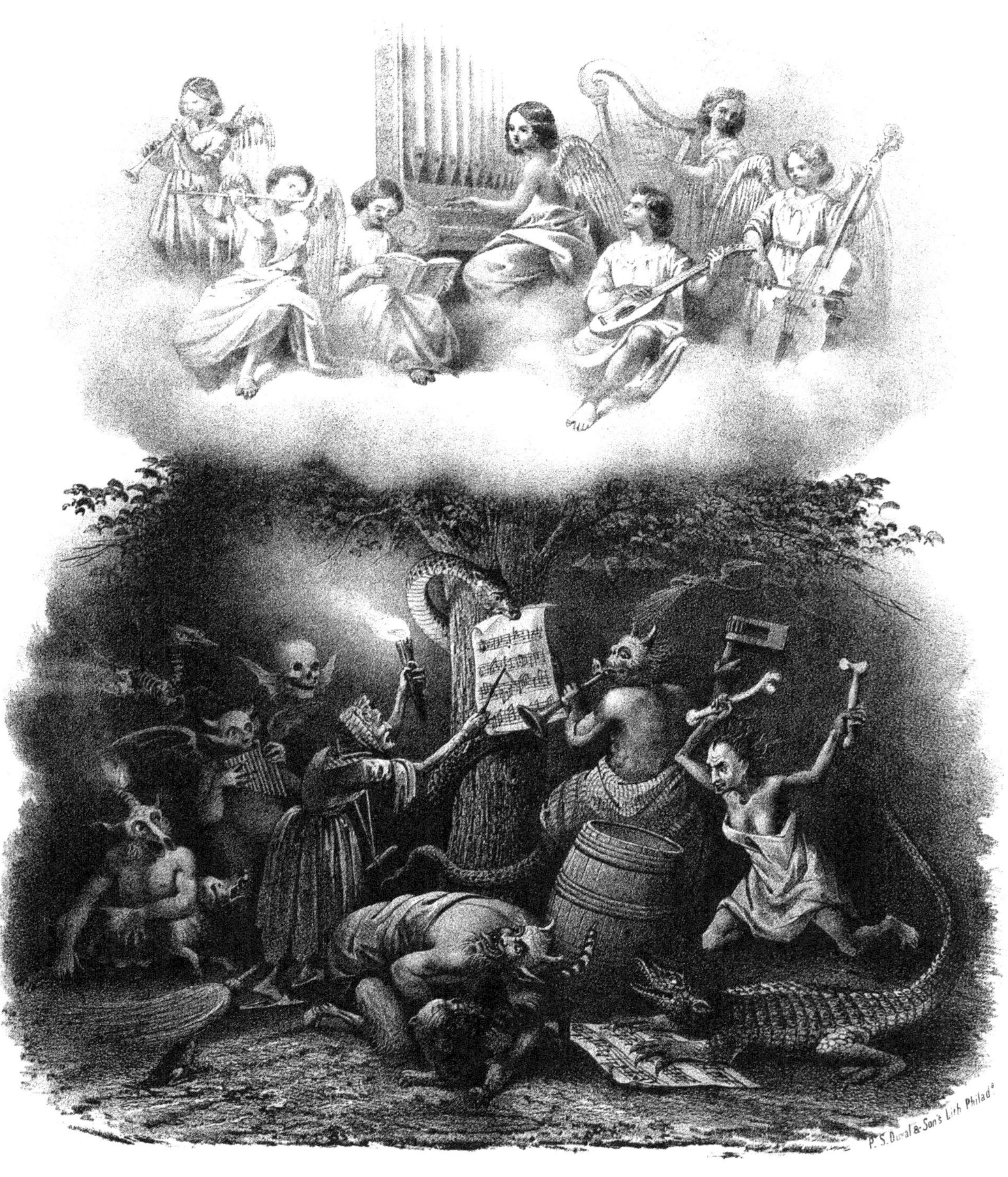

114. Angels playing music in heaven, harpies
playing music in Hell

115

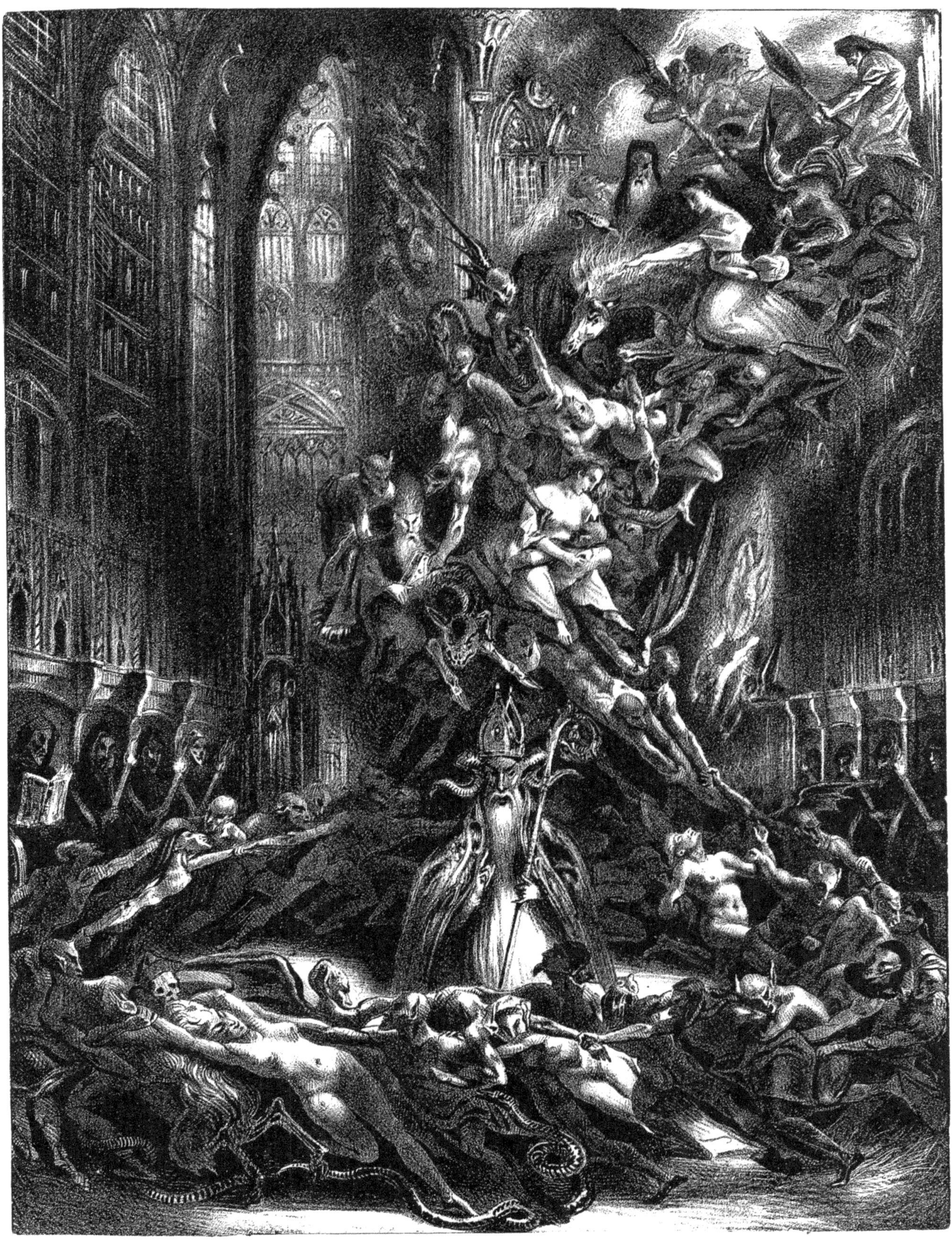

115. The Round of the Sabbath or Witches'
Sabbath Louis Boulanger French Publisher Frey
French 1835

116

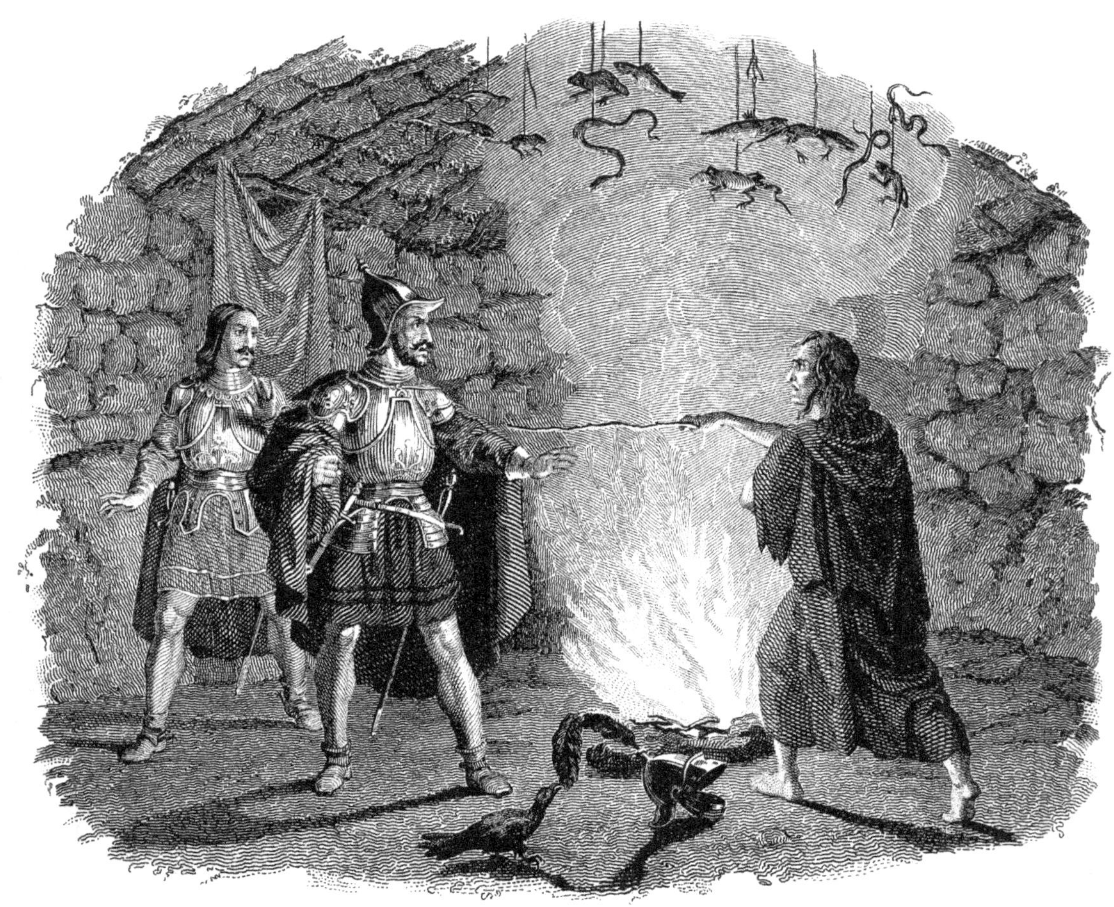

117

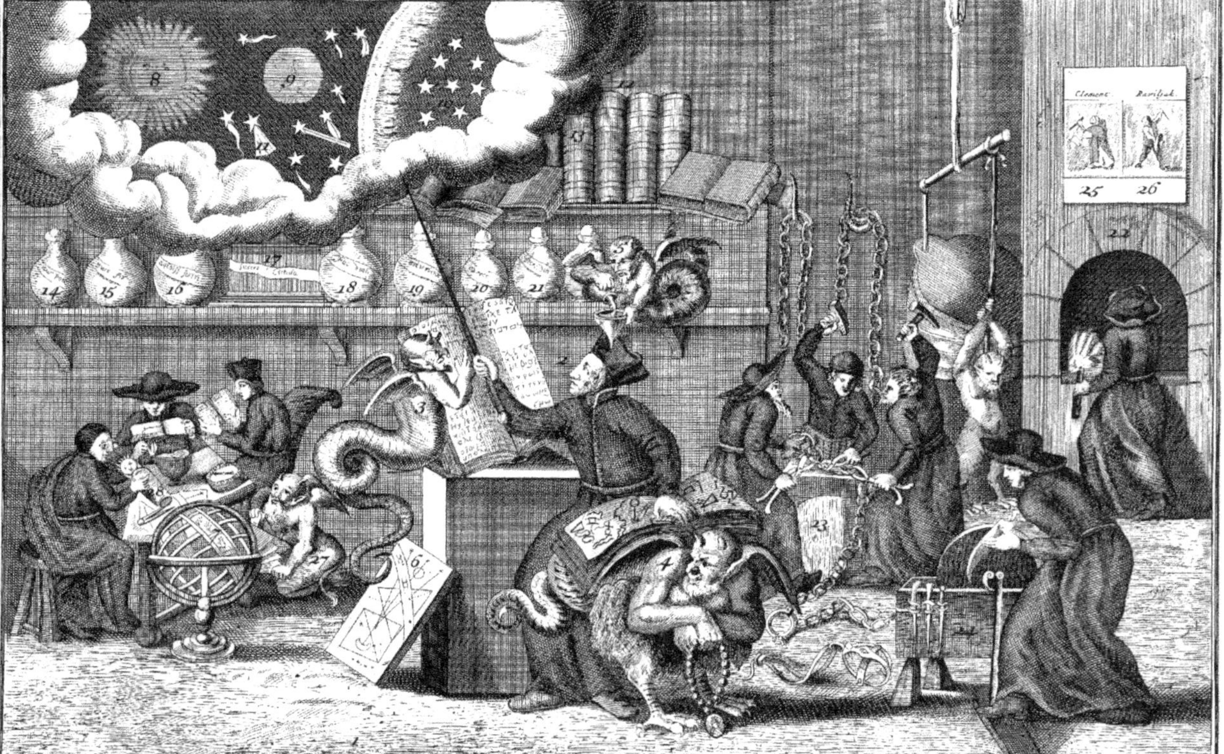

116. Two soldiers in the cabin of an alchemist by
Henricus Wilhelmus Couwenberg, 1830 – 1845

117. Father Peters's Laboratory, 1689, attributed
to Paul van Somer (II), 1689

118

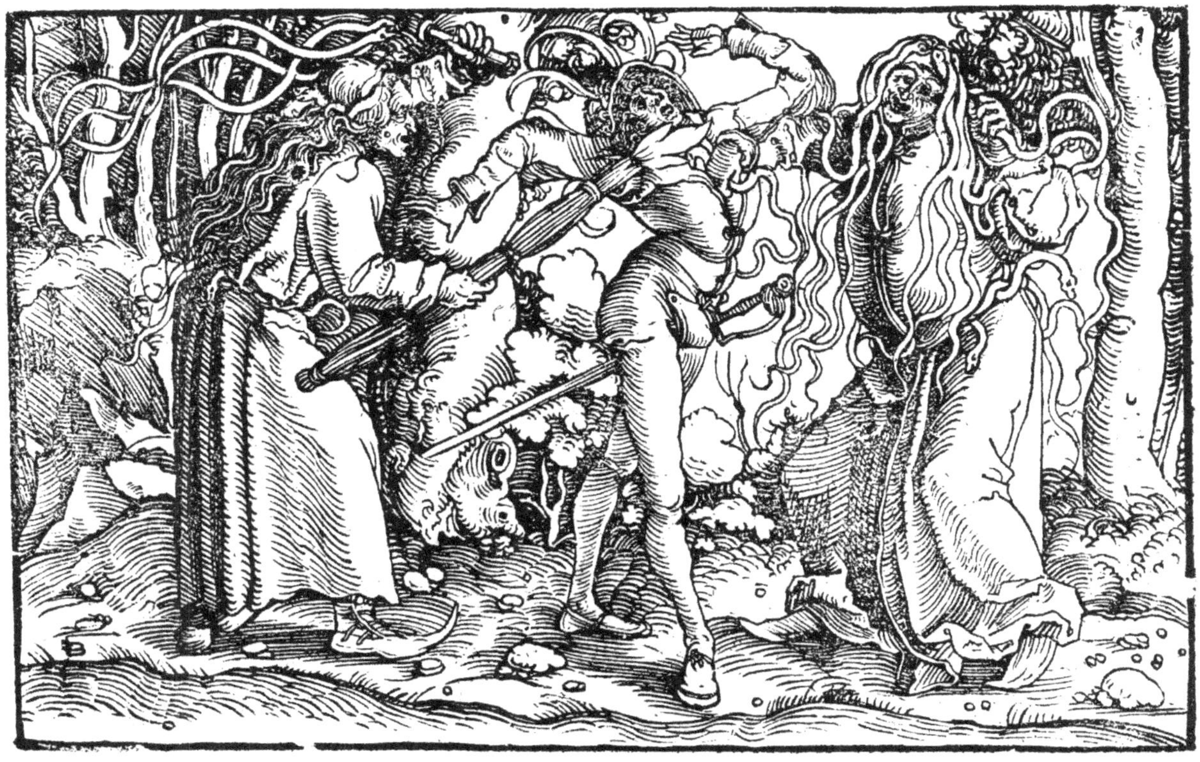

119

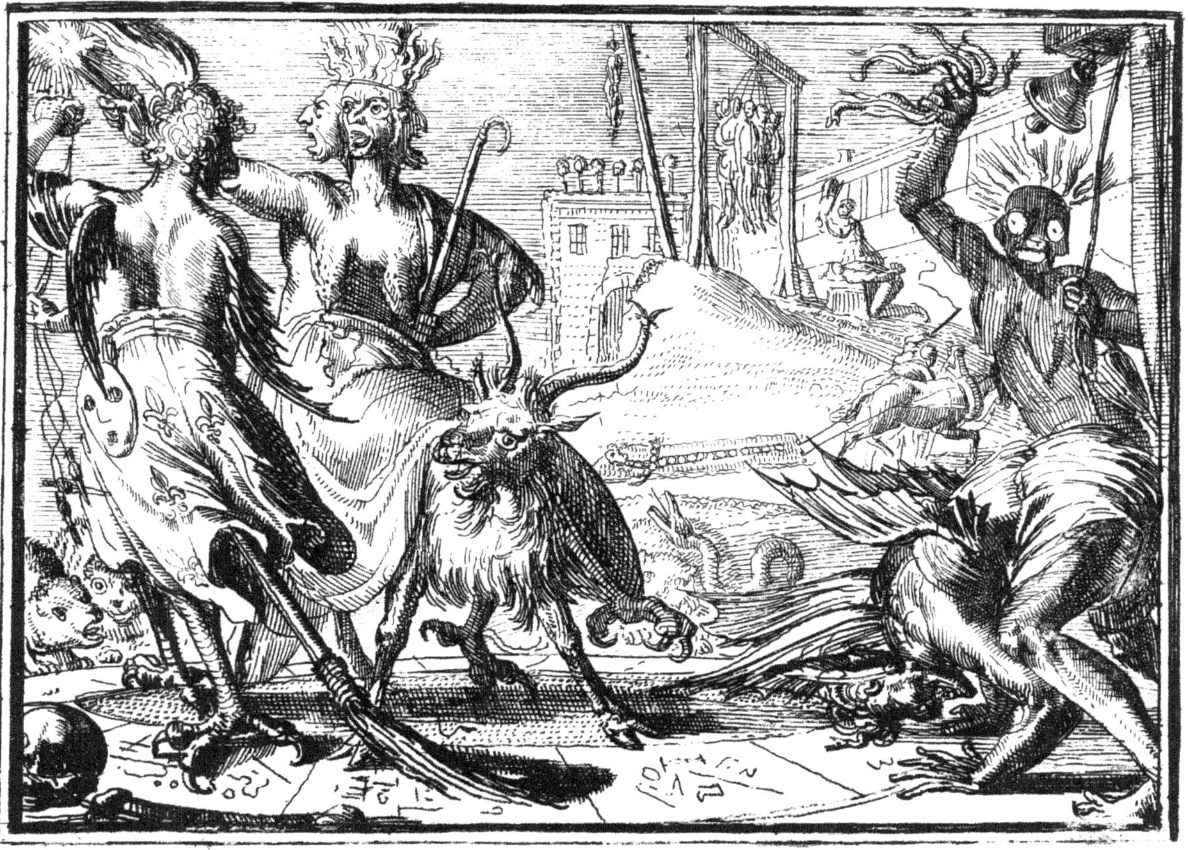

---

118. Young man and two gorgons, anonymous,
1500–1599

119. The Horlende Kollendans, on Tilburn, 1702,
Romeyn de Hooghe, 1702, Three witches at a
magic circle.

120

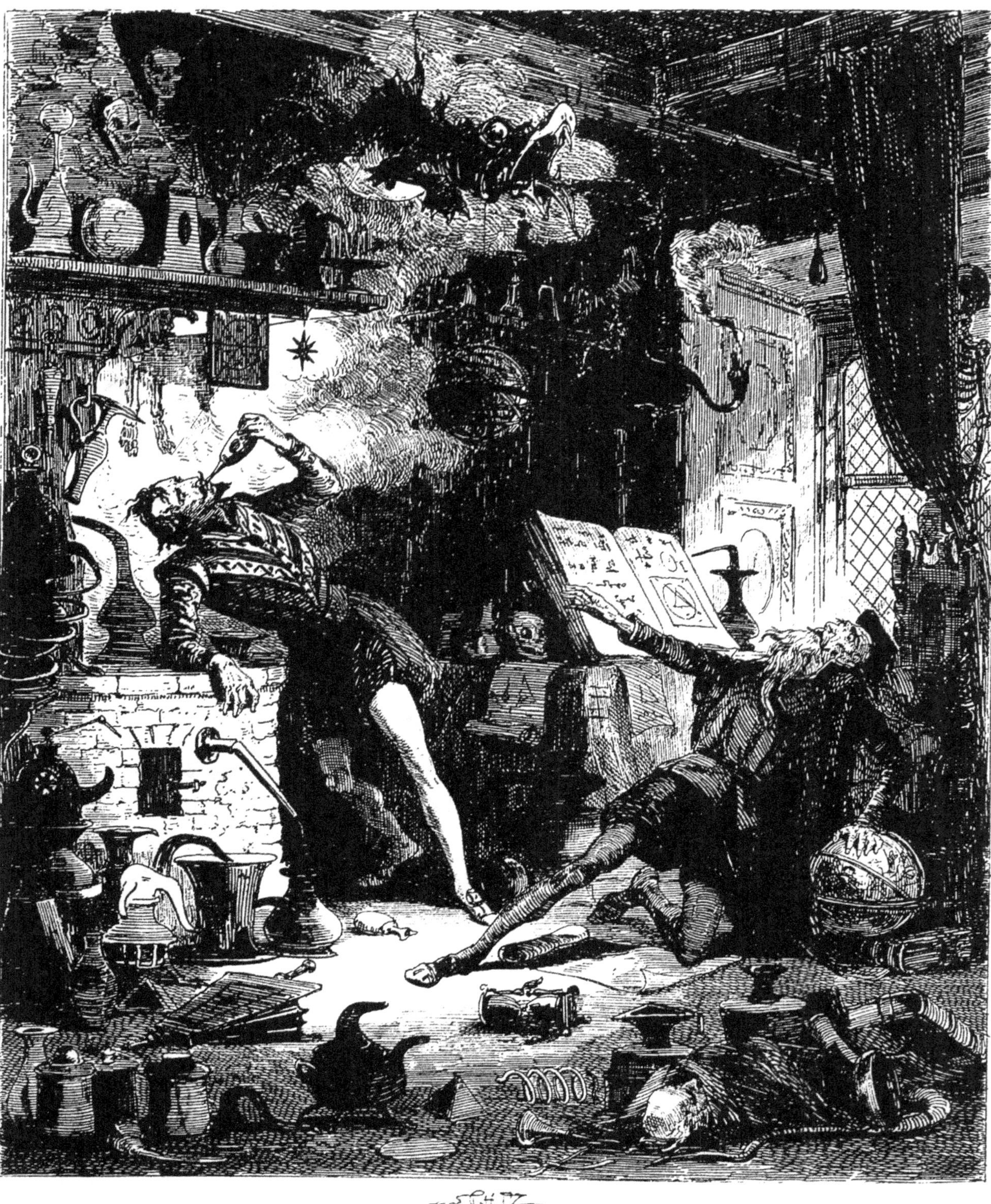

The Elixir of Long Life.

120. An alchemist's laboratory— a young man
drinks an elixir of life. Wood engraving by H.K.
Browne (Phiz), 1865.

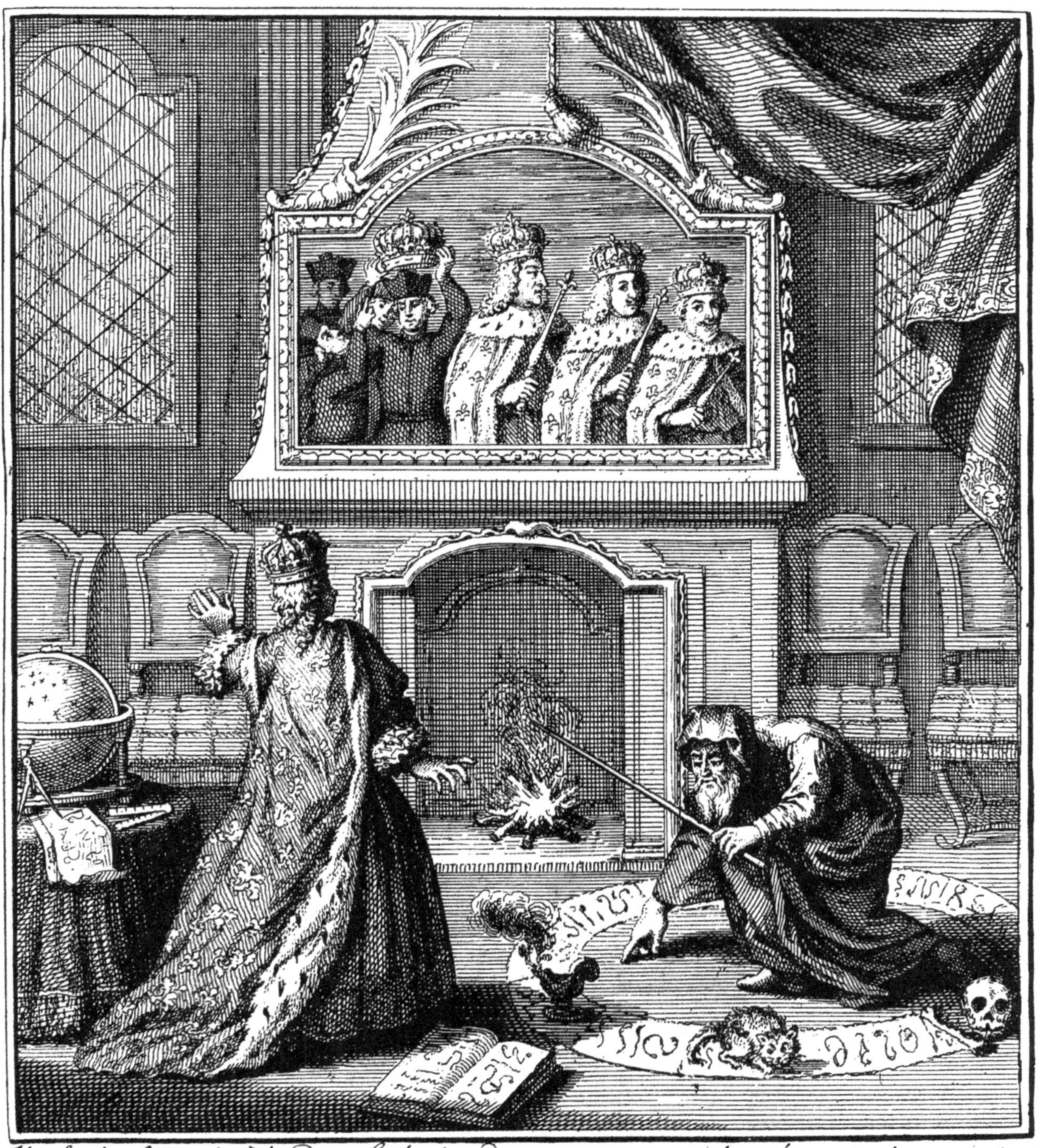

Un Sorcier fait voir à la Reine Catherine dans un miroir enchanté ceux qui regneroient
en France à l'avenir. Elle vit d'abord Henry IV, ensuite Louis XIII, après Louis XIV, &
enfin une troupe de Jésuites qui devoient abolir la Monarchie, & gouverner eux-mêmes. Ce
miroir se voit encore dans le Palais du Roi. Voÿ. l'Espion Turc Tom: IV. p: 353. Ed. de 1750.

121. Catharina de' Medici sees in the magic
mirror the future kings of France, anonymous,
1710 – 1780

122

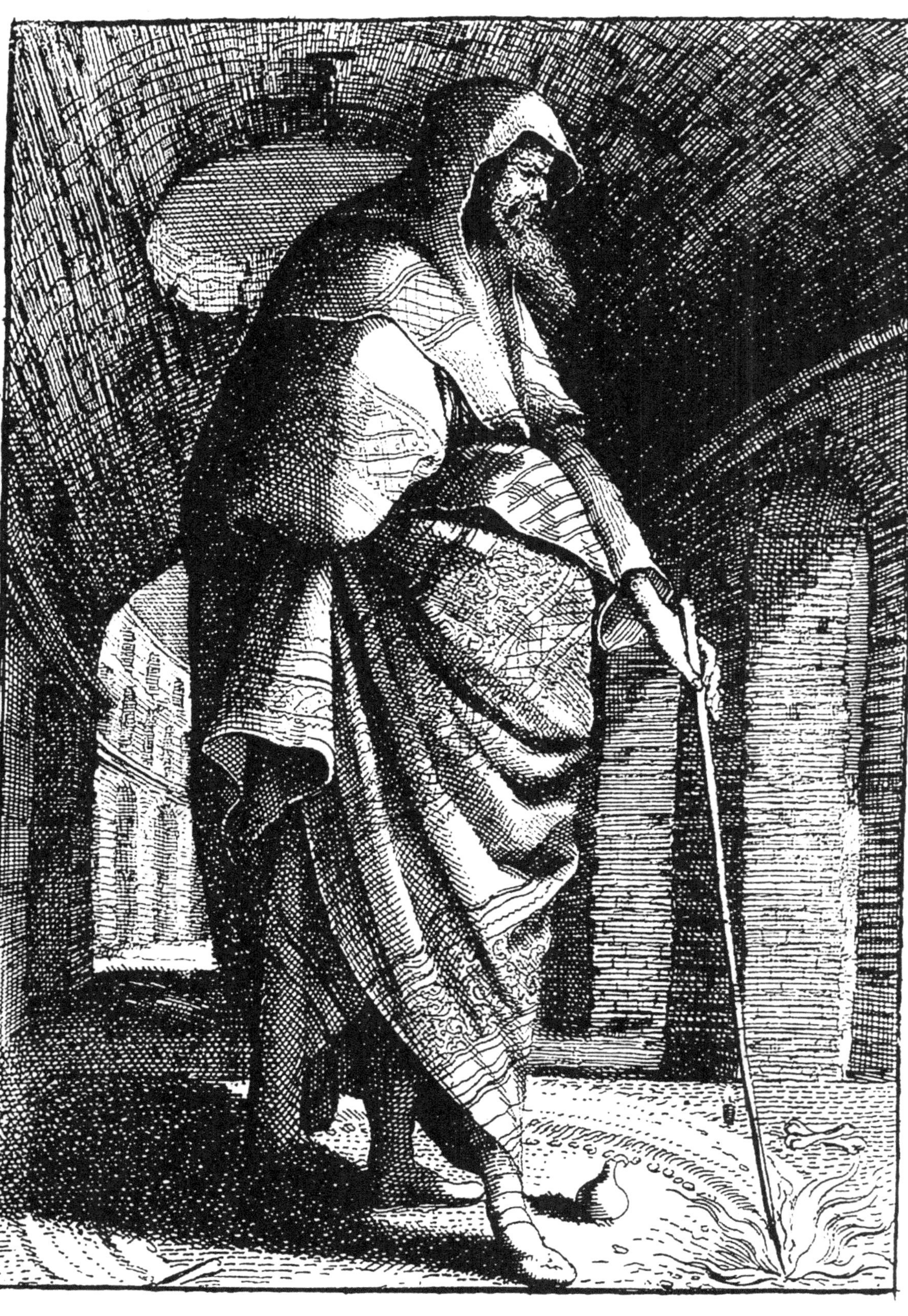

122. Magician in the hallway of a building,
Sébastien Leclerc (I) (mentioned on object),
1647 – 1701

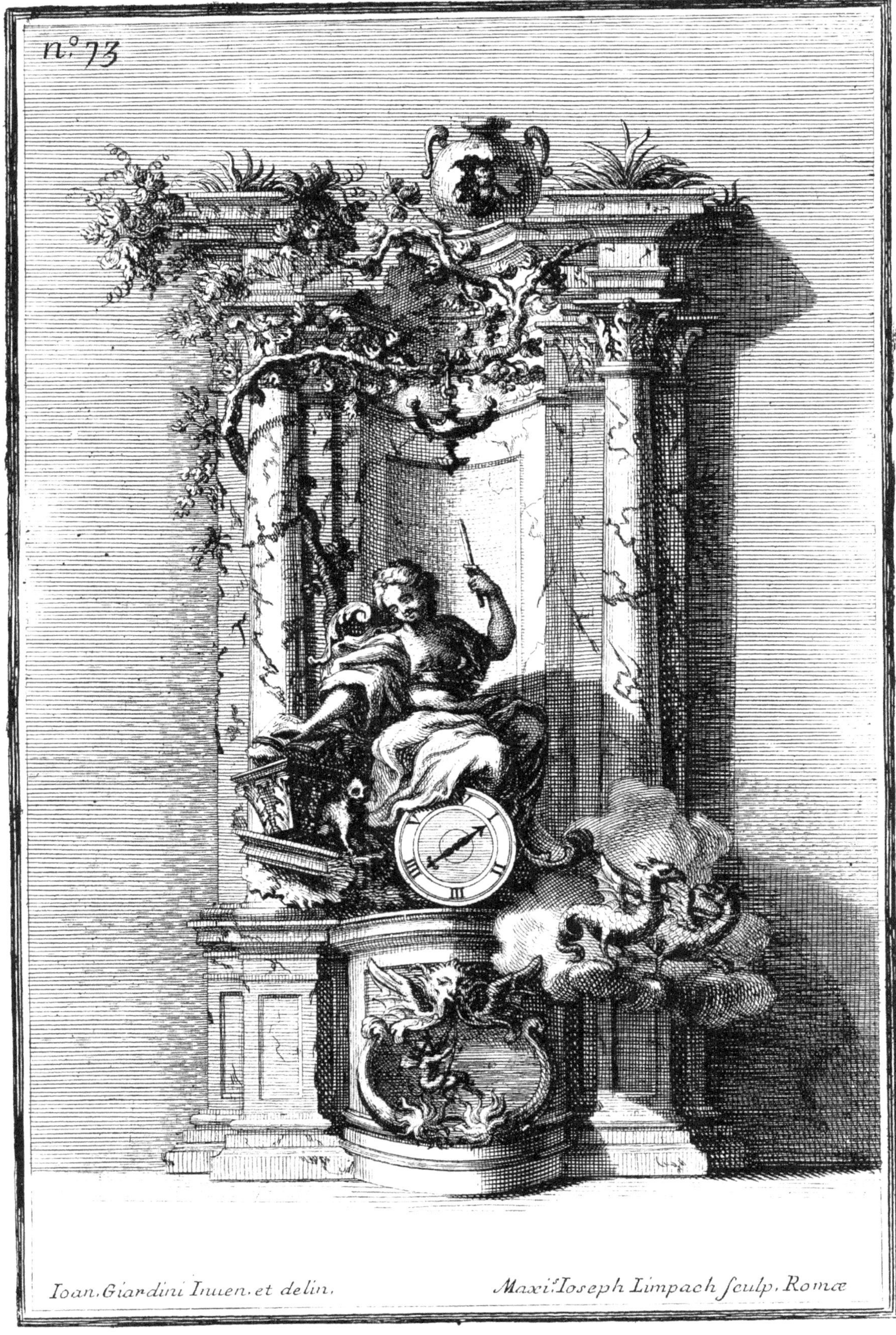

123. Clock with sorceress, Maximilian Joseph
Limpach (manned on object), 1714

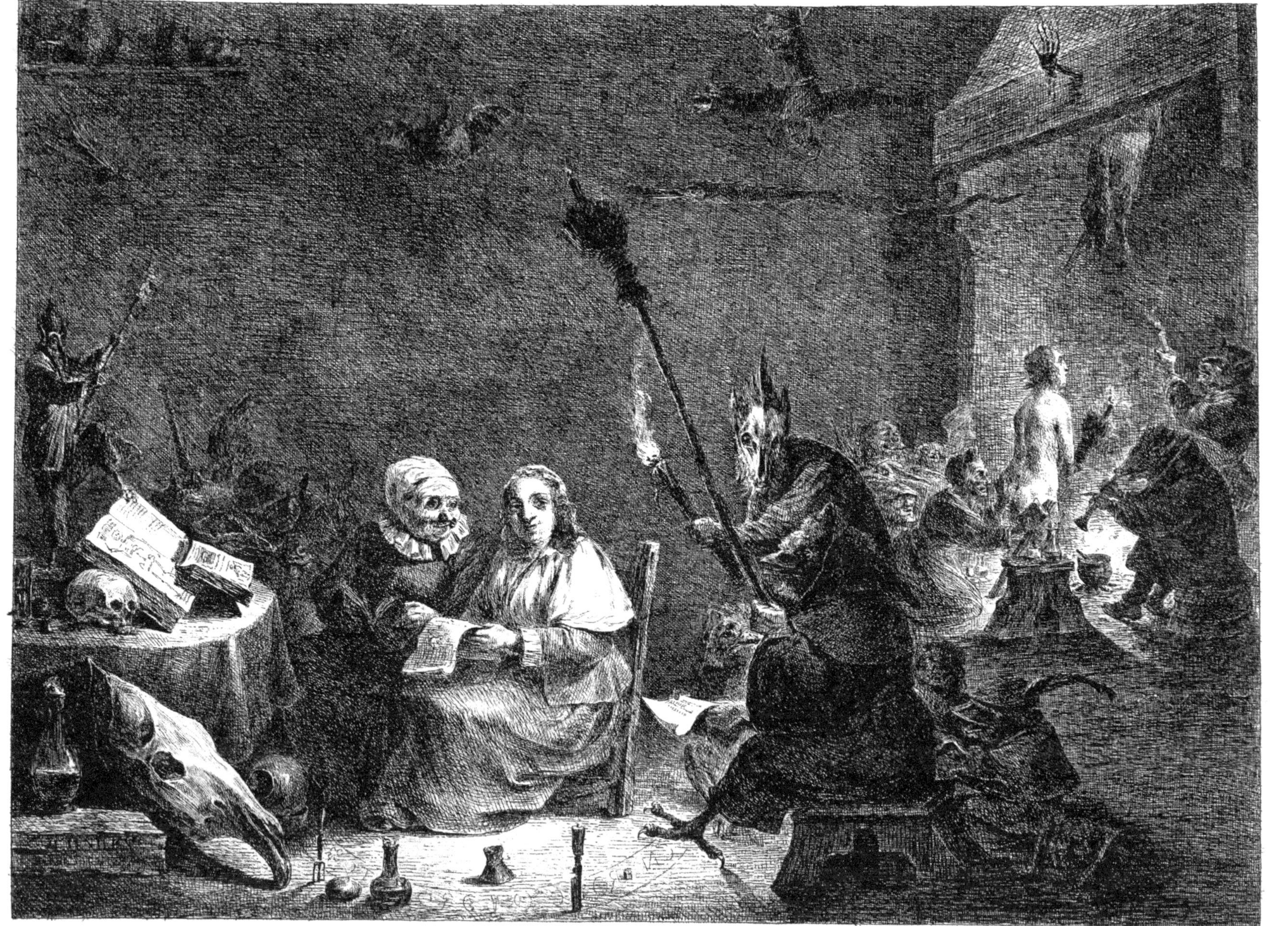

124. Departure for the Sabbath Baron Dominique
Vivant Denon French after David Teniers the
Younger Flemish

125

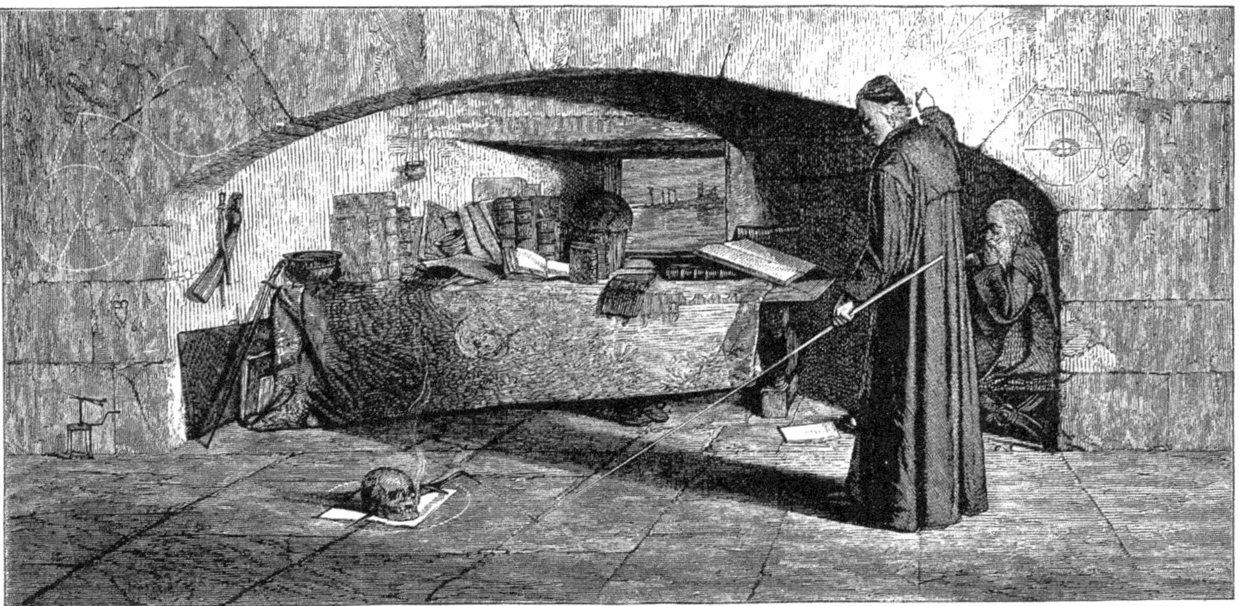

126

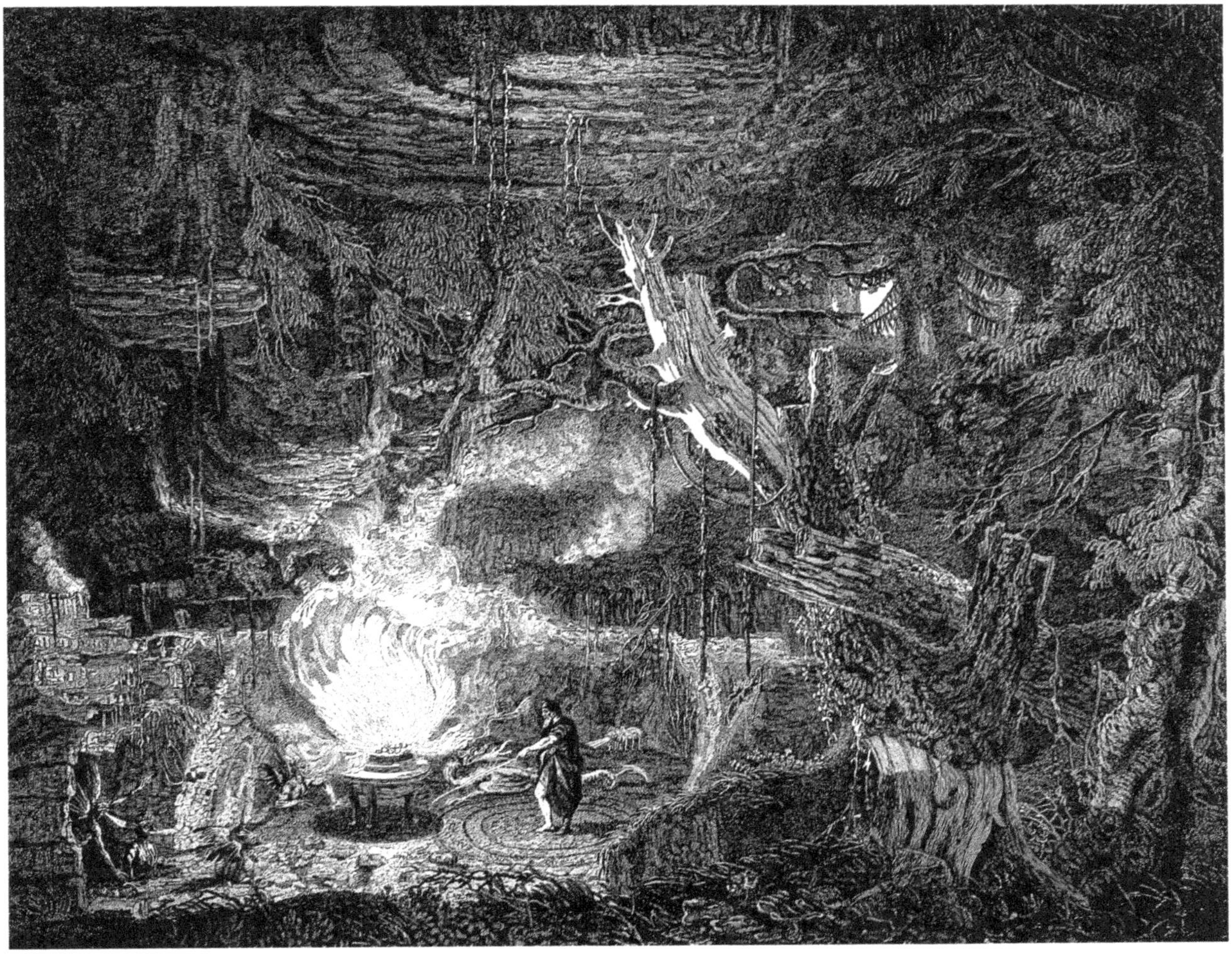

125. A wizard performing spells in his den. Wood engraving by S. Millar after himself.

126. A wizard casting spells from his magic circle by the light of his cauldron surrounded by creatures. Engraving by J. Wood, 1763

127

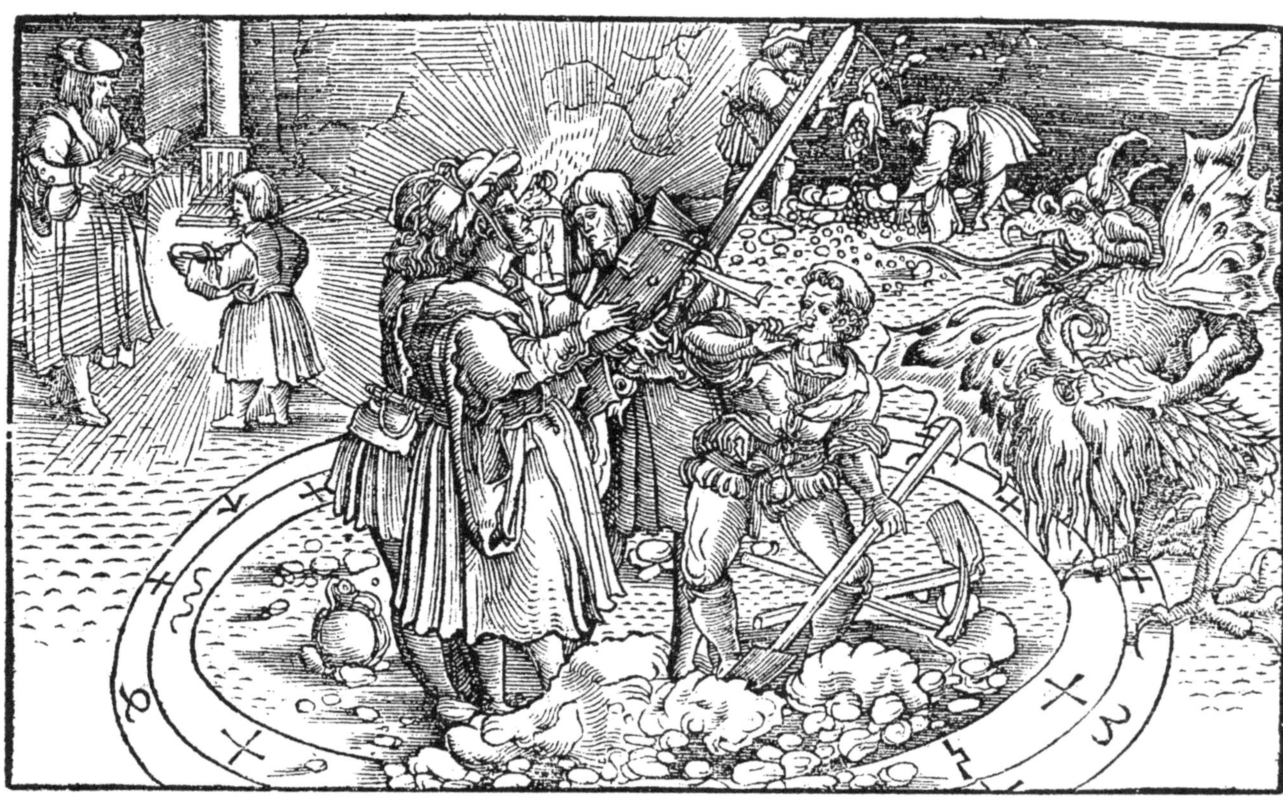

128

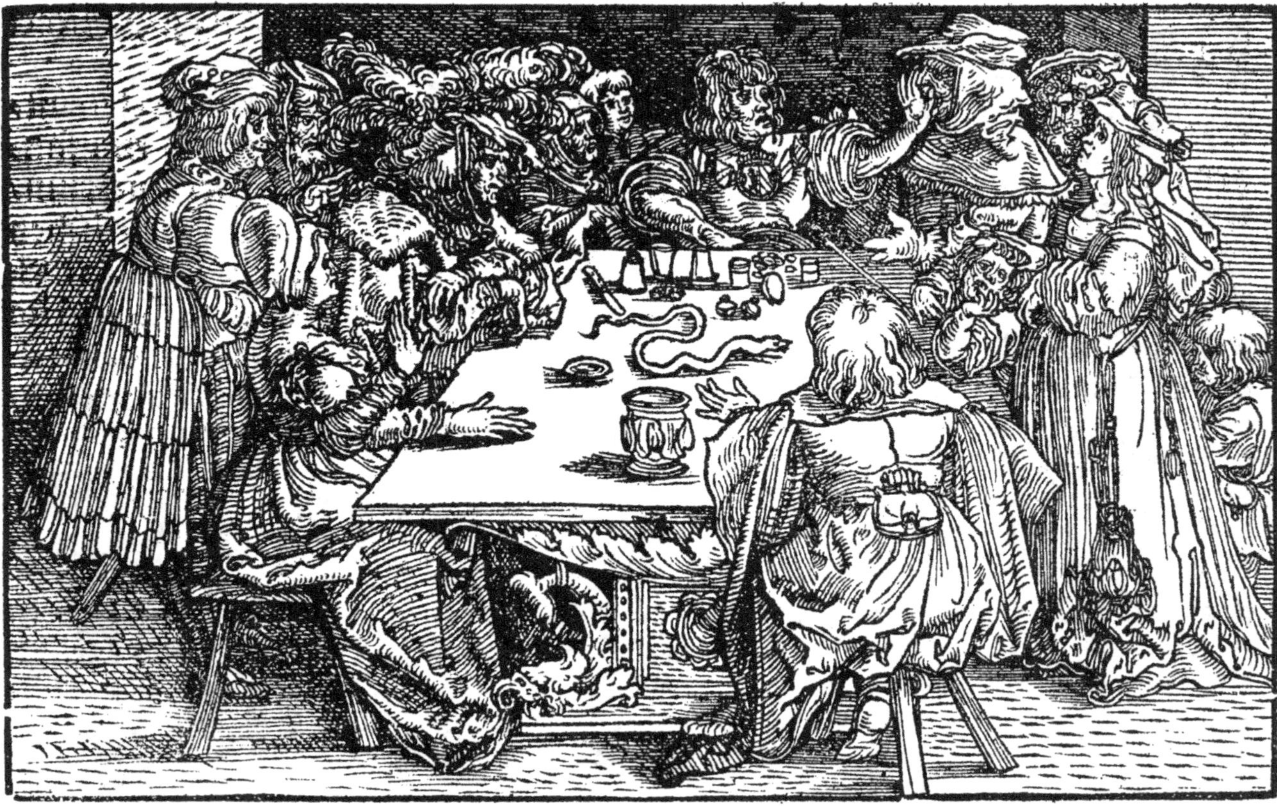

127. Magic circle with treasure diggers and a
devil, anonymous, after design by Hans Weiditz
(II), 1514 – 1532

128. Magician entertains his audience at a table,
anonymous, after design by Hans Weiditz (II),
1514 – 1532

129

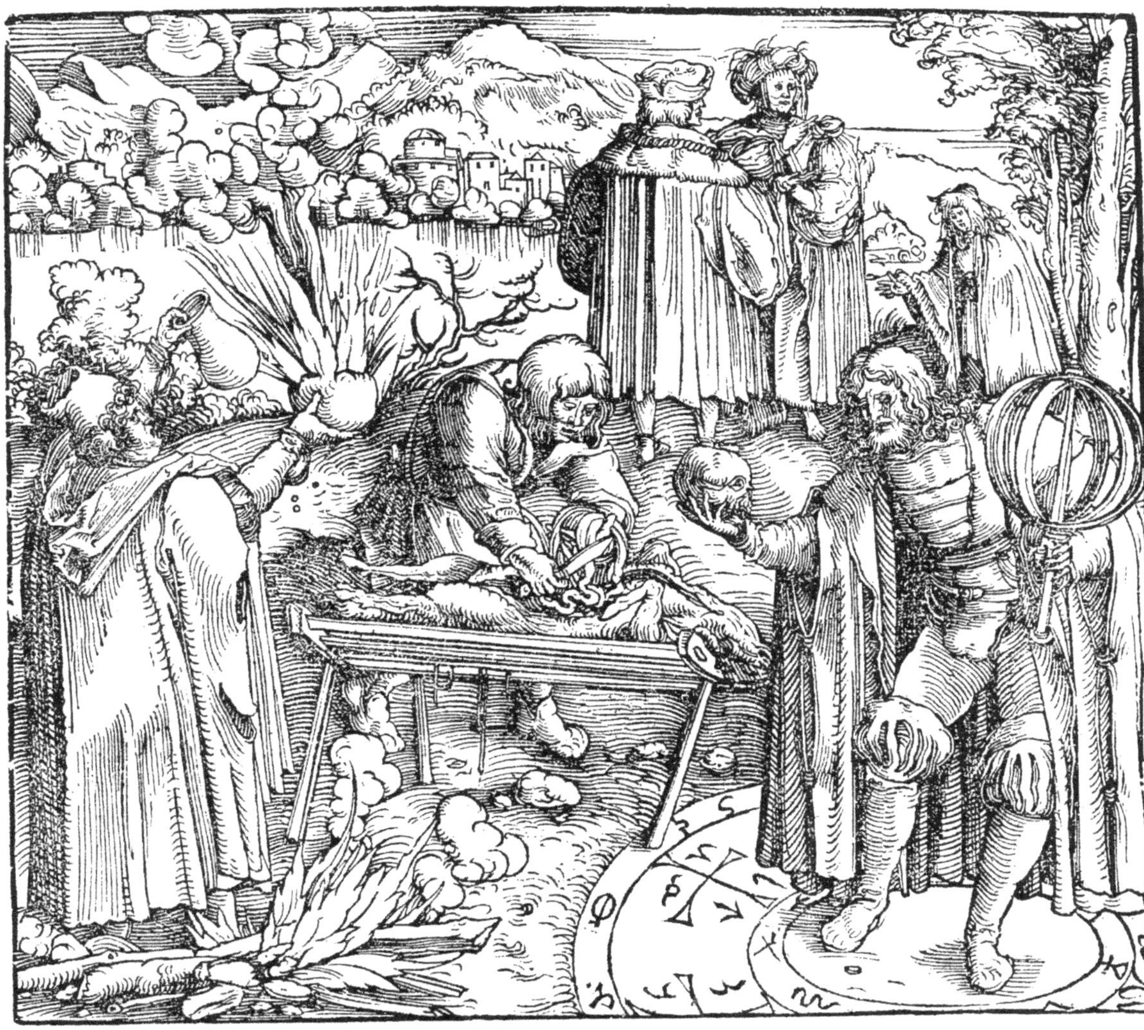

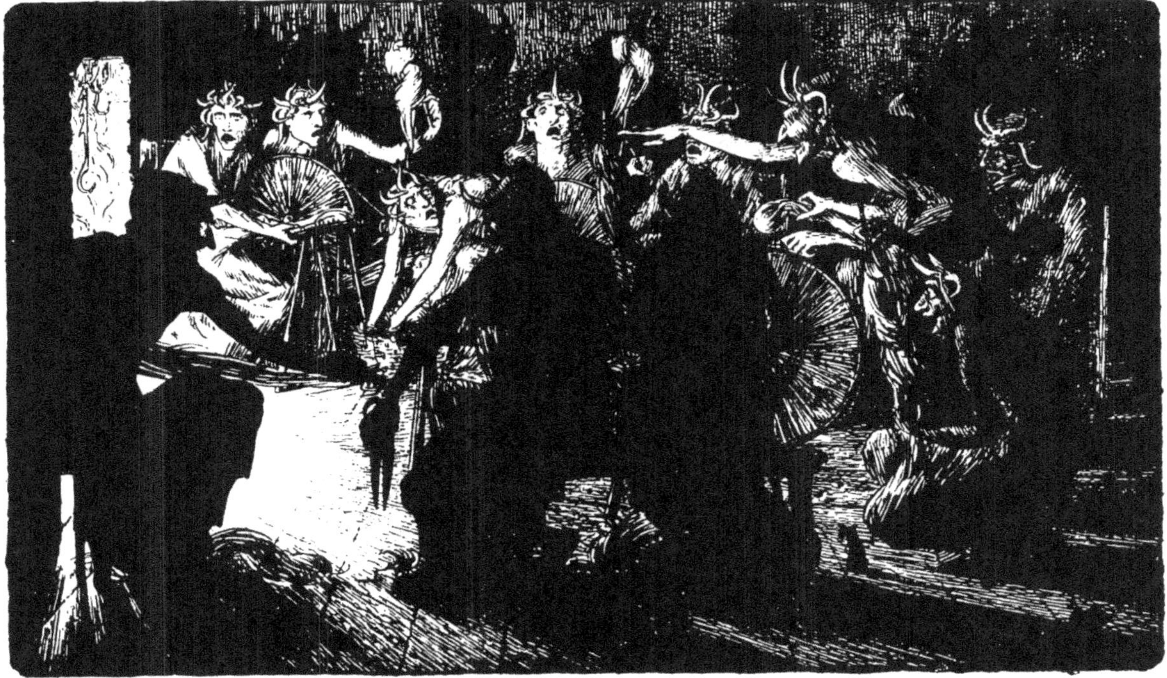

130

129. Seer, constor and alchemist, anonymous,
after design by Hans Weiditz (II), 1514 – 1532

130. The Horned Women, Celtic Fairy Tales by
Joseph Jacobs 1854–1916 and John Dickson
Batten, 1860–1932, 189

131

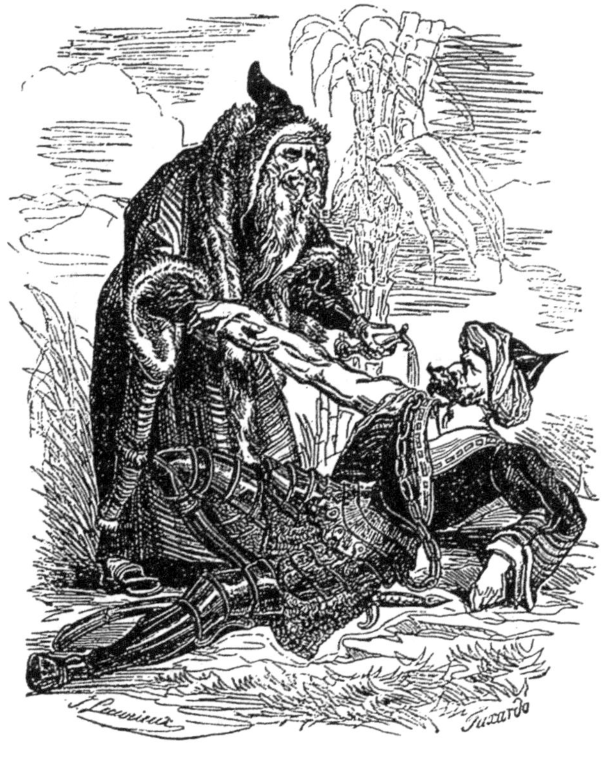

132

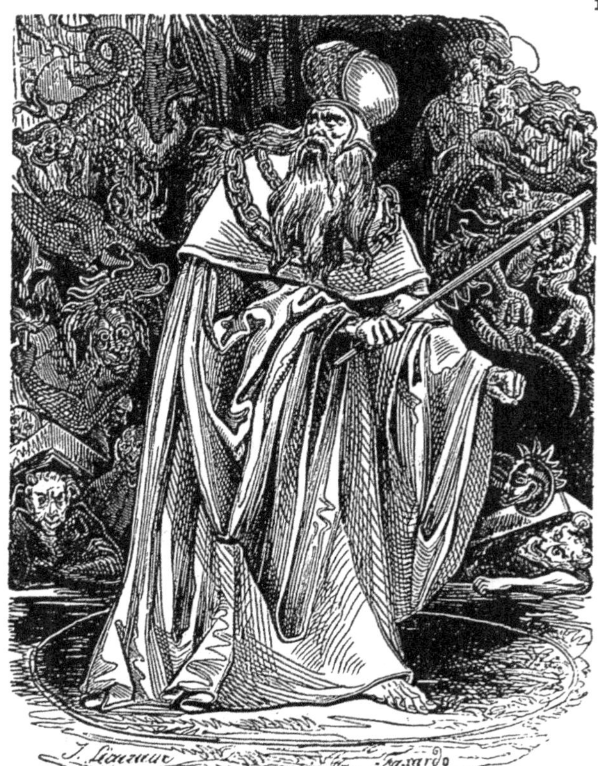

133

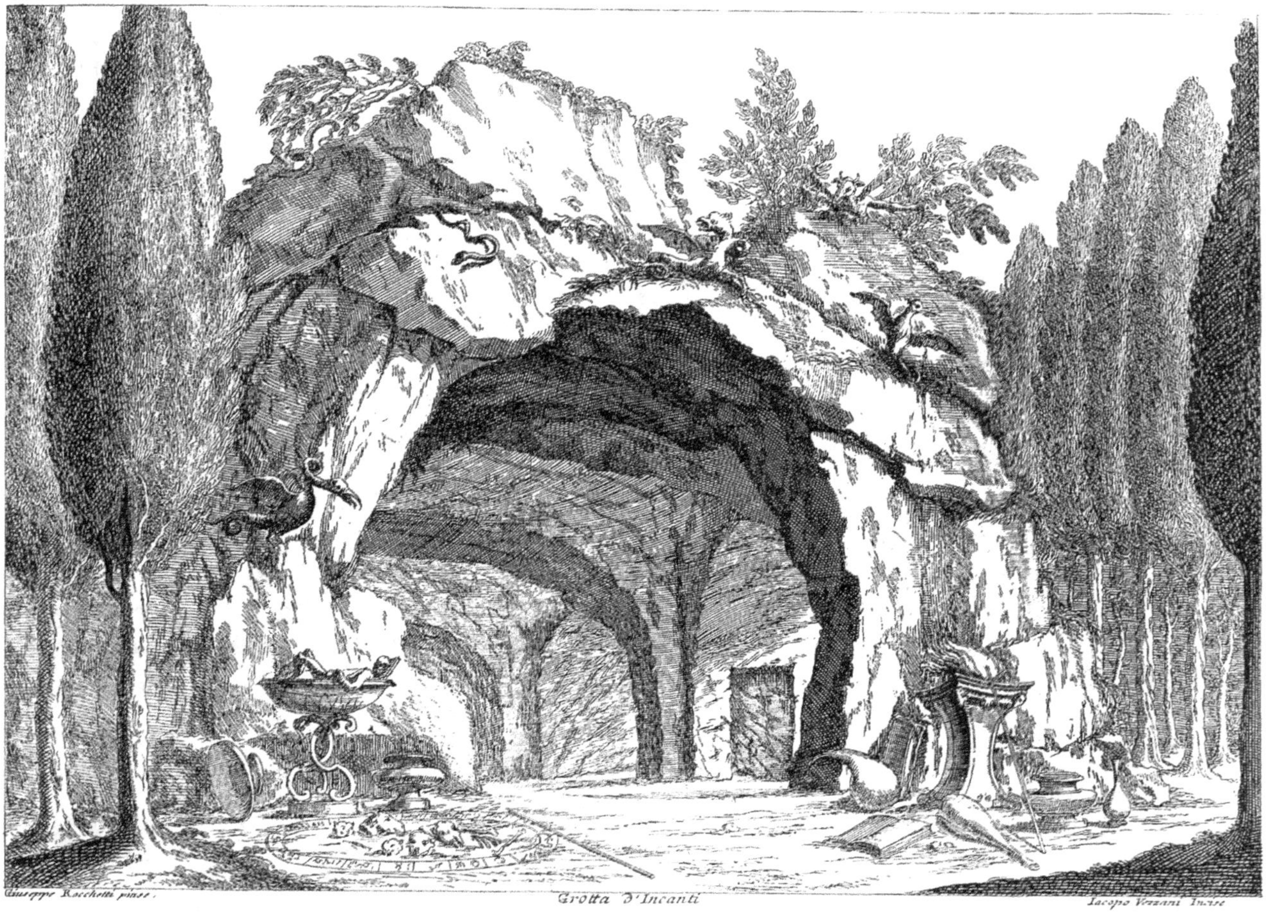

131. The sorcerer Ismen and Suleyman– an episode in Gerusalemme liberata by Tasso. Wood engraving by J.A. Faxardo, 1838

132. The sorcerer Isman with a wand in an enchanted forest, Wood engraving by J.A. Faxardo after JJ. Lecurieux, 1838

133. A grotto containing a magic circle, books and mythical creatures. Etching by J. Vezzani, 1728, after G. Rocchetti after P. Righini.

134

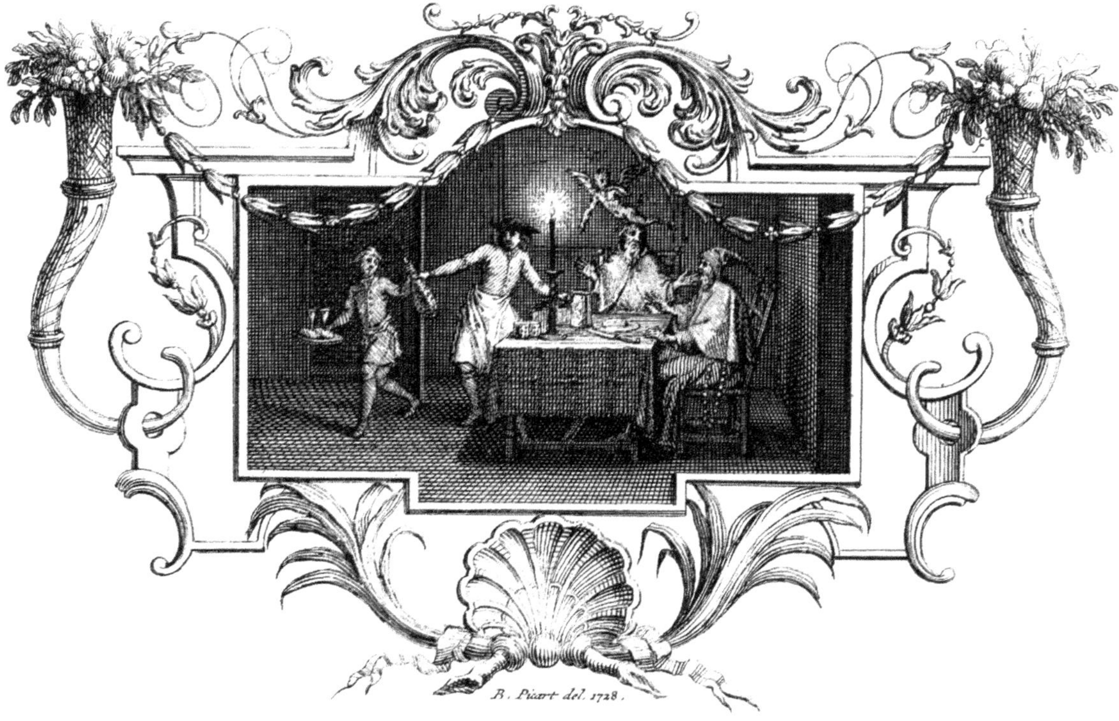

135

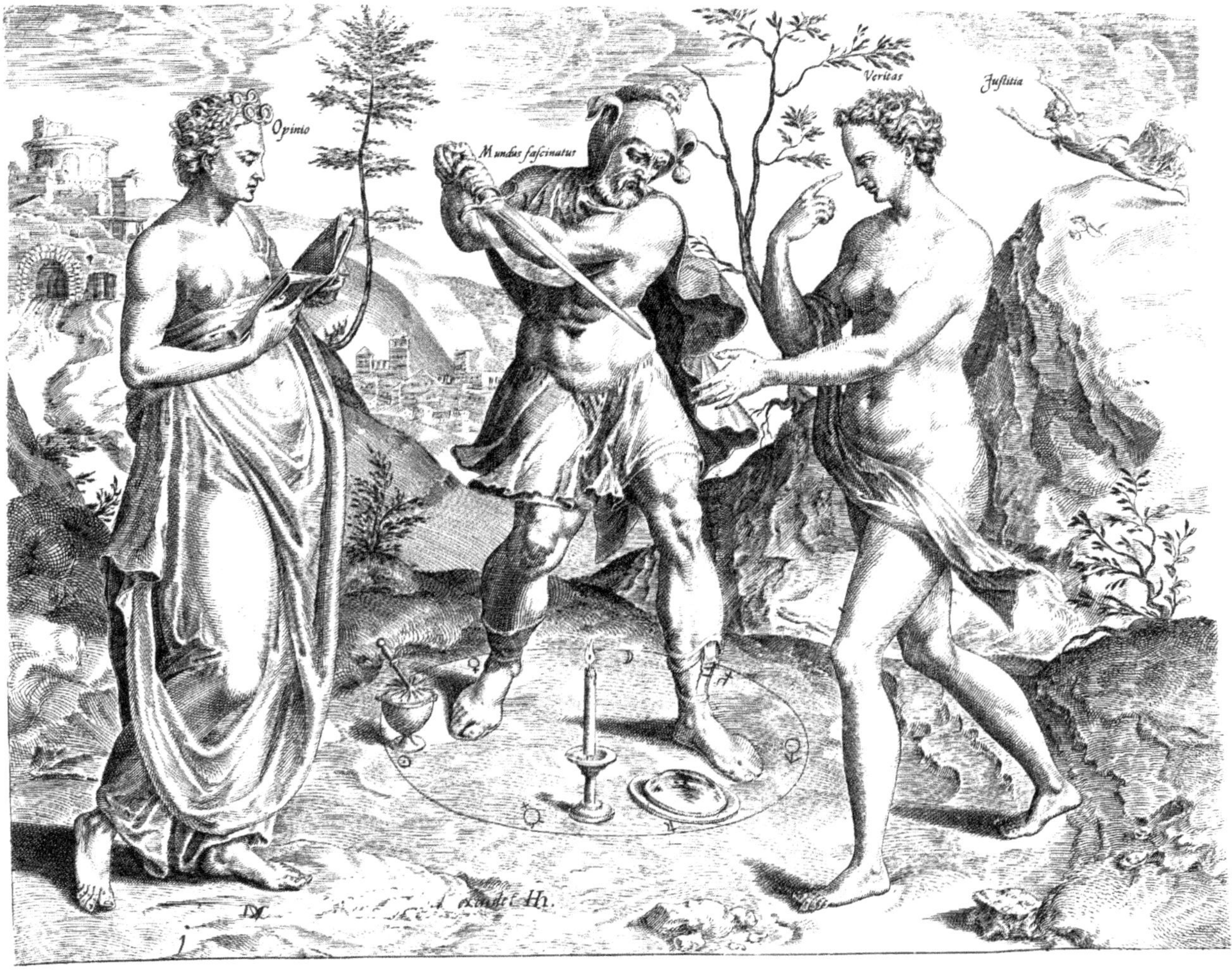

134. Wizards at a table and the appearance of a demon, workshop of Bernard Picart, 1728

135. Wrong conviction alienates the world from truth, Dirck Volckertsz. Coornhert (on object), 1575 – 1581

136

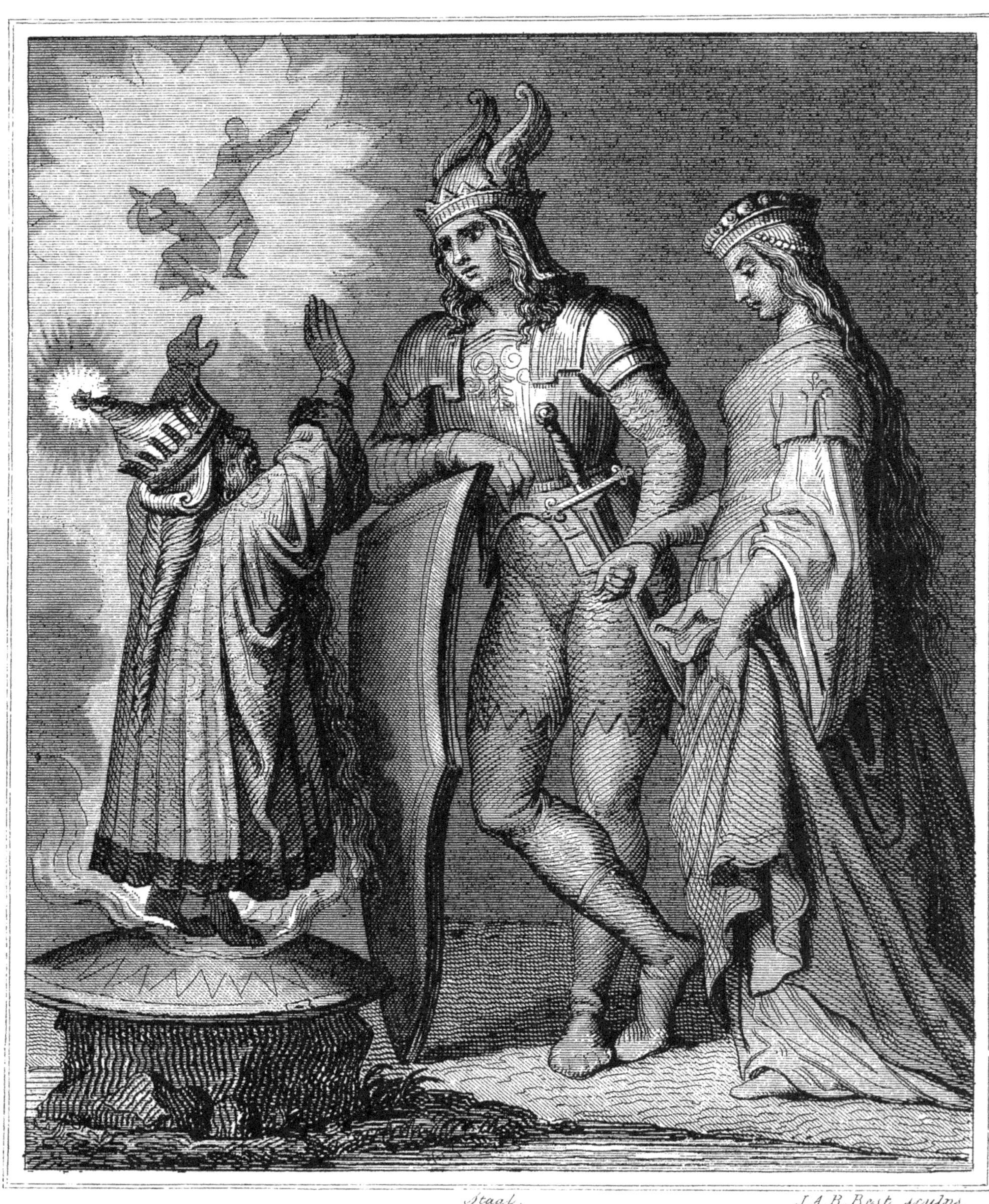

136. Small wizard and knight with lady, Johannes
Alexander Rudolf Best (on object), 1807 – 1855

137

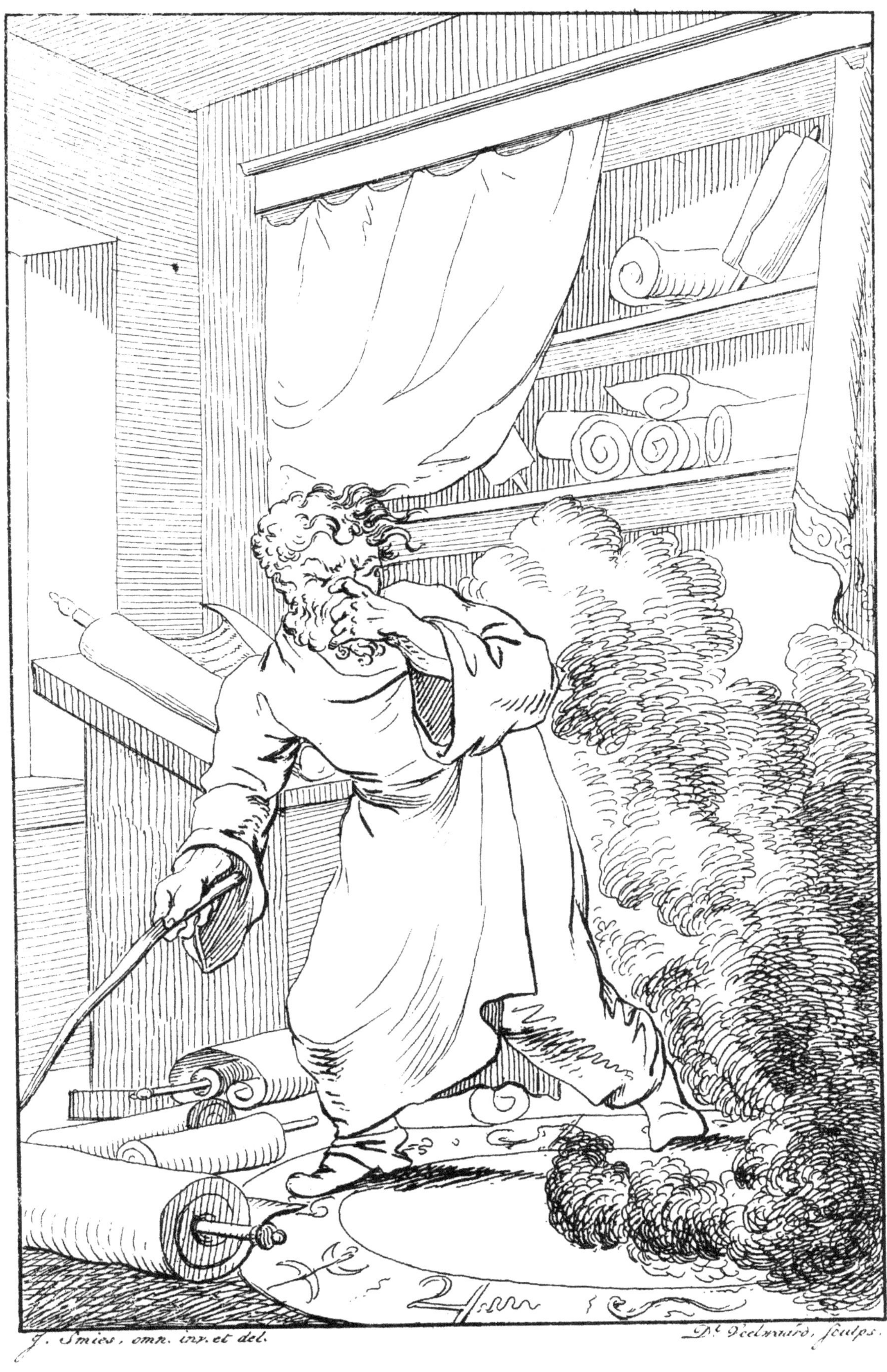

137. Wizard at work, Daniel Veelwaard (immed) (
on object), 1803

138

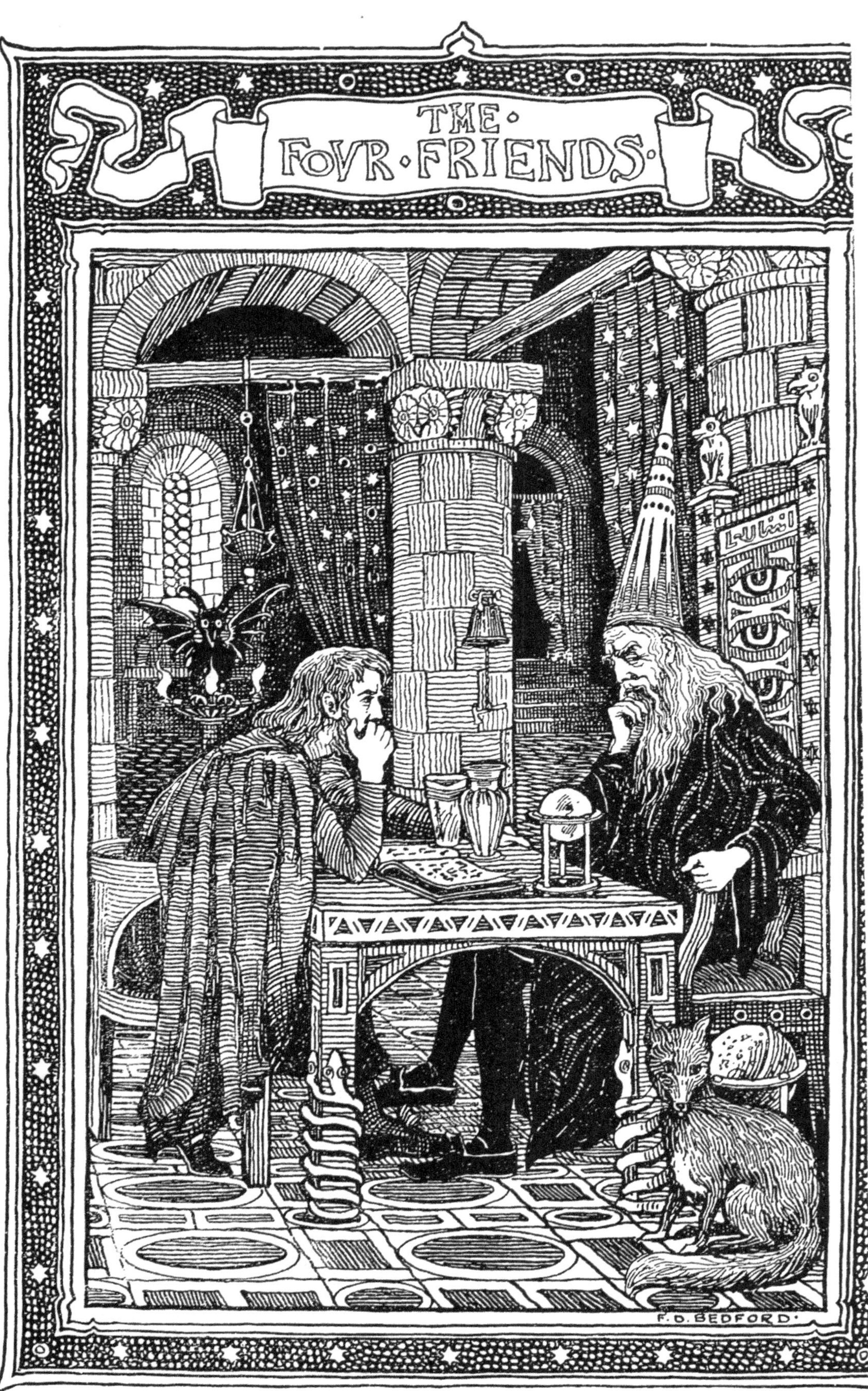

138. The Four Friends, from Old English Fairy Tales

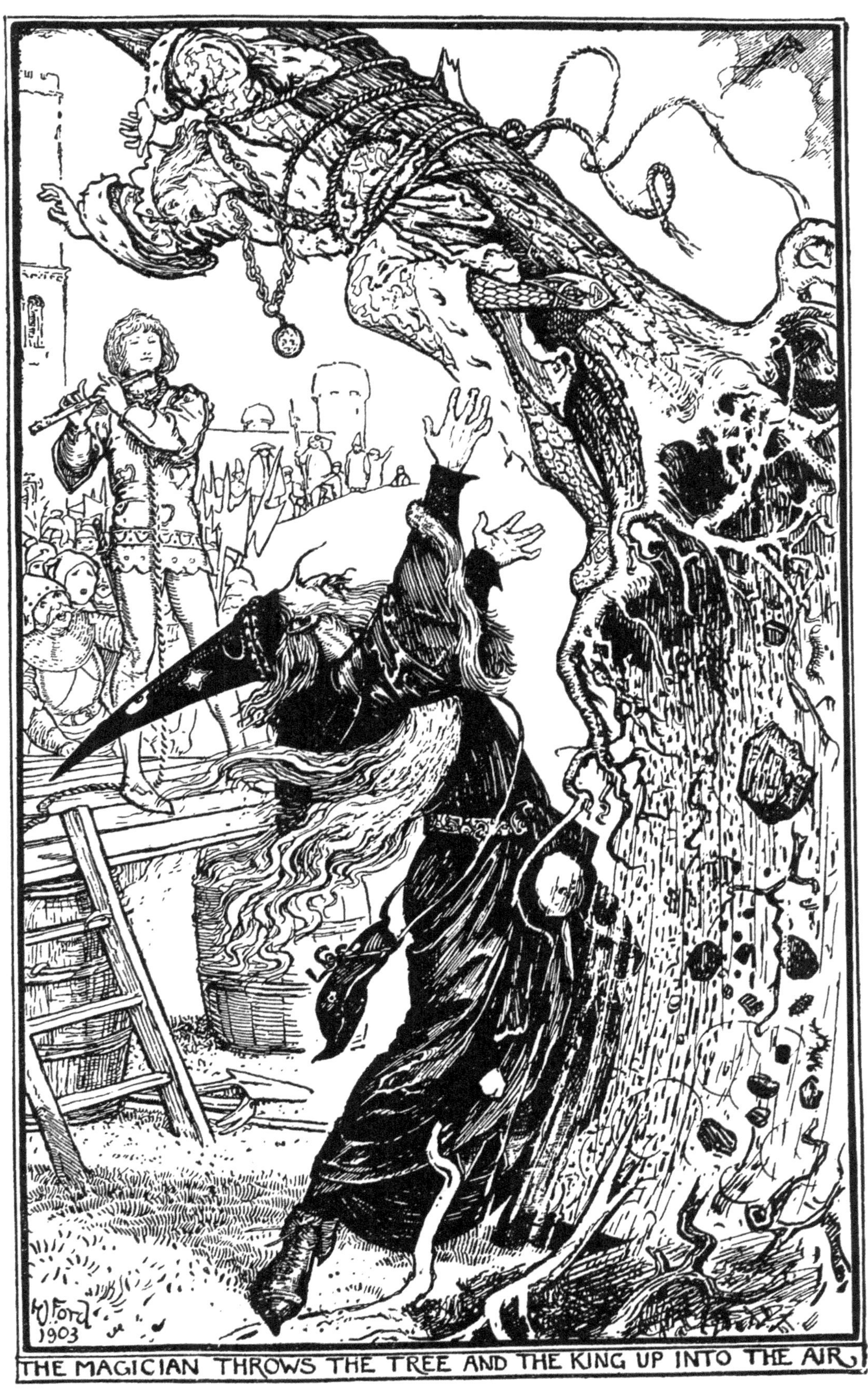

WITCHES & WIZARDS

139. The Magician Throws The Tree and The
King Up Into The Air, from The Crimson Fairy
Book, 1903

LIST OF ILLUSTRATIONS

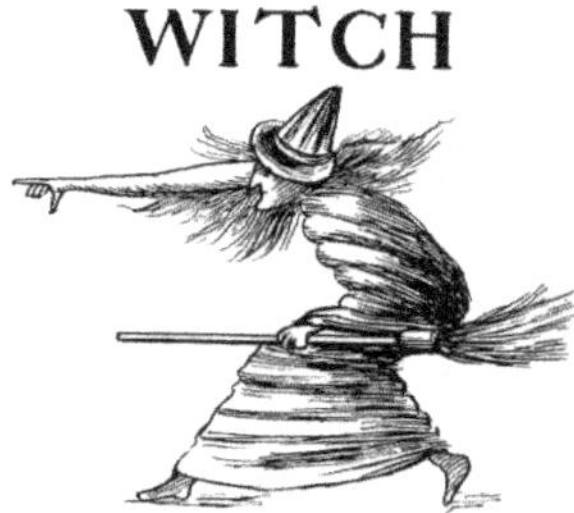

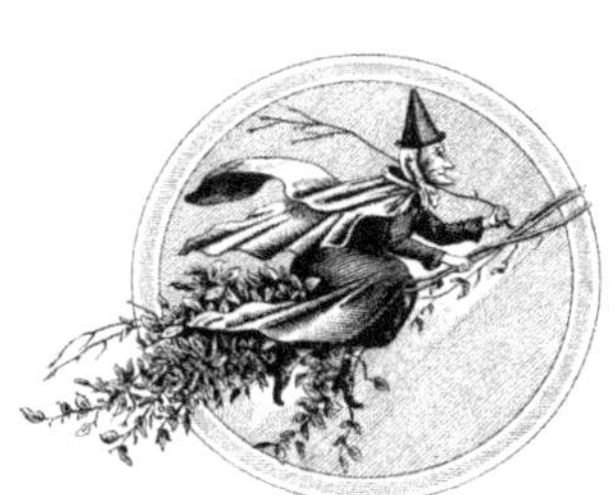

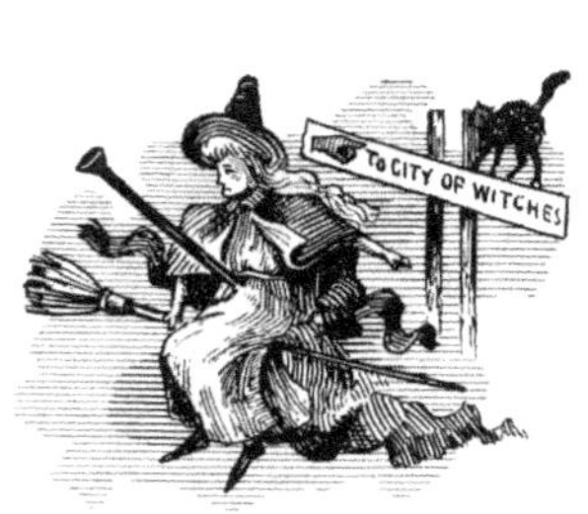

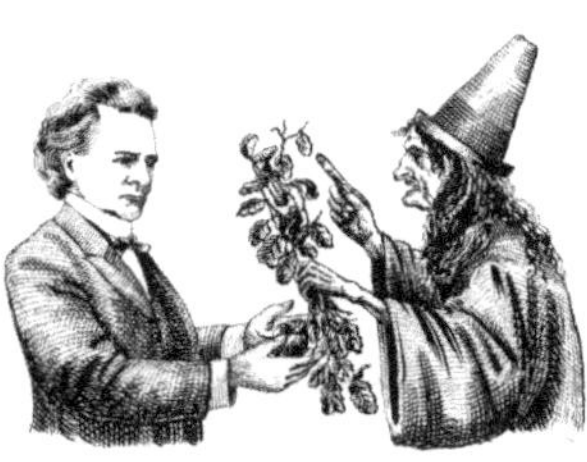

1. Saul by the witch of Endor, Caspar Luyken, 1712

2. Saul by the witch of Endor, Philip van Gunst (on object), 1685 - 1732

3. Saul by the witch of Endor, Quiryn Fonbonne (mentioned on object), c. 1690 - c. 1757

4. Saul and the witch of Endor, William Sharp (on object), 1788

5. Saul by the witch of Endor, Jacob Folkema (on object), 1791

6. Saul collapses as the witch of Endor conjures Samuel from the dead. Wood engraving after Schnorr von Carolsfeld, Julius, 1794-1872

7. Three witches appear to Macbeth and Banquo, James Caldwall (on object), Thomas Trotter, 1798

8. The witch of Endor conjures the ghost of Samuel; Saul bows before him on the right. Etching, 18th century.

9. The witch of Endor with a candle. Engraving by J. Kay, 1805, after A. Elsheimer. Elsheimer, Adam, 1578-1610.

10. Witches Sabbath, Spranger II

11. Witches Preparing for Sabbath Andries Stock Netherlandish

12. A witch casting spells over a steaming cauldron. Engraving by H.S. Thomassin after Demaretz.

13. Medea the sorceress, Louis Desplaces (on object), 1692 - 1738

14. Witch conjures demons for Willemynken, Boetius Adamsz. Bolswert, 1590 - 1627

15. Saul by the witch of Endor, Simon Fokke (on object), 1766.

16. A sorceress. Engraving by G.A. Periam, 1837, after F. Corbaux.   Corbaux, F. (Fanny) (1812-1883.)1837

17. Arrival at the witches' sabbath, Jacques Aliamet (on object), 1755-10

18. Le streghe, frontispiece, 1830

19. The Witches' Cauldron, 1810

20. Witches' sabbath, Claude Gillot (on object), 1683 - 1722

21. Damon visits the Lodippe witch, after design by Adriaen Pietersz van de Venne, 1637

22. Witches dance around the kettle, Daniel Nikolaus Chodowiecki, 1784

23. Witch, Unknown, 1897

24. Witch Jan van de Velde (II), 1626

25. A traveller being entranced by a witch disguised as a beautiful woman in the Alps. Engraving by T. Stocks after F. Meadows

26. Illustration of a witch from Walter Scott's 1830 book, Letters on Demonology and Witchcraft.

27. Illustration of Witches circling a church from Walter Scott's 1830 book, Letters on Demonology and Witchcraft.

28. Illustration from Walter Scott's 1830 book, Letters on Demonology and Witchcraft.

29. Witches 4 'The Ride Though The Murky Air, The Lancashire Witches, A Romance of Pendle Forest by W.H Ainsworth, J. Gilbert, illustrator, 1897

30. Witches 4 'The Incantation', The Lancashire Witches, A Romance of Pendle Forest by W.H Ainsworth, J. Gilbert, illustrator, 1897

31. Witches 3, The Lancashire Witches, A Romance of Pendle Forest by W.H Ainsworth, J. Gilbert, illustrator, 1897

32. Witches 1, The Lancashire Witches, A Romance of Pendle Forest by W.H Ainsworth, J. Gilbert, illustrator, 1897

33. Witches, The Lancashire Witches, A Romance of Pendle Forest by W.H Ainsworth, J. Gilbert, illustrator, 1897

34. Three witches attack the devil, Daniel Hopfer (I) (on object), 1505 - 1536

35. Medea calls on the gods and sees her chariot coming to her, René Boyvin (on object), 1563, The whole is framed by an ornamental list of putti, prophets, saters and nymphs.

36. Medea flees in a car pulled by dragons, René Boyvin (on object), 1563, The whole is framed by an ornamental list of putti and guirlandes.

37. Medea sacrifices a ram for the altar of Hecate and Hebe in front of Proserpina and Pluto, René Boyvin (on object), 1563

38. Medea cooks magic herbs in a kettle for Aeson, René Boyvin (on object), 1563

39. Medea restores Aeson's youth, Antonio Tempesta, 1606

40. Medea conjures up her chariot, Antonio Tempesta, 1606

41. Medea restores Aeson's youth, Virgil Solis, 1569

42. Medea draining the blood of Aeson in order to rejuvenate him with her special brew. Engraving

43. Macbeth consults the three witches; an apparition appears of a bloody child, who calls Macbeth's name three times. Engraving by W. Byrne, 1773, after E. Edwards., Edwards, Edward, 1738-1806.

44. Macbeth and Banquo meet the three witches on a heath; scene from Shakespeare's 'Macbeth'. Engraving by W. Bromley after J.H. Füssli (Fuseli). Fuseli, Henry, 1741-1825.

45. Macbeth Consulting the Witches, Eugène Delacroix, 1825

46. Macbeth and the Witches

47. Witches' sabbath, Jacques Aliamet (on object), 1755

48. Warrior and a witch, Arnold Houbraken (on object), 1681 - 1683

49. A naked witch carried on the shoulders of a monster sings from a choirbook held with pincers by two grotesque bishops while two apelike swimmers look on. Etching by F. Goya, 1796/1798

50. Two naked witches riding on a broomstick accompanied by an owl. Etching by F. Goya, 1796/1798.

51. Witch Riding Backwards on a Goat, Albrecht Durer

52. The Witches Hans Baldung (called Hans Baldung Grien) German, 1510

53. Witches meeting and performing spell. Etching by J.A.A. Pastelot.   Pastelot, Jean Amable Amédée, -1870.

54. The witch mistakes the chicken bone for Hans' finger, 1912

55. The Carcass by Agostino Veneziano, 1500 - 1536

56. Witches' Sabbath, attributed to workshop of Jacques de Gheyn (II), 1608 - 1612

57. Witches' Sabbath, Claude Gillot (mentioned on object), 1683 - 1722

58. The Witch by Joseph E. Cena, 1892

59. Macbeth seeing the three witches, with other horrifying visions. Etching after J. Reynolds, ca. 1786-1790, after W. Shakespeare

60. "De heksenketel in Rusland" (The Witches' Cauldron in Russia), Johan Braakensiek, 1905

61. Jeanne D'Arc, Charles-Abraham Chasselat (1782–1843)

62. Medea prays to Hecate, Crispain of the Passe (I), 1602 - 1607

63. A witches' sabbath. Spranger

CONCLUSION

The images curated in this collection span five centuries, yet the fascination they reflect shows no sign of fading. Witches and wizards have endured as artistic subjects precisely because they speak to something persistent in human experience — the desire to explain the unknown, to imagine power beyond the ordinary, and to give form to our deepest fears and desires.

We hope this archive has offered both inspiration and a deeper appreciation for the artists who shaped this tradition. Now the work passes to you.

ACKNOWLEDGMENTS

The works featured in this collection represent the extraordinary skill and imagination of artists, engravers, and printmakers working across five centuries. From Albrecht Dürer and Hans Baldung Grien in the early sixteenth century to Francisco Goya, Eugène Delacroix, and Arthur Rackham in later eras, each artist brought their own vision to subjects that captivated our imaginations.

Many of the works here are the product of anonymous hands, craftsmen and women whose names have been lost to time but whose artistry speaks clearly across the centuries. In the precision of a carved line or the patience of an illuminated border, their presence is still felt. It is to all of these makers, named and unnamed, that this collection is dedicated.

LEARN MORE

At Vault Editions, our mission is to provide the highest-quality reference materials for artists and designers, offering meticulously curated resources that inspire and empower creativity. If you've found value in this book, we invite you to explore more of our expertly crafted titles at vaulteditions.com, where you'll discover a world of visual inspiration and practical tools designed to elevate your creative work.

REVIEW THIS BOOK

As a family-owned and operated independent publisher, reviews are essential to the success of our business. Please leave an honest review of this book wherever you purchased it.

JOIN OUR COMMUNITY

Love bizarre and beautiful historical art? Join our community of 300K+ on Instagram — search @vault_editions for daily posts spanning natural history illustrations, mythical beasts, ornamental designs, and much more.

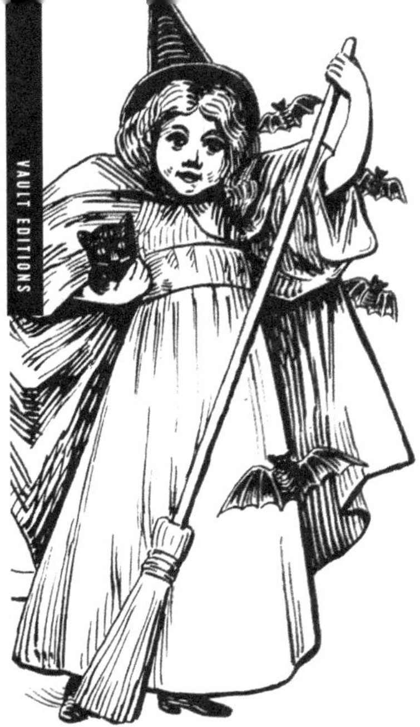

DOWNLOAD YOUR FILES

All images featured in this book are available to download as high-resolution files, ready for use in your creative projects. To access your files, visit the link below and enter the password provided.

The files are provided in high-resolution JPEG formats, suitable for both print and digital use. Each image has been individually restored and cleaned to ensure the finest possible quality,

preserving the detail and character of the original works while making them ready for modern creative applications.

Download yours now and get creating!

STEP ONE

Enter the following web address on a desktop or laptop computer in your web browser.

vaulteditions.com/pages/waw

STEP TWO

Enter the following password to access the download page:

w a w 7 3 2 4 5 9 s x d a

STEP THREE

Follow the prompts to access your high-resolution files.

CONTACT

For technical support, please email:
info@vaulteditions.com

Copyright © 2026
Vault Editions Ltd

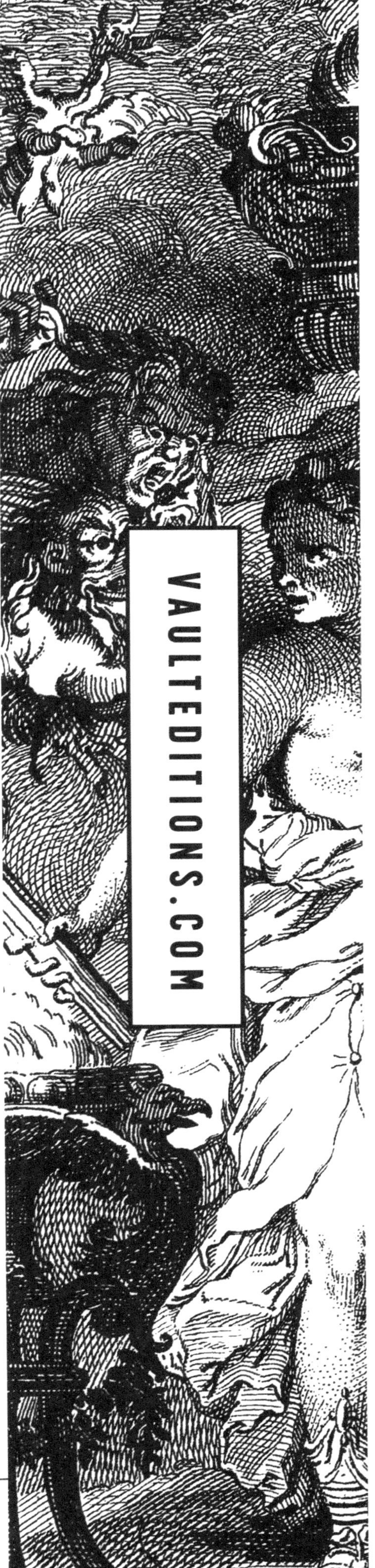

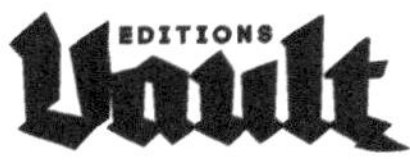

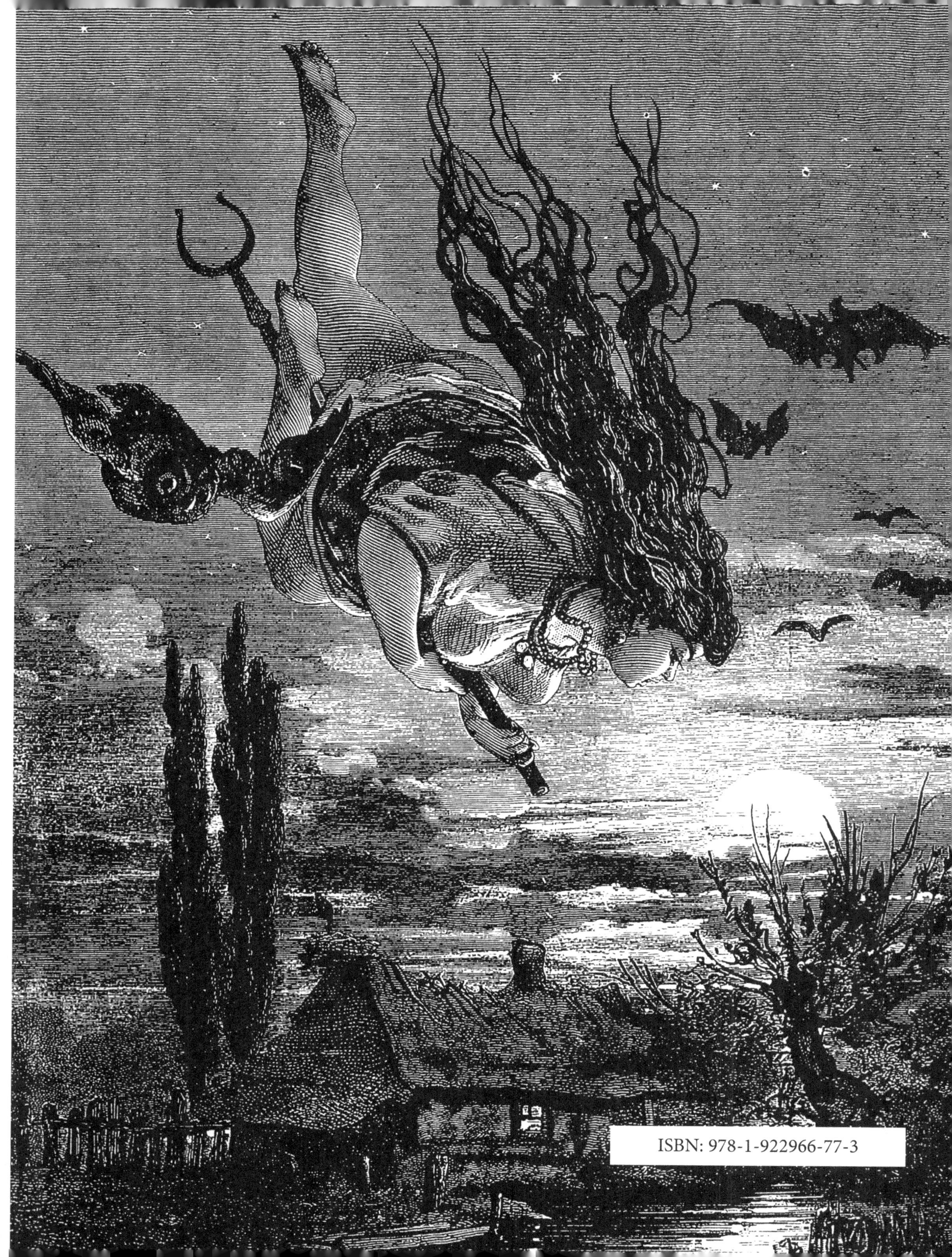
ISBN: 978-1-922966-77-3

www.ingramcontent.com/pod-product-compliance
Lightning Source LLC
Chambersburg PA
CBHW080521030726
47592CB00012B/3421